HALAL BUSINESS ONLINE

(Empowering Muslims to Build Wealth Online
While Upholding Islamic Values)

AFJAL KHAN

Copyright © 2024 Afjal Khan

All rights reserved.

ISBN: 9798341460706

DEDICATION

In the name of Allah, the Most Gracious, the Most Merciful.
This book is dedicated to every Muslim striving to balance worldly success with the eternal pursuit of the Hereafter. To the entrepreneurs and visionaries who build their businesses with integrity, guided by the principles of Islam, and who seek to uplift their communities through halal means.
To my family, whose unwavering support and prayers have been my strength, and to all who inspired and encouraged this journey.
May this work be a source of benefit for the Ummah, and may it serve as a reminder that true success is found in both wealth and faith, in this world and the next.
Bismillah.

CONTENTS

ACKNOWLEDGMENTS *1*

Chapter 1: Introduction to Halal Business *2*

Chapter 2: Digital Entrepreneurship: Opportunities and Challenges *20*

Chapter 3: Halal Finance: Building Wealth with Integrity *41*

Chapter 4: Ethical Marketing and Branding in Halal Business *61*

Chapter 5: The Role of Halal Compliance in Modern Business *82*

Chapter 6: Building Trust and Loyalty in Halal Business *103*

Chapter 7: Leadership and Ethical Governance in Halal Business *121*

Chapter 8: Building a Resilient and Sustainable Halal Business *140*

Chapter 9: Ethical Marketing and Promotion in Halal Business *159*

Chapter 10: Financial Integrity and Halal Business Operations *180*

Chapter 11: Ethical Leadership and Governance in Halal Business ... *199*

ACKNOWLEDGMENTS

Alhamdulillah, all praise and gratitude are due to Allah, the Most Gracious, the Most Merciful, for granting me the opportunity and strength to complete this book. Without His guidance, none of this would have been possible.

I would like to express my deep appreciation to my family for their endless support, patience, and encouragement throughout this journey. Their belief in my vision has been a constant source of motivation.

A heartfelt thanks to the scholars and mentors who have imparted their wisdom on Islamic business ethics, helping shape the foundation of this work. Your insights and teachings have been invaluable.

I also extend my gratitude to the Muslim entrepreneurs and business owners who shared their experiences, challenges, and successes, inspiring much of the content in this book. Your commitment to building businesses that honor both deen and dunya is a true testament to the strength of our Ummah.

To the readers, I am grateful for your interest and trust. May this book provide you with the knowledge and inspiration to build wealth in a way that is pleasing to Allah and beneficial to our communities.

Lastly, I would like to acknowledge everyone who contributed, directly or indirectly, to the completion of this book. Your support and encouragement have been instrumental in making this vision a reality.

Jazakumullahu Khairan. May Allah reward you all abundantly.

CHAPTER 1: INTRODUCTION TO HALAL BUSINESS

In a world dominated by rapid advancements in technology and a burgeoning global economy, the notion of business has taken on various forms. Amidst the hustle for wealth and success, the Muslim entrepreneur stands on sacred ground. Their journey is not merely about profits but about creating an impact while adhering to the ethical boundaries set by Islam. A halal business transcends beyond a regular enterprise; it is a reflection of faith, trust in Allah, and unwavering dedication to upholding moral and ethical standards.

The idea of halal, meaning permissible, extends far beyond dietary laws. Halal governs all aspects of life, including the financial and commercial endeavors of Muslims. A halal business is one where every step, every decision, and every transaction conforms to Islamic principles. This might sound like a daunting task in a world where haram (forbidden) activities, such as interest (riba) and unethical practices, are prevalent. Yet, the faithful Muslim entrepreneur finds solace and guidance in the Quran and Sunnah, both of which illuminate a path to success that is pure, blessed, and enduring.

The importance of halal business is rooted in the responsibility that every Muslim holds – to ensure that their wealth is earned lawfully and ethically. Islam places immense emphasis on transparency, honesty, and justice in business dealings. The Prophet Muhammad (PBUH) himself was known for his impeccable integrity in trade, and his example serves as the cornerstone for Muslim entrepreneurs today. He said, "The truthful and honest merchant will be with the Prophets, the truthful, and the martyrs" (Tirmidhi). This hadith highlights the noble status of those who conduct their business with integrity and faith.

In today's economic landscape, the demand for halal businesses is growing rapidly. The global Muslim population, estimated at over 1.8 billion, represents a substantial market for products and services that adhere to Islamic guidelines. From halal food to Islamic finance, ethical fashion, and education, opportunities abound for those who wish to build a business that not only thrives but also aligns with their faith. The Muslim entrepreneur is, therefore, in a unique position to lead, innovate, and inspire by showing the world that success can be achieved without compromising one's values.

Halal businesses operate on a set of core principles derived from the Quran and Sunnah. One of the foremost principles is honesty. A Muslim entrepreneur must always remain truthful in their dealings, avoiding any form of deceit or fraud. Allah commands in the Quran: "O you who have believed, do not consume one another's wealth unjustly or send it [in bribery] to the rulers in order that [they might aid] you [to] consume a portion of the wealth of the people in sin, while you know [it is unlawful]" (Quran 2:188). This verse reminds us that wealth, when earned unjustly, is void of blessings (barakah), and the consequences of such actions ripple not only through the individual's life but also through society.

Additionally, a halal business is rooted in fairness. This applies to every transaction and interaction with customers, employees, and partners. Whether in pricing, contracts, or wages, a Muslim entrepreneur ensures fairness and justice, fulfilling the rights of all parties involved. The Prophet Muhammad (PBUH) said, "Give the worker his wages before his sweat dries" (Ibn Majah), underscoring the importance of honoring one's commitments in business.

In a world filled with temptations and shortcuts, the Muslim entrepreneur walks a path of integrity. The temptation to engage in haram activities such as interest (riba), fraudulent marketing, or unethical investments is great, but the rewards of remaining steadfast in halal practices are far greater. Not only does a halal business invite the blessings of Allah, but it also builds trust within the community. Trust is the foundation upon which long-lasting and fruitful relationships are built, whether with customers, suppliers, or employees.

Moreover, a halal business is one that avoids any form of exploitation. This includes avoiding riba, the charging of interest, which is explicitly prohibited in Islam. The Prophet Muhammad (PBUH) cursed the one who takes riba, the one who gives it, and the one who records it (Muslim). Interest-based transactions are prevalent in modern economies, and it requires diligence and creativity to avoid them in business. However, Islamic finance offers alternatives such as profit-sharing (mudarabah) and joint ventures (musharakah), which allow businesses to flourish without engaging in haram activities.

Running a halal business requires more than just following the rules. It is about embodying Islamic values in every facet of the enterprise. The concept of ihsan, which means striving for excellence, plays a crucial role in Islamic entrepreneurship. A business that adheres to halal principles must also strive to provide excellent products and services, maintain ethical standards, and continuously seek improvement. The Prophet Muhammad (PBUH) said, "Verily, Allah loves that when anyone of you does a job, he should perfect it" (Al-Bayhaqi). This teaching encourages Muslim entrepreneurs to aim for the highest standards, not only in terms of product quality but also in their conduct and interactions.

Additionally, the success of a halal business is not measured solely by financial gain. It is measured by the impact it has on the community and the legacy it leaves behind. A Muslim entrepreneur should aim to benefit not just themselves but also their employees, customers, and society as a whole. The Prophet Muhammad (PBUH) emphasized the importance of charity and giving back to the community. In business, this can manifest as providing fair wages, creating jobs, and engaging in ethical practices that support the well-being of others. In essence, a halal business is one that contributes positively to the world while ensuring that its wealth is earned in a way that pleases Allah.

One of the key challenges that Muslim entrepreneurs face in today's global economy is the integration of Islamic principles into modern business practices. While the conventional business world often prioritizes profit over ethics, the Muslim entrepreneur must navigate this landscape with a different set of priorities. Profit is important, but it must never come at the cost of faith or integrity. This means avoiding businesses or practices that involve haram elements, such as alcohol, gambling, or interest-based investments, no matter how profitable they may appear.

Fortunately, the rise of ethical consumerism is paving the way for halal businesses to thrive. Consumers, both Muslim and non-Muslim, are becoming more conscious of where their products come from, how they are made, and the impact they have on society and the environment. This shift towards ethical consumption aligns perfectly with the values of halal businesses, which prioritize fairness, transparency, and social responsibility.

For a business to be considered truly halal, it must fulfill certain obligations. These obligations include paying zakat, the mandatory charity on wealth. Zakat is not just a financial obligation but a means of purifying one's wealth. By giving a portion of their earnings to those in need, Muslim entrepreneurs ensure that their wealth is not tainted by selfishness or greed. Allah says in the Quran, "Take from their wealth a charity by which you purify them and cause them increase, and invoke [Allah's blessings] upon them. Indeed, your invocations are reassurance for them" (Quran 9:103). This verse highlights the spiritual benefits of zakat and its role in ensuring that wealth is earned and distributed justly.

In addition to zakat, a halal business must also avoid any form of hoarding or monopolization. Islam encourages the circulation of wealth, ensuring that it benefits as many people as possible. The Prophet Muhammad (PBUH) said,

"He who monopolizes is a sinner" (Muslim). This teaching underscores the importance of fairness in trade and the responsibility that comes with wealth. By avoiding monopolistic practices and ensuring that goods and services are accessible to all, a Muslim entrepreneur contributes to a just and balanced economy.

As we reflect on the nature of halal business, it becomes clear that it is not just about following rules but about embodying values. These values—honesty, transparency, fairness, and social responsibility—form the foundation of a business that is not only profitable but also blessed. The concept of barakah, or divine blessings, is central to Islamic business practices. Barakah is not just about increasing wealth; it is about the quality of wealth and the peace and satisfaction that come with earning it in a halal way.

Muslim entrepreneurs who build their businesses on the principles of halal are setting themselves up for success, not just in this life but in the Hereafter. They are building legacies that will benefit them, their families, and their communities for generations to come. This is the ultimate goal of a halal business: to create wealth that is pure, ethical, and blessed, and to use that wealth in the service of Allah and humanity.

The journey of establishing a halal business may be filled with challenges, but it is also filled with rewards. One of the greatest rewards is the peace of mind that comes from knowing that every transaction, every deal, and every dollar earned is pleasing to Allah. This peace of mind cannot be bought with money; it is the result of living a life of integrity and purpose. For Muslim entrepreneurs, success is not just about financial gain—it is about earning Allah's pleasure and building a business that reflects the teachings of Islam.

The global market for halal products and services is expanding rapidly, providing ample opportunities for Muslim entrepreneurs to make a significant impact. From halal food and beverages to Islamic finance, fashion, and travel, the demand for halal products is increasing worldwide. Muslim consumers are looking for businesses that understand their values and provide products and services that align with their faith. This growing demand presents a unique opportunity for entrepreneurs to not only meet the needs of Muslim consumers but also to educate and engage non-Muslim consumers about the ethical and inclusive nature of halal business.

As more consumers become aware of the ethical and environmental benefits of halal products, the halal business landscape will continue to grow. The future of halal business lies in its ability to adapt to modern consumer demands while staying true to its Islamic roots. By leveraging technology, innovation, and ethical practices, Muslim entrepreneurs can create businesses that are not only profitable but also serve as beacons of integrity and faith in the marketplace.

A successful halal business is one that is built on trust, respect, and a commitment to serving others. It is a business that honors the principles of

Islam while embracing the opportunities of the modern world. For Muslim entrepreneurs, the path to success is clear: build a business that reflects your faith, treats others with fairness and respect, and contributes to the betterment of society. In doing so, you will not only achieve financial success but also earn the greatest reward of all—Allah's pleasure and blessings.

The heart of any halal business lies in its intention and purpose. A business born from sincere intentions to serve the community and earn halal income is one that is bound to prosper. The Muslim entrepreneur must always remember that the ultimate purpose of wealth in Islam is not merely personal gain but to serve a higher cause. Wealth, in the hands of the righteous, is a means of supporting family, uplifting the needy, and contributing to the welfare of the ummah (community).

In this regard, the concept of halal wealth takes on a spiritual dimension. Islam teaches that wealth is a test from Allah, a blessing that must be used responsibly. The Quran reminds us, "And know that your wealth and your children are but a trial, and that Allah has with Him a great reward" (Quran 8:28). This verse reflects the profound responsibility that comes with wealth and the need to ensure that it is earned and spent in ways that please Allah.

As Muslim entrepreneurs embark on the path of halal business, it is essential to constantly remind themselves of their role as custodians of wealth. They are not merely business owners but stewards of the resources Allah has granted them. This perspective shifts the focus from accumulating wealth for personal enjoyment to using it for the greater good. In essence, a halal business is not just about creating financial success—it is about fostering a meaningful, purposeful, and spiritually rewarding life.

To achieve this, Muslim entrepreneurs must cultivate a deep sense of taqwa (God-consciousness) in their business dealings. Taqwa serves as a compass, guiding them toward decisions that align with Islamic principles and steering them away from haram practices. This consciousness of Allah's presence in every transaction fosters a business environment rooted in honesty, transparency, and respect for the rights of others.

In practical terms, taqwa manifests in the way a business treats its employees, customers, and partners. It encourages the entrepreneur to act with integrity, even when no one is watching. It reminds them that success comes not only from hard work but from seeking Allah's pleasure in every aspect of the business. This sense of accountability to Allah is what sets a halal business apart from its conventional counterparts.

The Muslim entrepreneur's journey is a delicate balance between striving for worldly success and maintaining spiritual purity. In a world where haram (forbidden) practices are often disguised as lucrative opportunities, it can be challenging to stay true to one's faith. But the rewards of doing so are immense, both in this life and the Hereafter. The Prophet Muhammad (PBUH) emphasized the importance of lawful earnings when he said, "No one earns better than that which is from his own hands, and a man's spending on himself, his family, his children, and his servant is a charity" (Ahmad). This hadith underscores the nobility of earning halal income and spending it on oneself and others in a manner that benefits society.

Moreover, a halal business creates ripple effects within the community. By providing halal products and services, Muslim entrepreneurs contribute to the growth of the halal economy, benefiting consumers who seek to align their purchases with Islamic values. The halal economy is vast and includes sectors such as food, finance, fashion, tourism, pharmaceuticals, and more. As this market continues to grow, the need for businesses that adhere to Islamic guidelines becomes even more critical.

One of the most significant challenges facing Muslim entrepreneurs today is navigating the global marketplace while maintaining their commitment to halal principles. The global economy is interconnected, with supply chains spanning multiple countries and cultures. Ensuring that every aspect of the business complies with Islamic principles can be a complex task. However, with diligence and careful planning, it is entirely possible to operate within these constraints while remaining competitive in the marketplace.

One key factor is transparency in supply chains. Muslim entrepreneurs must ensure that the products they source and sell are free from haram elements. This requires thorough research, building relationships with trustworthy suppliers, and, where necessary, obtaining halal certifications. The transparency and honesty with which a business operates not only comply with Islamic principles but also build trust with customers.

Customers, both Muslim and non-Muslim, are increasingly looking for ethical businesses that prioritize transparency and fairness. This trend toward ethical consumerism aligns perfectly with the values of halal businesses. By positioning their products and services as halal, ethical, and environmentally friendly, Muslim entrepreneurs can attract a broader audience that shares these values.

In addition to sourcing products ethically, Muslim entrepreneurs must also pay attention to how they market their businesses. Islamic ethics place a high value on honesty and fairness in advertising. Deceptive marketing, false claims, and exaggerated benefits are all forms of dishonesty that Islam forbids. Allah warns in the Quran, "Woe to those who give less [than due], who, when they take a measure from people, take in full. But if they give by measure or by weight to them, they cause loss" (Quran 83:1-3). This verse serves as a reminder that honesty in business transactions is not just about the product itself but extends to how it is presented and sold.

Marketing in a halal business must reflect the same principles of honesty, transparency, and respect for the customer's rights. The entrepreneur should ensure that the claims made about the product or service are truthful and that the customer is fully informed about what they are purchasing. This not only complies with Islamic teachings but also enhances the reputation of the business, as customers appreciate transparency and ethical practices.

The rise of digital marketing has opened up new opportunities for Muslim entrepreneurs to promote their halal businesses. Social media, content marketing, and online advertising provide cost-effective ways to reach a global audience. However, these tools must be used responsibly, ensuring that the content shared is appropriate and aligns with Islamic values. Engaging with customers in a respectful and ethical manner online can build long-term relationships and foster brand loyalty.

Furthermore, the concept of halal extends beyond the products and services themselves to the way a business operates internally. A halal business must ensure that its employees are treated with dignity and fairness. Islam places great emphasis on workers' rights, and the Prophet Muhammad (PBUH) warned against exploitation, saying, "Your employees are your brothers, whom Allah has placed under your command. So, whoever has his brother under his command should feed him of what he eats and dress him of what he wears. Do not burden them beyond their capacity, but if you do so, then help them" (Bukhari). This hadith highlights the importance of treating employees with kindness, fairness, and respect.

A key aspect of running a halal business is the responsibility toward employees. Ensuring that they are paid fairly, treated justly, and provided with a safe working environment is not just a legal obligation but a religious one. The Prophet Muhammad (PBUH) emphasized the importance of fair wages, saying, "Give the worker his wages before his sweat dries" (Ibn Majah). This teaching applies not only to payment but to all aspects of how employees are treated in a halal business. A company that cares for its employees and respects their rights is one that is blessed with barakah and success.

Another important consideration in running a halal business is the avoidance of riba (interest). Riba is strictly prohibited in Islam, as it is seen as exploitative and unjust. The Quran strongly condemns riba, stating, "Allah has permitted trade and forbidden riba" (Quran 2:275). Muslim entrepreneurs must, therefore, avoid engaging in interest-based transactions, whether in borrowing, lending, or investing. This can be challenging in a world where interest-based financing is the norm, but alternatives such as Islamic finance provide solutions that align with halal principles.

Islamic finance operates on the basis of profit-sharing, risk-sharing, and ethical investing. By engaging with Islamic financial institutions, Muslim entrepreneurs can secure the funding they need for their businesses without compromising their faith. These institutions offer a range of halal financing options, including mudarabah (profit-sharing) and musharakah (joint ventures), which allow businesses to grow in a way that is compliant with Islamic principles.

The success of a halal business is not just measured by financial gains but by the positive impact it has on society. A business that adheres to Islamic principles benefits not only the entrepreneur but the entire community. It creates jobs, contributes to the local economy, and provides goods and services that meet the needs of the Muslim community. By operating within the framework of halal, Muslim entrepreneurs can build businesses that are not only profitable but also serve as models of integrity, fairness, and ethical leadership.

As we explore the concept of halal business, it is important to remember that success is not guaranteed by wealth alone. True success in a halal business comes from the combination of financial prosperity and spiritual fulfillment. A business that is built on the principles of halal invites Allah's blessings, or barakah, which is often intangible but manifests in ways that bring peace, satisfaction, and sustainability to the business. The concept of barakah is unique to Islamic teachings, emphasizing that wealth gained through halal means is not just beneficial in terms of quantity but also in the quality of its impact.

Barakah in a halal business is seen when wealth is used for good, when the business brings happiness and benefit to others, and when the entrepreneur feels a sense of contentment and purpose in their work. It is the unseen force that makes a business thrive, even when external factors suggest otherwise. Muslim entrepreneurs must, therefore, continuously seek Allah's guidance and blessings in their business endeavors, ensuring that their actions remain aligned with Islamic values.

In summary, the foundation of a halal business is built on a deep connection between faith and commerce. It is a journey of integrity, resilience, and unwavering dedication to upholding the teachings of Islam. As Muslim entrepreneurs navigate the complexities of modern business, they must remain grounded in their faith, trusting that success comes not from cutting corners or compromising on values but from adherence to the principles that Allah has set forth. By embodying honesty, transparency, and fairness, the Muslim entrepreneur earns not only financial success but also spiritual rewards that far outweigh the material gains of this world. The peace of mind that comes from knowing that every transaction, every decision, and every effort in the business is aligned with halal principles is a gift beyond measure.

A crucial aspect of ensuring that a business remains halal is constant self-reflection and accountability. Muslim entrepreneurs must regularly assess their business practices and ensure that they remain compliant with Islamic teachings. This involves looking at every part of the business, from how products are sourced to how profits are shared. It also requires keeping an open line of communication with scholars and experts in Islamic finance to ensure that the business continues to adhere to the evolving guidelines of what is permissible and what is not.

One of the areas where self-reflection is particularly important is in dealing with competition. In the fast-paced world of modern business, competition can sometimes lead entrepreneurs to take shortcuts or engage in unethical practices to stay ahead. However, Islam teaches that rizq (sustenance) is ultimately in the hands of Allah. As the Prophet Muhammad (PBUH) said, "No soul will die until it has received all of its provision" (Ibn Majah). This hadith serves as a reminder that no amount of unethical behavior will bring lasting success. Trust in Allah's plan, combined with ethical business practices, ensures that the rizq comes in the best and purest form.

For Muslim entrepreneurs, this means focusing on providing the best products and services while maintaining a competitive edge without compromising on Islamic principles. Trusting in Allah's plan does not mean avoiding hard work or innovation, but it does mean that one should not resort to haram methods out of fear of losing business. The Quran reassures us: "And whoever fears Allah – He will make for him a way out and will provide for him from where he does not expect" (Quran 65:2-3). This verse emphasizes that Allah will provide for those who remain conscious of Him and adhere to His laws, even in the most challenging times.

In this light, Muslim entrepreneurs must view their business not just as a means of generating income but as a platform for embodying the highest ethical standards in their industry. The trust that is built through halal practices is invaluable. Customers, employees, and partners respect and appreciate businesses that operate with transparency and integrity, and this trust often leads to long-term success. The reputation of being a halal business, especially in industries where competition is fierce, can be a significant differentiator. Consumers are increasingly looking for businesses they can trust, and a business that is upfront about its adherence to halal principles will naturally attract both Muslim and non-Muslim customers who value ethical practices.

Beyond the direct consumer base, Muslim entrepreneurs must also consider their broader impact on society. Islam teaches us to be responsible stewards of the Earth, to treat people with kindness and fairness, and to ensure that wealth is circulated in a way that benefits the community. The Prophet Muhammad (PBUH) said, "The best of people are those who bring the most benefit to others" (Daraqutni). This hadith underscores the idea that a business's success is not just measured in profits but in the positive impact it has on the lives of others.

For instance, businesses that focus on ethical sourcing, fair wages, and environmentally sustainable practices are in a unique position to lead by example. By demonstrating that profitability and ethics can go hand-in-hand, they inspire other businesses to follow suit. Moreover, they contribute to the larger movement of ethical consumerism, where customers seek out businesses that prioritize moral and social responsibility over mere profit.

One practical way to embody these principles is through corporate social responsibility (CSR). CSR initiatives can take various forms, from charitable donations to community engagement projects, from reducing environmental impact to providing educational opportunities for employees and customers. By integrating these initiatives into the fabric of the business, Muslim entrepreneurs can ensure that their success is shared with the wider community and that their business contributes to the greater good.

In addition to CSR, another significant aspect of running a halal business is financial responsibility. Islam places a strong emphasis on managing wealth wisely, avoiding extravagance, and ensuring that financial practices are in line with Islamic teachings. This includes avoiding debt, particularly interest-based debt, as riba (interest) is strictly forbidden in Islam. The Quran states, "Those who consume interest cannot stand [on the Day of Resurrection] except as one stands who is being beaten by Satan into insanity. That is because they say, 'Trade is [just] like interest.' But Allah has permitted trade and has forbidden interest" (Quran 2:275).

In modern business environments, avoiding interest can be challenging, especially when many financial institutions are based on interest-bearing loans and financing. However, Islamic finance provides alternatives that allow businesses to grow without compromising on their principles. Profit-sharing models, such as mudarabah and musharakah, allow businesses to obtain financing in a way that is halal. Additionally, Islamic banks and financial institutions are increasingly offering Shariah-compliant products that help Muslim entrepreneurs manage their finances while adhering to Islamic principles.

Being financially responsible also means keeping meticulous records of business transactions, ensuring that all earnings and expenditures are transparent and accountable. This not only helps in maintaining a halal business but also ensures that the business is well-organized and able to meet its legal and financial obligations. Proper financial management is essential for the long-term success of any business, and for a halal business, it is particularly important as it demonstrates a commitment to honesty and accountability.

Moreover, the Quran and Hadith emphasize the importance of giving back to society through zakat and sadaqah. Zakat is a mandatory form of charity that purifies wealth, while sadaqah is voluntary charity that further increases barakah in one's earnings. The Prophet Muhammad (PBUH) said, "Charity does not decrease wealth" (Muslim), highlighting the idea that giving back to others only increases the blessings in one's wealth. For Muslim entrepreneurs, zakat is not just a religious obligation but also a way to ensure that their business contributes to the well-being of others, particularly those in need.

When we consider the long-term goals of a halal business, one of the most important aspects is leaving behind a legacy of goodness. A successful halal business is not just about generating wealth for the present but about building something that will benefit future generations. This idea of leaving a positive legacy is deeply rooted in Islamic teachings. The Prophet Muhammad (PBUH) said, "When a person dies, his deeds are cut off except for three: ongoing charity, knowledge that is benefited from, or a righteous child who prays for him" (Muslim).

For Muslim entrepreneurs, building a halal business that benefits others can be a form of ongoing charity (sadaqah jariyah). By creating jobs, supporting ethical causes, and ensuring that wealth is distributed justly, the entrepreneur leaves behind a legacy that continues to generate blessings long after they have passed. The intention behind every business decision, therefore, should not only be focused on short-term gains but also on long-term impact.

In practical terms, this means that Muslim entrepreneurs must think about succession planning and how to ensure that their business remains halal even after they are no longer actively involved. This may involve training and mentoring the next generation of leaders within the company, ensuring that they are equipped with both the skills and the ethical foundation needed to carry on the business in accordance with Islamic principles. It may also mean setting up charitable trusts or foundations that ensure the business continues to support important causes long into the future.

Furthermore, a halal business must consider its environmental impact. Islam teaches that humans are stewards of the Earth and that we have a responsibility to protect the environment for future generations. The Quran says, "It is He who has made you successors upon the earth" (Quran 35:39). This verse reminds us that the resources of the Earth are a trust from Allah and must be used responsibly. Muslim entrepreneurs, therefore, have a duty to implement sustainable practices in their businesses, whether that means reducing waste, using eco-friendly materials, or supporting initiatives that protect the environment.

In conclusion, a halal business is not merely a means of earning a living—it is an opportunity to embody the highest values of Islam and to make a lasting impact on the world. The Muslim entrepreneur who adheres to halal principles is not only building a business but also participating in the creation of a just and ethical society. The success of a halal business is measured not only in financial terms but in the barakah it brings to the lives of everyone it touches—from employees and customers to the wider community and even the environment.

As Muslim entrepreneurs continue to navigate the complexities of the modern business world, they must remain steadfast in their commitment to halal principles. This requires not only knowledge and diligence but also a deep sense of purpose and a desire to seek Allah's pleasure in every aspect of their business. In doing so, they ensure that their efforts are rewarded both in this world and in the Hereafter, creating a legacy of success, faith, and integrity that will endure for generations to come.

A business that is deeply rooted in the concept of halal understands that it is not just operating in a vacuum of profit and loss. It operates within a framework of moral responsibility, religious obligation, and social contribution. The concept of halal is so vast and comprehensive that it becomes a way of life for the Muslim entrepreneur. This is particularly important in a world where many have lost sight of ethical business practices, where shortcuts and questionable dealings often lead to temporary gains but long-term instability.

Islam teaches that every aspect of a Muslim's life should be connected to the greater good, including their business ventures. In doing so, the Muslim entrepreneur is not only seeking financial success but also fulfilling the higher purpose of living in accordance with Allah's commands. A halal business becomes a vessel through which one can achieve personal growth, contribute to the community, and seek Allah's pleasure.

A successful halal business rests on several pillars. One of the most critical pillars is trust, known as *amanah* in Islamic terms. Trust is the foundation of any relationship, whether it be between an employer and employee, a seller and buyer, or a business partner and investor. Allah has placed an immense emphasis on the concept of trust in business transactions. The Quran says, "Indeed, Allah commands you to render trusts to whom they are due and when you judge between people to judge with justice" (Quran 4:58). A Muslim entrepreneur must understand that maintaining trust is not just a business necessity but a religious obligation. Breaking this trust can lead to both worldly consequences, such as losing customers and damaging one's reputation, and spiritual consequences that impact one's relationship with Allah.

In today's digital world, where information travels at lightning speed, maintaining trust has become more challenging. A single mistake, a poor decision, or an unethical transaction can quickly go viral, tarnishing the reputation of the business. This makes the commitment to halal principles even more crucial for Muslim entrepreneurs. By consistently adhering to Islamic guidelines, they create a solid foundation of trust that protects their business from these challenges. Trust is also what fosters long-term relationships with customers and clients, who, once satisfied with the honesty and integrity of the business, often become loyal patrons.

Another key pillar of a halal business is fairness, or *adl*, which permeates every aspect of the business, from how products are priced to how employees are treated. Fairness is central to Islamic teachings, and it is an essential quality that every Muslim entrepreneur must cultivate. The Prophet Muhammad (PBUH) was known for his fairness in trade, even before he became a Prophet. His dealings were marked by honesty and justice, earning him the nickname "Al-Amin," meaning the trustworthy. This attribute of fairness attracted people to do business with him, knowing that they would never be cheated or treated unfairly.

A Muslim entrepreneur today must strive to embody this same fairness in their business. Whether it is in negotiating contracts, paying wages, or setting prices, fairness ensures that the rights of all parties involved are respected. The Quran repeatedly emphasizes the importance of fairness and justice in all dealings: "O you who have believed, be persistently standing firm for Allah, witnesses in justice, and do not let the hatred of a people prevent you from being just. Be just; that is nearer to righteousness" (Quran 5:8). Fairness, therefore, is not simply a business strategy—it is an act of worship, a way of drawing closer to Allah.

For the modern Muslim entrepreneur, fairness also extends to the larger community. A halal business should aim to uplift and support the communities in which it operates. This can be done by creating jobs, paying fair wages, and ensuring that employees work in a safe and respectful environment. A fair business also supports local suppliers, engages in ethical sourcing, and avoids practices that exploit workers or harm the environment. In this way, fairness is not only about the internal workings of the business but also about how the business impacts society at large.

The global halal industry has seen tremendous growth in recent years, and with this growth comes increased responsibility for those operating within it. Entrepreneurs must be vigilant in maintaining the integrity of their halal practices, ensuring that they are not merely using the halal label as a marketing tool but truly embodying the principles behind it. The halal certification process, while important, is just one part of running a halal business. What truly defines a halal business is the daily commitment to honesty, transparency, and fairness in all dealings.

The growth of the halal market has been driven by a variety of factors, including the increasing awareness among Muslim consumers about the importance of aligning their consumption habits with their faith. This shift has created a demand for businesses that not only sell halal products but also operate in a way that is consistent with Islamic values. This presents a unique opportunity for Muslim entrepreneurs to tap into a growing market while simultaneously setting a new standard for ethical business practices.

However, tapping into this market requires more than just offering halal-certified products. Muslim entrepreneurs must also ensure that their business operations, marketing strategies, and customer service reflect the values of halal. The Quran instructs, "And do not consume one another's wealth unjustly or send it [in bribery] to the rulers in order that [they might aid] you [to] consume a portion of the wealth of the people in sin, while you know [it is unlawful]" (Quran 2:188). This verse highlights the importance of avoiding exploitation and ensuring that all business practices are conducted ethically.

Muslim entrepreneurs must also be mindful of how they present their products and services. Honesty in marketing is a critical aspect of maintaining halal practices. Deceptive advertising, misleading claims, and manipulation of customer emotions are all forms of dishonesty that are prohibited in Islam. The Prophet Muhammad (PBUH) said, "He who deceives is not of us" (Muslim). This hadith serves as a stark reminder that even seemingly harmless marketing tactics that involve deception can have serious spiritual consequences.

Instead of relying on deceptive tactics, Muslim entrepreneurs should focus on building strong relationships with their customers through trust, authenticity, and transparency. Consumers today are more informed and discerning than ever before, and they are increasingly looking for brands that they can trust. By being upfront about the products being sold, their origins, and their benefits, Muslim entrepreneurs can build a loyal customer base that values integrity over gimmicks.

One of the challenges of running a halal business in the modern world is navigating the complexities of the global supply chain. The rise of globalization has made it easier than ever to source products and materials from all corners of the world, but it has also introduced new challenges in ensuring that these products comply with halal standards. For Muslim entrepreneurs, this means being vigilant in verifying the halal status of the products they sell and the ingredients they use.

This vigilance can sometimes require going beyond simply trusting suppliers' certifications. Entrepreneurs may need to conduct their own research, engage with suppliers directly, and, in some cases, visit manufacturing facilities to ensure that the products they are selling truly meet halal standards. This level of diligence is not just about maintaining the integrity of the business but also about protecting the trust that has been placed in the business by its customers.

Transparency is key in this process. If there is any doubt about the halal status of a product, it is the responsibility of the entrepreneur to either refrain from selling it or to be upfront with customers about the uncertainty. The Prophet Muhammad (PBUH) taught us, "Leave that which makes you doubt for that which does not make you doubt" (Tirmidhi). This hadith encourages us to avoid anything that may be questionable or lead to doubt in our dealings. For the Muslim entrepreneur, this means ensuring that every product and transaction is free from any uncertainty regarding its permissibility.

Furthermore, running a halal business is not just about avoiding haram; it is about actively seeking out barakah (blessings) in every aspect of the business. Barakah is the divine blessing that brings prosperity, growth, and sustainability to a business. It is not something that can be measured in financial terms alone, but its presence is felt in the smooth running of operations, the satisfaction of employees, the loyalty of customers, and the overall harmony of the business. A business that operates with integrity, fairness, and faithfulness to halal principles naturally attracts barakah, which in turn leads to long-term success.

The concept of barakah is central to the Islamic worldview of business. It reminds the Muslim entrepreneur that success is not solely the result of hard work or clever strategies, but rather it is a gift from Allah that comes to those who conduct their affairs in accordance with His guidance. The Prophet Muhammad (PBUH) said, "Wealth does not decrease by giving charity. Allah increases the honor of one who forgives, and no one humbles himself for the sake of Allah except that Allah raises him in status" (Muslim). This hadith encapsulates the idea that barakah comes not from hoarding wealth but from using it in ways that benefit others.

For the Muslim entrepreneur, this means that the business should not only focus on generating profits but also on contributing to the welfare of society. Giving back through charity, supporting community initiatives, and ensuring that the business has a positive social impact are all ways to invite barakah into the business. This principle of giving back is not just a recommendation but a religious obligation in the form of zakat. Zakat is not merely a tax on wealth; it is a means of purifying one's earnings and ensuring that the blessings of Allah continue to flow into the business.

Muslim entrepreneurs must also remember that seeking barakah extends to how they treat their employees. Fair wages, respectful treatment, and creating a positive work environment are all essential elements of a halal business. The Prophet Muhammad (PBUH) said, "Your employees are your brothers, whom Allah has placed under your command. So, whoever has his brother under his command should feed him of what he eats and dress him of what he wears. Do not burden them beyond their capacity, but if you do so, then help them" (Bukhari). This hadith highlights the responsibility that business owners have toward their employees, treating them with kindness and fairness.

A halal business that cares for its employees, its customers, and its community is one that reflects the principles of Islam in every facet. The success of such a business is not only measured in financial terms but in the satisfaction, well-being, and happiness it brings to everyone connected to it. A business that operates with this holistic approach to success is one that will not only thrive but will leave a lasting legacy of goodness and integrity.

The Muslim entrepreneur's journey is one that requires constant vigilance, self-reflection, and a commitment to living out the principles of Islam in every aspect of life. It is not an easy path, but it is a path that is filled with blessings, both in this world and the Hereafter. By adhering to halal principles, Muslim entrepreneurs have the opportunity to create businesses that are not only profitable but also serve as beacons of ethical leadership in a world that is in desperate need of integrity.

As we look ahead to the future of halal business, it is clear that Muslim entrepreneurs have a unique opportunity to shape the global economy in ways that are aligned with Islamic values. The demand for halal products and services is growing, and with this demand comes the responsibility to ensure that these businesses are truly reflective of the principles of Islam. The Muslim entrepreneur who remains steadfast in their commitment to halal principles will find success not only in their business but in their faith, as they contribute to the betterment of society and seek the pleasure of Allah.

A halal business is not just a theoretical concept but a living, breathing manifestation of Islamic values in the marketplace. It is a testament to the fact that one can succeed in this world without compromising on their faith. For the Muslim entrepreneur, this understanding forms the bedrock of their business operations. Each decision, whether small or large, is guided by the principles of halal, ensuring that the business remains pure and ethical in all its dealings.

At its core, a halal business is built on integrity. Integrity is more than just being honest in business transactions; it is about being true to one's values, regardless of the challenges or temptations that arise. The Muslim entrepreneur must always remember that their business is a reflection of their faith, and every action taken within the business should be aligned with the teachings of Islam. This level of integrity creates a business environment that fosters trust, loyalty, and respect from both customers and employees.

One of the key challenges that Muslim entrepreneurs face today is staying true to halal principles in a world where haram practices often seem easier or more profitable. For instance, many conventional businesses rely heavily on interest-based financing, deceptive marketing practices, or exploitative labor to maximize profits. These methods may bring short-term gains, but they ultimately lead to long-term instability and spiritual harm. For the Muslim entrepreneur, the path to success may sometimes seem longer or more difficult, but it is a path that is filled with barakah (blessings) and peace of mind.

The Quran reminds us that wealth earned through haram means is devoid of blessings: "O you who have believed, do not consume usury, doubled and multiplied, but fear Allah that you may be successful" (Quran 3:130). This verse serves as a stark warning to those who seek wealth through impermissible means, reminding them that true success lies in earning wealth in a way that is pleasing to Allah. The Muslim entrepreneur who adheres to this principle will find that their business is not only profitable but also sustainable in the long run, as it is built on a foundation of honesty and fairness.

Fairness is a fundamental principle in Islamic business ethics, and it applies to every aspect of a halal business. Whether it is in pricing products, paying employees, or dealing with suppliers, fairness must always be at the forefront of the entrepreneur's mind. The Prophet Muhammad (PBUH) said, "The just will be with Allah on thrones of light, to the right of the Merciful, Exalted be He, those who are just in their rulings and are fair with their families and those under their authority" (Muslim). This hadith highlights the immense reward that awaits those who act justly in all their affairs, including in their business dealings.

One way that fairness manifests in a halal business is through transparent pricing. In a world where many businesses engage in price gouging or hidden fees, the Muslim entrepreneur must ensure that their pricing is fair and transparent. Customers should know exactly what they are paying for, without any hidden costs or deceptive practices. This level of transparency not only complies with Islamic teachings but also builds trust with customers, leading to long-term loyalty and success.

Another important aspect of fairness in business is the treatment of employees. Islam places great emphasis on the rights of workers, and it is the responsibility of the business owner to ensure that employees are treated with dignity and respect. This includes paying fair wages, providing a safe working environment, and respecting the rights of workers to rest and have time for worship. The Quran states, "And do not withhold from the people the things that are their due, and do not commit abuse on the earth, spreading corruption" (Quran 11:85). This verse serves as a reminder that withholding the rights of others, whether through unfair wages or exploitation, is a grave sin in Islam.

The Muslim entrepreneur must also be mindful of the importance of work-life balance for their employees. Islam encourages moderation in all things, and this includes the amount of time spent working. Overworking employees or expecting them to sacrifice their personal lives for the sake of the business goes against the principles of fairness and balance that Islam teaches. By respecting the personal time and needs of employees, the Muslim entrepreneur creates a work environment that is not only productive but also filled with barakah.

The concept of fairness in a halal business extends beyond employees and customers to the broader community. A business that operates in accordance with Islamic principles has a responsibility to contribute positively to the society in which it operates. This can be done through charitable giving, supporting local initiatives, and ensuring that the business's impact on the environment is minimal. Islam teaches that wealth is a trust from Allah, and it must be used in ways that benefit not only the individual but the entire community. The Quran says, "And spend [in the way of Allah] from what We have provided you before death approaches one of you and he says, 'My Lord, if only You would delay me for a brief term so I would give charity and be among the righteous'" (Quran 63:10). This verse emphasizes the importance of giving back and using wealth in ways that are pleasing to Allah.

For the Muslim entrepreneur, giving back to the community is not just a way to earn rewards in the Hereafter but also a way to build goodwill and strengthen the business's reputation. Customers are more likely to support businesses that they perceive as being socially responsible and ethical. By engaging in charitable activities, supporting local causes, and ensuring that the business operates in an environmentally sustainable way, the Muslim entrepreneur not only benefits the community but also enhances the long-term success of their business.

One area where Muslim entrepreneurs can have a significant impact is in the realm of ethical consumerism. As consumers become more conscious of the ethical and environmental impact of their purchases, there is a growing demand for businesses that prioritize sustainability, fair trade, and social responsibility. This trend aligns perfectly with the values of halal businesses, which are built on the principles of fairness, honesty, and responsibility. By positioning their business as one that is not only halal but also ethical and socially responsible, Muslim entrepreneurs can tap into a growing market of consumers who are looking for products and services that align with their values.

In conclusion, the foundation of a halal business is built on the principles of honesty, fairness, transparency, and social responsibility. These values are not just abstract concepts but practical guidelines that shape every aspect of the business, from how products are sourced to how employees are treated. The Muslim entrepreneur who adheres to these principles is not only building a profitable business but also creating a legacy of integrity and faith that will benefit them in this world and the Hereafter.

A halal business is more than just a means of earning a living—it is a way of fulfilling one's obligations to Allah, contributing to the well-being of society, and leaving a positive impact on the world. The path of halal business may be challenging at times, but it is a path that is filled with blessings and rewards. By remaining steadfast in their commitment to halal principles, Muslim entrepreneurs can achieve success in both this life and the Hereafter, knowing that their efforts are pleasing to Allah and beneficial to all those around them.

The global halal market is growing rapidly, and with it comes the opportunity for Muslim entrepreneurs to lead the way in ethical and socially responsible business practices. By staying true to the teachings of Islam and maintaining a commitment to integrity and fairness, Muslim entrepreneurs can build businesses that not only thrive but also inspire others to do the same. The future of halal business is bright, and it is up to the next generation of Muslim entrepreneurs to carry forward the legacy of honesty, fairness, and social responsibility that has been passed down through the teachings of Islam.

CHAPTER 2: DIGITAL ENTREPRENEURSHIP: OPPORTUNITIES AND CHALLENGES

In the vast, ever-changing world of modern commerce, few transformations have been as profound and sweeping as the rise of digital entrepreneurship. The dawn of the digital age has opened doors that once seemed inaccessible, allowing entrepreneurs to establish, grow, and scale businesses with unprecedented ease. For Muslim entrepreneurs, this offers a unique opportunity: the ability to create halal businesses that operate globally, all while adhering to Islamic principles. The digital sphere, while vast and sometimes complex, is a frontier where faith and commerce can harmoniously coexist.

At its core, digital entrepreneurship involves using online platforms and digital technologies to create business opportunities. It covers a range of activities, from selling products and services online to offering educational content and digital tools. The beauty of digital entrepreneurship lies in its accessibility. One does not need vast financial resources or physical infrastructure to get started. Instead, with the right mindset, skills, and tools, an individual can reach a global audience from the comfort of their own home.

The Muslim entrepreneur must recognize the immense potential that the digital world holds, not only for personal gain but also as a platform to spread goodness, offer valuable services, and help uplift the ummah. Digital entrepreneurship, when approached with the right intention (*niyyah*), becomes more than just a business venture; it becomes a means of fulfilling Islamic values, benefiting others, and earning halal income.

For many entrepreneurs, the first step into the digital world is e-commerce. Whether through setting up an online store, joining a marketplace, or leveraging social media platforms, e-commerce provides a direct and accessible route to selling goods and services to a global audience. With e-commerce, geographical boundaries are erased, and the entrepreneur can operate in markets they may never have physically entered. However, as Muslim entrepreneurs embark on this journey, they must ensure that their offerings, pricing, and marketing methods all align with halal principles. Every transaction, every interaction, and every deal must be transparent, honest, and free from exploitation.

The digital landscape is full of opportunity, but it is not without its challenges. For the Muslim entrepreneur, these challenges are twofold: navigating the complexities of the digital world while also ensuring that every action taken remains in accordance with Islamic teachings. The Quran provides clear guidance on the importance of honesty and integrity in business: "And do not mix the truth with falsehood or conceal the truth while you know [it]" (Quran 2:42). In the digital sphere, this verse takes on a deeper meaning. With the anonymity that the internet often affords, it can be tempting for entrepreneurs to engage in deceptive practices, but the Muslim entrepreneur must rise above these temptations.

One of the most significant challenges faced by digital entrepreneurs is the competition. The barrier to entry in the digital world is low, which means that there are often thousands, if not millions, of businesses offering similar products and services. This creates a highly competitive environment where standing out can be difficult. However, for the Muslim entrepreneur, this challenge is also an opportunity. By building a business that is grounded in halal principles and ethical practices, one can differentiate themselves from the masses. Customers, particularly in today's world, are increasingly looking for businesses that they can trust. By demonstrating a commitment to integrity, honesty, and fairness, the Muslim entrepreneur can build a loyal customer base that values these qualities over price or convenience.

Another challenge in digital entrepreneurship is maintaining transparency in every aspect of the business. This includes being upfront with customers about product quality, pricing, and shipping times. Islam emphasizes the importance of honesty in all transactions, and the digital entrepreneur must ensure that their website, product descriptions, and customer interactions are free from any form of deceit. The Prophet Muhammad (PBUH) said, "He who deceives is not of us" (Muslim). This powerful statement serves as a reminder that even in the competitive world of digital business, there is no room for dishonesty. Success, in the Islamic sense, is not just about profit but about ensuring that one's dealings are pleasing to Allah.

The rise of social media has provided an unparalleled platform for digital entrepreneurs to engage with potential customers, build their brand, and promote their products and services. Platforms such as Instagram, Facebook, LinkedIn, and YouTube have become essential tools for businesses to reach their target audience. However, social media also presents unique challenges. In a space where image often trumps substance, and where marketing can sometimes blur the line between truth and exaggeration, the Muslim entrepreneur must be particularly cautious.

Islam teaches that every word we speak, every action we take, and every interaction we have is recorded and will be accounted for. The Quran states, "Not a word does he (or she) utter, but there is a watcher by him ready (to record it)" (Quran 50:18). For the digital entrepreneur, this means being mindful of how they present their business on social media. It can be tempting to exaggerate the benefits of a product or service in order to gain more customers, but this would go against the principles of halal business. The Muslim entrepreneur must ensure that all marketing efforts are truthful, honest, and respectful, avoiding any form of manipulation or deceit.

Moreover, social media offers an opportunity for Muslim entrepreneurs to build a community around their brand. By sharing not only their products but also their values, stories, and principles, they can attract a loyal following that resonates with their message. This is particularly important in the context of halal business, where the values of trust, honesty, and fairness are paramount. Social media allows the Muslim entrepreneur to demonstrate these values in action, creating a strong bond with their audience based on mutual respect and shared ideals.

One of the most exciting opportunities in digital entrepreneurship is the ability to create and sell digital products. These products, such as online courses, eBooks, software, and subscription services, are not only scalable but can also be delivered instantly to a global audience. For the Muslim entrepreneur, digital products offer a unique opportunity to share valuable knowledge, skills, and services with others while earning halal income. However, as with any business venture, the creation and sale of digital products must adhere to Islamic principles.

The key to success in digital entrepreneurship lies in continuous learning and adaptation. The digital world is constantly evolving, with new technologies, platforms, and trends emerging regularly. For the Muslim entrepreneur, staying informed and adapting to these changes is essential for remaining competitive. However, this learning must always be grounded in the principles of Islam. The Quran encourages us to seek knowledge and grow: "And say: My Lord, increase me in knowledge" (Quran 20:114). This verse serves as a reminder that the pursuit of knowledge is not only a means of improving one's business but also a form of worship when done with the right intention.

In the realm of digital entrepreneurship, learning takes many forms. It involves keeping up with the latest digital marketing strategies, understanding the changing needs of the target audience, and staying informed about the tools and platforms that can help streamline the business. It also means being aware of the challenges and pitfalls that come with operating in the digital space. For instance, data privacy has become a significant concern for consumers, and businesses are expected to handle customer information with the utmost care. The Muslim entrepreneur must ensure that their business complies with all data protection laws and respects the privacy of their customers, as Islam teaches us to protect the rights and dignity of others.

Another important aspect of digital entrepreneurship is building strong partnerships. In the digital world, collaborations with influencers, affiliates, or other businesses can significantly boost visibility and reach. However, the Muslim entrepreneur must be cautious in choosing partners. Partnerships should only be formed with individuals or businesses that share similar values and principles. The Quran warns us, "And cooperate in righteousness and piety, but do not cooperate in sin and aggression" (Quran 5:2). This verse highlights the importance of aligning with others who also prioritize righteousness and ethical behavior. A partnership with a business or individual that engages in haram practices can tarnish the reputation of the entrepreneur and their brand.

One of the greatest advantages of digital entrepreneurship is the flexibility it offers. Unlike traditional businesses that often require a physical presence, a digital business can be operated from anywhere in the world, at any time. This flexibility allows Muslim entrepreneurs to structure their businesses in a way that accommodates their religious obligations, such as the five daily prayers, fasting during Ramadan, and other acts of worship. The freedom to work remotely also enables entrepreneurs to spend more time with family, engage in charitable activities, and pursue personal growth, all while running a successful business.

However, with this flexibility comes the responsibility of managing time effectively. Digital entrepreneurship requires discipline and focus, as the boundaries between work and personal life can easily blur. Islam teaches us the importance of balance in all aspects of life, including how we manage our time. The Prophet Muhammad (PBUH) said, "Take advantage of five before five: your youth before your old age, your health before your sickness, your wealth before your poverty, your free time before your preoccupation, and your life before your death" (Hakim). This hadith serves as a reminder to use one's time wisely and to ensure that business activities do not consume the time that should be dedicated to family, worship, and self-care.

For the Muslim entrepreneur, achieving balance is not only a personal goal but also a business strategy. A business that is built on burnout and overwork is unlikely to succeed in the long term. By prioritizing self-care, maintaining a healthy work-life balance, and staying connected to one's faith, the entrepreneur can create a sustainable business that thrives both financially and spiritually.

Additionally, digital entrepreneurship allows Muslim entrepreneurs to reach and serve a diverse global audience. The internet breaks down geographical barriers, allowing businesses to connect with customers from all corners of the world. This global reach offers immense potential for growth and expansion, but it also comes with the responsibility of respecting cultural differences and understanding the needs of diverse markets. The Quran teaches us that diversity is a sign of Allah's creation: "And among His Signs is the creation of the heavens and the earth, and the variation in your languages and your colors; verily in that are Signs for those who know" (Quran 30:22). For the digital entrepreneur, this means approaching business with cultural sensitivity, ensuring that marketing messages, products, and services are inclusive and respectful of different backgrounds and traditions.

In the ever-evolving world of digital entrepreneurship, one of the most significant challenges is staying ahead of technological advancements. New tools and platforms are being introduced at an unprecedented rate, each offering new ways to streamline business operations, enhance customer engagement, or increase efficiency. For the Muslim entrepreneur, navigating this technological landscape requires both diligence and discernment. Not every technological innovation aligns with the values of halal business, and it is essential to assess each tool or platform carefully before integrating it into the business.

For example, artificial intelligence (AI) and machine learning have transformed how businesses operate, offering automation solutions that save time and reduce costs. However, there are ethical considerations to take into account when using AI, particularly in terms of data privacy and decision-making processes. Islam places great emphasis on the rights of individuals, including their right to privacy. The Quran says, "And do not spy or backbite each other. Would one of you like to eat the flesh of his brother when dead? You would detest it" (Quran 49:12). This verse highlights the importance of respecting the privacy of others, a principle that must be upheld in the digital world. Muslim entrepreneurs must ensure that any AI tools or platforms they use comply with privacy laws and respect the confidentiality of their customers' data.

Another technological advancement that has impacted digital entrepreneurship is blockchain. Originally developed as the underlying technology for cryptocurrencies, blockchain offers a decentralized, transparent, and secure way to manage transactions. While the permissibility of cryptocurrencies is still a topic of debate among Islamic scholars, the underlying blockchain technology has the potential to revolutionize many aspects of business, including supply chain management, contract enforcement, and even financial transactions. For Muslim entrepreneurs, exploring the potential of blockchain while adhering to Islamic principles is a path that could lead to new opportunities in the halal digital economy.

Ultimately, the key to success in digital entrepreneurship is the ability to adapt to changes while remaining grounded in Islamic values. The digital world is fast-paced and constantly changing, but the principles of halal business remain timeless. By staying true to these principles, Muslim entrepreneurs can navigate the complexities of digital entrepreneurship with confidence, knowing that their efforts are pleasing to Allah and beneficial to others.

In the realm of digital entrepreneurship, one of the most important elements is maintaining trust with customers. Trust, or *amanah*, is a cornerstone of any successful business, but in the digital world, where face-to-face interactions are often absent, it becomes even more crucial. Customers must feel confident that the products or services they purchase will be delivered as promised, that their personal information will be protected, and that they are being treated fairly. In Islam, maintaining trust is not just a good business practice—it is a religious obligation. The Quran says, "Indeed, Allah commands you to render trusts to whom they are due" (Quran 4:58).

For the Muslim entrepreneur, building trust online requires transparency and communication. Customers should always be informed about what they are purchasing, how long it will take to receive their goods, and what to expect from the product or service. If there are delays, issues, or unexpected challenges, it is essential to communicate openly with the customer and offer solutions. The Prophet Muhammad (PBUH) emphasized the importance of fulfilling promises, saying, "The signs of a hypocrite are three: When he speaks, he lies; when he makes a promise, he breaks it; and when he is entrusted, he betrays that trust" (Bukhari). Fulfilling promises, whether in digital or physical transactions, is central to maintaining trust in the business.

Moreover, building trust online also means safeguarding the privacy and data of customers. In the digital age, data is one of the most valuable commodities, and many businesses collect personal information to enhance their services or target their marketing efforts. However, Islam teaches that the privacy of individuals must be respected. The Quran warns against invading the privacy of others, stating, "Do not spy on one another" (Quran 49:12). For digital entrepreneurs, this means ensuring that all data collected is done so with the explicit consent of the customer and that the data is stored securely. There must be clear policies in place regarding data protection, and customers should be informed about how their information will be used.

Trust is not just built through policies and practices; it is also built through consistency. A digital business that consistently delivers high-quality products or services, meets its deadlines, and treats customers with respect will naturally foster trust and loyalty. In a world where customers have many options to choose from, trust can often be the deciding factor in whether a customer returns or seeks out another business. For Muslim entrepreneurs, maintaining this trust is not only a business necessity but also a reflection of their commitment to Islamic ethics.

One of the most significant opportunities presented by digital entrepreneurship is the ability to create and sell digital products. These products, which include eBooks, online courses, software, and digital downloads, offer a scalable way to generate income. Unlike physical products, which require inventory, shipping, and logistical management, digital products can be delivered instantly to a global audience with minimal overhead costs. For the Muslim entrepreneur, this represents an ideal way to earn halal income while reaching a wide audience.

However, as with any business venture, the creation and sale of digital products must adhere to Islamic principles. The Prophet Muhammad (PBUH) said, "The best of you are those who learn the Quran and teach it" (Bukhari). This hadith highlights the importance of sharing knowledge, but it also implies that the knowledge shared must be beneficial, truthful, and aligned with Islamic teachings. For entrepreneurs who create digital products, this means ensuring that the content they produce is accurate, ethical, and beneficial to the customer.

The process of creating digital products begins with identifying a need or gap in the market. Whether it is an educational course, a software tool, or an artistic product, the entrepreneur must ask themselves how their offering will benefit others. In Islam, business is not just about making money—it is about contributing to the well-being of society. The Quran says, "Help one another in acts of piety and righteousness" (Quran 5:2). A successful digital entrepreneur understands that their product should solve a problem, fulfill a need, or offer value to the customer in a way that aligns with the values of piety and righteousness.

Additionally, when selling digital products, it is essential to maintain transparency about what the customer is purchasing. The Prophet Muhammad (PBUH) said, "The buyer and the seller have the option of cancelling or confirming the bargain unless they separate, and if they spoke the truth and made clear the defects of the goods, then they would be blessed in their bargain" (Bukhari). This hadith emphasizes the importance of transparency in transactions. If the digital product has limitations, restrictions, or specific requirements, these must be communicated clearly to the customer before the purchase is made.

For Muslim entrepreneurs who are exploring the world of digital products, subscription-based models offer another avenue for success. Subscription models, where customers pay a recurring fee to access content or services, have become increasingly popular in the digital world. Platforms like Netflix, Audible, and various online learning sites have leveraged subscription models to build long-term relationships with customers while generating consistent revenue. For Muslim entrepreneurs, this model can be adapted to create halal subscription services, such as Islamic education platforms, health and wellness programs, or ethical lifestyle products.

One of the key benefits of subscription-based businesses is the ability to build a loyal customer base. By offering valuable, regularly updated content, entrepreneurs can create ongoing relationships with their subscribers, providing them with a steady stream of revenue. However, the subscription model must be implemented in a way that is transparent and fair. Customers should always be informed about what they are subscribing to, how much it will cost, and how they can cancel their subscription if they choose to. Islam emphasizes fairness and justice in all dealings, and this applies to subscription services as well.

Another important consideration in the digital world is the rise of affiliate marketing. Affiliate marketing allows entrepreneurs to earn commissions by promoting other businesses' products or services. This can be a highly profitable model for digital entrepreneurs who have built a loyal audience or have a strong online presence. However, as with any business model, affiliate marketing must be approached with caution to ensure that the products being promoted are halal and that the promotion is done ethically. The Prophet Muhammad (PBUH) said, "A truthful and trustworthy merchant is associated with the Prophets, the upright, and the martyrs" (Tirmidhi). This hadith reminds us that honesty and trustworthiness are essential in all business dealings.

In affiliate marketing, Muslim entrepreneurs must carefully vet the products or services they promote to ensure that they are in line with Islamic values. Promoting products that are haram, such as alcohol, gambling, or interest-based financial products, is strictly prohibited. Additionally, the entrepreneur must be transparent with their audience, clearly stating that they may receive a commission if a purchase is made through their affiliate links. Transparency, honesty, and fairness are all critical components of ethical affiliate marketing.

Another significant opportunity for digital entrepreneurs is the ability to leverage content marketing. Content marketing involves creating and sharing valuable, relevant content to attract and engage a target audience. This content can take many forms, including blog posts, videos, social media updates, and podcasts. The goal of content marketing is to build trust and authority in a particular niche, ultimately leading to increased sales and customer loyalty.

For Muslim entrepreneurs, content marketing provides a unique opportunity to share not only their products but also their values, principles, and knowledge. By creating content that is aligned with Islamic teachings, entrepreneurs can build a strong connection with their audience based on shared beliefs and values. This approach not only fosters trust but also differentiates the entrepreneur from competitors who may focus solely on promoting products.

When engaging in content marketing, it is essential to remember that the content produced should be valuable, informative, and truthful. The Prophet Muhammad (PBUH) said, "Speak good or remain silent" (Bukhari). This hadith serves as a guiding principle for digital entrepreneurs who are creating content. Every piece of content shared should be beneficial, whether it is educating the audience, offering helpful tips, or providing insights into a particular industry. Content marketing should never be used as a means of manipulation or deceit.

Furthermore, content marketing allows Muslim entrepreneurs to demonstrate their commitment to ethical business practices. By sharing behind-the-scenes insights into how their business operates, showcasing their transparency in sourcing products, or highlighting their charitable initiatives, entrepreneurs can build a brand that is not only profitable but also respected for its integrity. The Quran encourages us to "enjoin what is right and forbid what is wrong" (Quran 3:104), and content marketing offers a platform for entrepreneurs to promote goodness and ethical behavior in the marketplace.

In addition to content marketing, email marketing remains one of the most effective tools for digital entrepreneurs. Email marketing allows businesses to communicate directly with their audience, offering personalized messages, product updates, and special promotions. However, like all forms of marketing, email marketing must be done ethically. Customers should only receive emails if they have given their consent, and the content of the emails should be truthful, respectful, and free from any form of manipulation.

When using email marketing, it is important to remember that the Prophet Muhammad (PBUH) encouraged kindness and respect in all interactions. He said, "Whoever believes in Allah and the Last Day should speak a good word or remain silent" (Muslim). This hadith applies to all forms of communication, including email marketing. The messages sent to customers should always be polite, clear, and respectful. Additionally, entrepreneurs must provide an easy way for customers to unsubscribe if they no longer wish to receive emails. Forcing customers to remain on an email list or bombarding them with excessive messages is not only poor business practice but also goes against the principles of respect and fairness in Islam.

One of the emerging trends in digital entrepreneurship is the rise of online marketplaces. Platforms such as Amazon, Etsy, and eBay allow entrepreneurs to sell their products to a global audience without the need to create their own e-commerce site. For Muslim entrepreneurs, online marketplaces provide a unique opportunity to reach a large customer base while maintaining a halal business. However, there are specific challenges that come with selling on these platforms, including competition, fees, and the need to comply with platform policies.

When selling on online marketplaces, it is essential to ensure that all products listed comply with halal standards. This may require thorough research into suppliers, manufacturers, and ingredients. Additionally, Muslim entrepreneurs must be transparent in their product descriptions, providing accurate information about what customers can expect. The Prophet Muhammad (PBUH) said, "The best among you are those who have the best manners and character" (Bukhari). This hadith emphasizes the importance of good character in all interactions, including those with customers on online platforms.

Another critical consideration for entrepreneurs who sell on online marketplaces is maintaining ethical pricing practices. The Quran warns against exploitation, stating, "Give full measure and do not be of those who cause loss" (Quran 26:181). This verse highlights the importance of fairness in pricing. Entrepreneurs must ensure that their prices are reasonable and reflect the true value of the product. Engaging in price gouging or unfair pricing practices not only harms the customer but also goes against the principles of fairness and justice in Islam.

In addition to selling on online marketplaces, many digital entrepreneurs are exploring the world of dropshipping. Dropshipping is a business model where the entrepreneur sells products without holding any inventory. Instead, when a customer makes a purchase, the entrepreneur forwards the order to a supplier who ships the product directly to the customer. This model allows entrepreneurs to start a business with minimal upfront costs, making it an attractive option for those entering the digital space.

However, the dropshipping model presents unique challenges for the Muslim entrepreneur. One of the primary concerns is ensuring that the products being sold are halal. Since the entrepreneur does not physically handle the products, there is a greater risk of selling items that do not meet halal standards. To mitigate this risk, it is essential to carefully vet suppliers and ensure that they provide halal-certified products. The Quran says, "O mankind, eat from whatever is on earth [that is] lawful and good" (Quran 2:168). This verse underscores the importance of ensuring that everything sold or consumed is both halal and wholesome.

Additionally, dropshipping often involves long shipping times, particularly if products are sourced from international suppliers. Entrepreneurs must be transparent with their customers about shipping times and any potential delays. Islam teaches that honesty in business dealings is paramount, and this includes being upfront about the logistics of fulfilling orders. The Prophet Muhammad (PBUH) said, "He who is not trustworthy has no faith" (Ahmad). For the digital entrepreneur, trustworthiness means being transparent about every aspect of the business, including shipping times, product quality, and returns.

In the dropshipping model, customer service becomes especially important. Since the entrepreneur is acting as a middleman between the customer and the supplier, they must ensure that any issues, such as defective products or late shipments, are resolved quickly and fairly. The entrepreneur is responsible for ensuring that the customer has a positive experience, even if the issue lies with the supplier. Providing excellent customer service not only aligns with Islamic values but also helps build a strong reputation in the competitive world of digital business.

Digital entrepreneurship offers boundless potential for those who are willing to embrace its opportunities, but along with this potential comes the weighty responsibility of operating with integrity, especially in a world where the lines between ethical and unethical practices can blur. For the Muslim entrepreneur, ensuring that every facet of their business is compliant with Islamic principles requires constant vigilance and dedication. The Quran reminds us of the importance of acting righteously, "Whoever does righteousness, whether male or female, while he is a believer — We will surely cause him to live a good life" (Quran 16:97). A halal business, grounded in faith and principles, ultimately results in a life that is enriched not just by financial success but by spiritual contentment.

A key factor in maintaining the halal integrity of a digital business is the careful selection of payment gateways and financial partners. Many conventional financial systems operate on the basis of interest (riba), which is explicitly forbidden in Islam. The Quran states, "Allah has permitted trade and has forbidden riba" (Quran 2:275). For Muslim entrepreneurs, this means avoiding financial arrangements that involve interest-bearing loans or payment processing systems that include riba-based fees. Fortunately, there are several halal-compliant alternatives in the digital space, including Islamic banks and fintech platforms that offer interest-free services.

The importance of ethical financial management extends beyond just avoiding riba. It also involves transparency in billing practices, fair pricing, and ensuring that customers are not burdened by hidden fees or unjust charges. The Prophet Muhammad (PBUH) said, "The best earnings are those that are earned by a man's own hands, and every permissible transaction" (Ahmad). This hadith encourages entrepreneurs to earn their income through honest and permissible means, ensuring that all financial dealings are just and transparent.

Moreover, the digital entrepreneur must be mindful of the platforms they use to sell their products or services. Some online platforms and marketplaces may engage in practices that are contrary to Islamic values, such as promoting haram products or supporting industries that exploit vulnerable populations. As Muslim entrepreneurs, it is our responsibility to research the platforms we associate with and ensure that they align with our values. By partnering with ethical platforms, we not only protect our business from engaging in haram practices but also support a global economy that prioritizes justice and fairness.

In the realm of digital entrepreneurship, customer engagement is paramount. The internet has made it easier than ever for businesses to interact with their customers directly, offering personalized experiences and building long-term relationships. For the Muslim entrepreneur, customer engagement is not just about creating a transactional relationship — it's about building trust, offering value, and treating customers with the dignity and respect that Islam commands. The Prophet Muhammad (PBUH) said, "None of you truly believes until he loves for his brother what he loves for himself" (Bukhari). This hadith serves as a guiding principle for entrepreneurs, encouraging them to always act in the best interest of their customers.

One way to enhance customer engagement in the digital space is through personalized marketing strategies. By tailoring content, product recommendations, and promotions to meet the unique needs of individual customers, businesses can create a more meaningful connection with their audience. However, it is essential that this personalization is done ethically. Customers' data should be collected only with their explicit consent, and they should have full control over how their information is used. Islam places a high value on privacy and personal autonomy, and this must be respected in all business dealings.

Social media platforms provide an excellent opportunity for Muslim entrepreneurs to engage with their audience on a deeper level. These platforms allow businesses to showcase their products, share their values, and interact with customers in real time. For many businesses, social media has become a vital tool for building brand loyalty and fostering a sense of community. However, with this visibility comes the responsibility to maintain ethical conduct. The Prophet Muhammad (PBUH) said, "A true believer is one from whom people feel safe and who spares them from harm" (Tirmidhi). This hadith highlights the importance of being a source of benefit and safety to others, which applies to both online and offline interactions.

In the digital world, where negative comments and criticisms can easily spiral out of control, it is essential for Muslim entrepreneurs to respond to feedback with patience and kindness. The Prophet Muhammad (PBUH) was known for his impeccable character, even in the face of hostility, and this serves as an example for all entrepreneurs navigating the challenges of customer relations in the digital age. Responding to criticism with grace and offering solutions rather than defensiveness can turn a negative situation into a positive one, fostering trust and loyalty from customers.

Beyond social media, email marketing remains one of the most effective tools for nurturing customer relationships in the digital space. A well-executed email marketing campaign allows businesses to keep their customers informed about new products, special offers, and important updates. However, as with all forms of communication, email marketing must be done ethically. Customers should only be added to an email list with their explicit permission, and they should have the option to unsubscribe at any time without hassle. The Prophet Muhammad (PBUH) said, "Whoever does not show mercy to the people, Allah will not show mercy to him" (Tirmidhi). This hadith reminds us of the importance of showing kindness and consideration to others, even in seemingly small matters such as email marketing.

One of the key benefits of email marketing is the ability to create a personalized experience for the customer. By segmenting the email list based on customer preferences and purchase history, businesses can send targeted messages that are relevant to each individual. This not only increases the likelihood of a sale but also strengthens the relationship between the customer and the brand. However, personalization should always be done in a way that respects the customer's privacy and autonomy. Islam teaches us to respect the rights of others, and this extends to how we handle their personal information.

As the digital landscape continues to evolve, one of the most exciting developments is the rise of mobile commerce. With the majority of consumers now using smartphones to browse, shop, and engage with businesses, it is essential for entrepreneurs to optimize their digital presence for mobile devices. A mobile-friendly website, easy-to-use apps, and seamless payment options are no longer optional — they are necessary for success in the digital marketplace. However, the convenience of mobile commerce should never come at the expense of ethical business practices. Muslim entrepreneurs must ensure that their mobile platforms are secure, accessible, and free from any haram elements.

In addition to mobile commerce, the growing trend of influencer marketing presents another opportunity for digital entrepreneurs. Influencer marketing involves partnering with individuals who have a large following on social media to promote products or services. While this can be an effective way to reach new customers, it must be approached with caution. Muslim entrepreneurs should only partner with influencers who share their values and adhere to halal standards. Promoting haram products or aligning with influencers who engage in unethical behavior can damage the reputation of the business and go against the principles of Islamic entrepreneurship.

As Muslim entrepreneurs navigate the world of digital marketing, it is essential to remember the concept of *niyyah* — intention. In Islam, intention is everything. The Prophet Muhammad (PBUH) said, "Actions are but by intentions, and every man shall have only that which he intended" (Bukhari). This hadith reminds us that our success in both this world and the Hereafter is determined not only by what we do but by why we do it. For the digital entrepreneur, this means ensuring that every marketing strategy, every promotion, and every interaction is done with the intention of earning halal income and benefiting others.

One of the key challenges in digital marketing is maintaining a balance between promoting products and staying true to Islamic values. In a world where aggressive marketing tactics often dominate, Muslim entrepreneurs must resist the temptation to engage in manipulative or deceptive practices. The Quran instructs us, "And do not mix the truth with falsehood or conceal the truth while you know [it]" (Quran 2:42). This verse serves as a powerful reminder that honesty should always be at the forefront of our marketing efforts. By building a brand that is known for its integrity, transparency, and ethical conduct, Muslim entrepreneurs can foster long-term success and build a loyal customer base.

Another important aspect of digital entrepreneurship is the concept of sustainability. Islam teaches us to be responsible stewards of the Earth and to avoid wastefulness in all forms. The Quran says, "Indeed, the wasteful are brothers of the devils, and ever has Satan been to his Lord ungrateful" (Quran 17:27). For Muslim entrepreneurs, this means adopting sustainable practices in their digital businesses. Whether it's reducing the environmental impact of packaging, sourcing ethical products, or supporting fair trade initiatives, sustainability should be an integral part of any halal business.

The digital world offers unique opportunities for entrepreneurs to contribute to the growing movement of ethical consumerism. More and more consumers are seeking out businesses that prioritize environmental and social responsibility, and this aligns perfectly with the values of halal entrepreneurship. By offering products and services that are not only halal but also environmentally friendly and ethically sourced, Muslim entrepreneurs can differentiate themselves in the market and appeal to a broader audience.

In addition to sustainability, the concept of charity and giving back is central to Islamic entrepreneurship. The Prophet Muhammad (PBUH) said, "Charity does not decrease wealth" (Muslim). This hadith highlights the spiritual and financial benefits of giving back to those in need. For the digital entrepreneur, incorporating charity into the business model is not only a way to earn rewards in the Hereafter but also a powerful way to build a positive brand image and foster customer loyalty.

There are many ways that digital entrepreneurs can incorporate charitable giving into their businesses. Some may choose to donate a portion of their profits to charitable causes, while others may create products or services that directly support a specific cause. For example, an online store selling ethical fashion could donate a percentage of each sale to organizations that support fair labor practices. By aligning the business with charitable initiatives, Muslim entrepreneurs can create a sense of purpose and fulfillment that goes beyond financial success.

The rise of crowdfunding platforms has also made it easier for digital entrepreneurs to support charitable causes. Crowdfunding allows businesses to raise funds for specific projects or initiatives by collecting small contributions from a large number of people. For Muslim entrepreneurs, this presents an opportunity to engage their community in meaningful ways, whether by raising funds for a new product launch, supporting a charitable initiative, or expanding the business. However, it is important to ensure that all crowdfunding efforts are transparent and ethical, with clear communication about how the funds will be used.

Crowdfunding can also be used to support innovative Islamic projects. For example, entrepreneurs could raise funds to create digital platforms that offer Islamic education, ethical investment opportunities, or halal products. By leveraging the power of the digital community, Muslim entrepreneurs can contribute to the growth of the global halal economy while earning halal income.

One of the key benefits of digital entrepreneurship is the ability to scale a business quickly and efficiently. With the right tools and strategies, a small digital business can grow into a global enterprise in a relatively short amount of time. However, scaling a business must be done thoughtfully and ethically. Rapid growth can sometimes lead to cutting corners or sacrificing quality in order to meet demand. The Prophet Muhammad (PBUH) said, "Allah loves that when any one of you does something, you should excel in it" (Al-Bayhaqi). This hadith reminds us that excellence in our work is an act of worship, and we should never compromise on quality, even in the pursuit of growth.

As businesses grow, it becomes increasingly important to establish a strong team that shares the same values and commitment to halal principles. Hiring employees, freelancers, or contractors who understand and respect the values of the business is crucial for maintaining the integrity of the brand. The Prophet Muhammad (PBUH) said, "The best among you are those who have the best manners and character" (Bukhari). For the digital entrepreneur, this means building a team that not only has the skills to help the business succeed but also the character and values to ensure that the business remains true to its Islamic foundation.

In addition to building a strong team, Muslim entrepreneurs must also focus on creating a positive work culture. A halal business is one that treats its employees with dignity and fairness, offering them a safe and respectful work environment. This includes providing fair wages, opportunities for growth, and a healthy work-life balance. The Prophet Muhammad (PBUH) emphasized the importance of treating workers fairly, saying, "Give the worker his wages before his sweat dries" (Ibn Majah). By treating employees with kindness and respect, entrepreneurs can build a strong, motivated team that contributes to the long-term success of the business.

As the business grows, it is also essential to maintain ethical financial practices. Scaling a business often requires investment, but Muslim entrepreneurs must ensure that any financial arrangements are halal and free from riba (interest). Islamic finance offers many alternatives to conventional interest-based loans, such as profit-sharing models and venture capital arrangements. By seeking out halal financing options, entrepreneurs can ensure that their business growth remains in line with Islamic principles.

Another key consideration when scaling a business is maintaining customer satisfaction. As the business grows, it becomes more challenging to maintain the same level of personalized service and attention to detail. However, customer satisfaction should never be sacrificed for the sake of growth. The Prophet Muhammad (PBUH) said, "The most beloved of people to Allah are those who are most beneficial to the people" (Daraqutni). This hadith emphasizes the importance of benefiting others, and for entrepreneurs, this means ensuring that every customer receives the highest level of service, even as the business expands.

The importance of maintaining a strong ethical foundation becomes even more critical as the business expands into new markets. For Muslim entrepreneurs, expanding into international markets presents unique challenges and opportunities. Different cultures, legal systems, and consumer preferences require careful consideration to ensure that the business remains halal in all aspects. The Quran says, "O mankind, indeed We have created you from male and female and made you peoples and tribes that you may know one another" (Quran 49:13). This verse reminds us of the importance of understanding and respecting cultural differences, especially in the global marketplace.

When entering new markets, it is essential to conduct thorough research to understand the local customs, regulations, and consumer expectations. For example, some markets may have specific halal certification requirements that differ from those in the entrepreneur's home country. Ensuring that the business complies with local halal standards is essential for maintaining trust and credibility with customers.

Additionally, when expanding into new markets, it is important to ensure that the marketing and branding efforts are culturally sensitive and respectful. What resonates with customers in one region may not be effective or appropriate in another. By taking the time to understand the needs and preferences of each market, Muslim entrepreneurs can build strong relationships with customers and create a brand that is both globally recognized and locally relevant.

The digital world also offers opportunities for entrepreneurs to diversify their revenue streams. Many successful digital businesses have multiple income sources, including product sales, affiliate marketing, online courses, and digital subscriptions. For Muslim entrepreneurs, diversifying income streams can provide financial stability and reduce reliance on any single revenue source. However, it is essential to ensure that all income streams are halal and in line with Islamic principles. The Prophet Muhammad (PBUH) said, "Halal is clear, and haram is clear, and between them are unclear matters that are unknown to most people" (Bukhari). This hadith serves as a reminder that when in doubt, it is best to avoid any business practice that may be questionable or haram.

By diversifying income streams, digital entrepreneurs can create a resilient business model that is better equipped to withstand economic fluctuations and market changes. This resilience not only benefits the entrepreneur but also allows the business to continue providing value to customers and supporting employees, even in challenging times.

In addition to diversifying income streams, Muslim entrepreneurs should also consider the role of innovation in their digital business. Innovation is not only encouraged in Islam but is also essential for staying competitive in the fast-paced digital world. The Prophet Muhammad (PBUH) said, "Verily, actions are judged by their intentions" (Bukhari). This hadith emphasizes that the intention behind innovation must be to improve the business, benefit customers, and contribute to the greater good.

Innovation can take many forms, from developing new products and services to improving internal processes and customer experiences. For example, digital entrepreneurs can explore the use of artificial intelligence (AI) to enhance customer support, streamline operations, or personalize marketing efforts. However, as with all technological advancements, Muslim entrepreneurs must ensure that the use of AI and other innovations aligns with halal principles. This includes respecting customer privacy, ensuring transparency in decision-making processes, and avoiding any practices that may be exploitative or unjust.

Moreover, innovation in digital entrepreneurship should also focus on creating positive social and environmental impact. The Quran teaches us to "do good as Allah has done good to you" (Quran 28:77). This verse reminds us of the importance of using our resources and talents to benefit others. For the digital entrepreneur, this means exploring innovative ways to reduce the environmental footprint of the business, support ethical labor practices, and contribute to the well-being of society.

As Muslim entrepreneurs continue to navigate the challenges and opportunities of digital entrepreneurship, it is essential to remain grounded in the principles of Islam. The digital world may be fast-paced and constantly changing, but the values of honesty, fairness, and responsibility remain timeless. By staying true to these principles, Muslim entrepreneurs can create businesses that are not only successful in the worldly sense but are also blessed with barakah, benefiting both the entrepreneur and the wider community.

The digital marketplace, vast and borderless, offers an unparalleled platform for Muslim entrepreneurs to promote their products and services while remaining true to Islamic values. Yet, as the digital world continues to evolve, so too must the strategies employed by those seeking to carve out a space in this competitive environment. For the Muslim entrepreneur, success in this space is not just measured by profit margins or the number of customers acquired but by the barakah (blessing) that comes from running a business aligned with Islamic ethics.

As Muslim entrepreneurs grow their digital businesses, one key area that often requires attention is customer service. In the digital world, where physical interaction is minimal, customer service can make or break a business. Providing prompt, efficient, and kind customer service is more than just a business strategy; it is a reflection of Islamic values. The Prophet Muhammad (PBUH) emphasized the importance of kindness and empathy, stating, "He who is deprived of kindness is deprived of goodness" (Muslim). For the digital entrepreneur, this means ensuring that every interaction with customers, whether through email, social media, or live chat, is handled with care, respect, and attentiveness.

Customer service is also an opportunity to build loyalty and trust. In the absence of face-to-face interactions, customers rely heavily on the quality of service they receive to form their impressions of a business. Responding promptly to inquiries, addressing concerns with patience, and going above and beyond to resolve issues can leave a lasting positive impression. This not only encourages repeat business but also fosters a reputation for excellence in the marketplace.

In the digital sphere, word-of-mouth spreads quickly, and businesses that fail to provide adequate customer service risk damaging their reputation. Negative reviews, complaints, and public criticisms can circulate online, potentially deterring new customers. As Muslim entrepreneurs, it is crucial to be proactive in resolving customer issues and to approach every situation with humility and a desire to serve. The Quran advises, "And the servants of the Most Merciful are those who walk upon the earth humbly, and when the ignorant address them harshly, they say [words of] peace" (Quran 25:63). This verse serves as a reminder to respond to negativity with calmness and composure, ensuring that the business remains a source of positive engagement, even in challenging situations.

In addition to providing exceptional customer service, digital entrepreneurs must also focus on building a strong brand presence. A brand is more than just a logo or a color scheme; it is the embodiment of the values, mission, and vision of the business. For Muslim entrepreneurs, building a brand that reflects Islamic principles is crucial to attracting and retaining a loyal customer base. A halal business should not only promote its products or services but also its commitment to fairness, transparency, and ethical behavior.

Branding in the digital space requires a consistent and cohesive strategy. Every aspect of the business, from the website design to social media posts, should align with the brand's core values. Consistency in messaging, tone, and visual elements helps to build trust with customers and creates a memorable and recognizable brand identity. The Prophet Muhammad (PBUH) said, "Allah loves that when you do anything, you do it with excellence" (Bukhari). This hadith encourages entrepreneurs to strive for excellence in all aspects of their business, including branding and marketing.

One way to strengthen a brand is through storytelling. Storytelling allows entrepreneurs to connect with their audience on a deeper level by sharing the story behind their business, the challenges they've overcome, and the values that drive them. For Muslim entrepreneurs, storytelling provides an opportunity to showcase the ethical foundation of their business, highlighting how their products or services align with Islamic teachings. This not only differentiates the brand from competitors but also fosters a sense of authenticity and trust.

Another critical component of branding is authenticity. In a digital world filled with advertisements and marketing messages, customers are increasingly drawn to brands that are genuine and transparent. Muslim entrepreneurs must ensure that their brand remains authentic by staying true to their values and principles. This means avoiding deceptive marketing tactics, being honest about the benefits and limitations of their products, and maintaining a clear and open line of communication with their customers.

A major part of building an authentic brand in the digital space is transparency, particularly when it comes to product sourcing and ethical practices. Consumers today are more conscious of where their products come from and how they are made. They want to know that the brands they support are committed to sustainability, ethical labor practices, and environmental responsibility. For Muslim entrepreneurs, this presents an opportunity to showcase their commitment to ethical business practices that align with Islamic values.

Islam teaches us to be stewards of the Earth and to avoid exploitation in all its forms. The Quran says, "And do not commit abuse on the earth, spreading corruption" (Quran 2:60). For the digital entrepreneur, this means ensuring that their supply chain is free from exploitation, that their products are sourced ethically, and that they are doing their part to minimize the environmental impact of their business. By being transparent about these practices, Muslim entrepreneurs can build a brand that is not only halal but also sustainable and socially responsible.

Transparency is also crucial when it comes to pricing. In Islam, fair and honest pricing is a core principle of halal business. The Prophet Muhammad (PBUH) said, "The one who cheats us is not one of us" (Muslim). This hadith emphasizes the importance of honesty in all transactions, including how prices are set. Digital entrepreneurs must ensure that their prices are fair and reflect the true value of their products or services. Engaging in price manipulation, overcharging, or hiding costs goes against the principles of halal business and can damage the trust that customers have in the brand.

In the digital world, where customers may not have the opportunity to physically inspect a product before purchasing, transparency in product descriptions is essential. Muslim entrepreneurs must provide accurate and detailed information about their products, ensuring that customers know exactly what they are buying. If a product has any defects or limitations, these should be clearly communicated to the customer before the purchase is made. The Quran instructs, "O you who have believed, do not consume one another's wealth unjustly" (Quran 4:29). This verse serves as a reminder that honest and transparent business dealings are a fundamental aspect of Islamic entrepreneurship.

In the world of digital entrepreneurship, maintaining a competitive edge requires continuous innovation and improvement. The digital marketplace is constantly evolving, with new technologies, platforms, and consumer preferences emerging at a rapid pace. For the Muslim entrepreneur, staying competitive means being open to innovation while remaining grounded in Islamic principles. The Quran encourages us to seek knowledge and strive for excellence: "Say, 'My Lord, increase me in knowledge'" (Quran 20:114).

One area of innovation that is particularly relevant to digital entrepreneurship is the rise of artificial intelligence (AI) and automation. AI tools can be used to streamline operations, enhance customer experiences, and personalize marketing efforts. For example, chatbots can provide instant customer support, AI algorithms can analyze customer data to offer personalized product recommendations, and automation tools can help manage social media accounts and email campaigns. However, as with all technological advancements, it is important to ensure that these tools are used ethically and in line with Islamic values.

When using AI and automation, Muslim entrepreneurs must prioritize transparency and fairness. Customers should be informed when they are interacting with an AI system, and their data must be handled responsibly and securely. Islam places a high value on privacy and protecting the dignity of individuals, and this must be reflected in how businesses use AI and data. The Quran warns against prying into the affairs of others: "And do not spy or backbite each other" (Quran 49:12). For digital entrepreneurs, this means ensuring that customer data is never misused or exploited for personal gain.

Innovation also extends to how businesses approach their products and services. Muslim entrepreneurs should constantly be looking for ways to improve their offerings, whether through better quality, new features, or more efficient processes. The Prophet Muhammad (PBUH) encouraged continuous improvement, saying, "Whoever seeks to complete something perfectly and puts in the effort, Allah will perfect his work" (Al-Bukhari). This hadith serves as a reminder that striving for excellence in all aspects of business is a form of worship, and by seeking to innovate and improve, entrepreneurs can achieve both worldly success and spiritual fulfillment.

Another important aspect of digital entrepreneurship is building strong, lasting relationships with customers. In the absence of physical stores, digital entrepreneurs must rely on online interactions to build trust and loyalty with their audience. This requires a proactive approach to customer engagement, ensuring that customers feel valued and heard at every stage of their journey. The Prophet Muhammad (PBUH) said, "The believer is one who is sociable, and there is no good in one who is not sociable" (Tabarani). This hadith encourages Muslims to be approachable and sociable, traits that are essential in the world of digital business.

One way to foster these relationships is through the creation of an online community. Social media platforms, forums, and email newsletters provide an excellent opportunity for entrepreneurs to build a sense of community around their brand. By creating spaces where customers can engage with the business, ask questions, share feedback, and connect with other customers, entrepreneurs can strengthen their relationships and build a loyal following. This community-building approach not only enhances the customer experience but also creates opportunities for word-of-mouth marketing, as satisfied customers are more likely to recommend the brand to others.

Another strategy for building lasting relationships is through customer feedback. Asking customers for their input, whether through surveys, reviews, or direct conversations, shows that the business values their opinions and is committed to continuous improvement. However, it is important to act on this feedback in a meaningful way. The Prophet Muhammad (PBUH) said, "The best of people are those who are most beneficial to others" (Daraqutni). For the digital entrepreneur, this means using customer feedback to make improvements that benefit the customer and enhance the overall experience.

As the business grows, it is essential to maintain the same level of personalized service and attention that helped establish the business in the first place. Scaling a business does not mean sacrificing quality or customer satisfaction. In fact, as the business expands, it becomes even more important to ensure that every customer interaction reflects the values of fairness, transparency, and kindness that are central to Islamic entrepreneurship. By remaining committed to these values, Muslim entrepreneurs can build businesses that are not only successful in the digital marketplace but are also blessed with barakah and long-term success.

CHAPTER 3: HALAL FINANCE: BUILDING WEALTH WITH INTEGRITY

In the grand mosaic of commerce and finance, few elements are as fundamental and transformative as the concept of wealth. Throughout human history, the pursuit of financial stability has driven empires, inspired revolutions, and shaped societies. Yet, in the pursuit of wealth, a line must be drawn between ethical accumulation and reckless ambition. For Muslim entrepreneurs, this line is drawn clearly by the divine laws of halal finance, an extraordinary guide that promises both prosperity and spiritual well-being. To understand the gravity of halal finance is to understand the moral weight that wealth carries and the duties it imposes.

Wealth in Islam is not a forbidden or frowned-upon pursuit. On the contrary, earning a livelihood is seen as a noble endeavor, a means through which individuals can provide for their families, support their communities, and contribute to the welfare of society at large. Yet, while the pursuit of wealth is permitted, it is bound by the moral and ethical limits set forth by Islamic principles. Halal finance is not simply about the absence of riba (interest); it is about fostering a financial system that is just, equitable, and grounded in mutual benefit.

At its heart, the concept of halal finance is a rejection of exploitation, whether it be through interest-bearing loans, deceptive practices, or monopolistic control. The Prophet Muhammad (PBUH) emphasized fairness in transactions and warned against the dangers of riba, declaring, "Allah has cursed the one who consumes riba, the one who gives it, the one who records it, and the two witnesses" (Muslim). This strong condemnation highlights the spiritual consequences of engaging in financial practices that lead to exploitation and inequality.

In today's world, where financial markets are often driven by speculation, greed, and the unrelenting pursuit of profit at any cost, halal finance offers a powerful alternative. It reminds us that wealth is a trust from Allah and must be earned and managed in ways that uphold justice, fairness, and compassion. For Muslim entrepreneurs, understanding and adhering to the principles of halal finance is not only a religious obligation but a way to ensure that their wealth is blessed with barakah and that their businesses contribute to the greater good.

The prohibition of riba is one of the most well-known aspects of halal finance, and it is a principle that sets Islamic finance apart from conventional financial systems. Riba, or interest, is seen as a form of exploitation, as it allows the lender to profit from the borrower's need without providing any real value or benefit. In Islam, wealth should be earned through trade, investment, and productive enterprise — activities that generate value and contribute to the betterment of society. The Quran states, "Allah has permitted trade and has forbidden riba" (Quran 2:275), drawing a clear distinction between ethical commerce and exploitative practices.

For Muslim entrepreneurs, avoiding riba can be challenging, especially in today's global financial system, where interest-based loans and investments are ubiquitous. However, Islamic finance offers several alternatives that allow businesses to grow and thrive without compromising their principles. One of the most common alternatives to conventional loans is the concept of mudarabah, a profit-sharing agreement where the financier provides the capital and the entrepreneur provides the expertise and management. Profits are shared between the two parties, but if the business incurs a loss, the financier bears the financial loss, while the entrepreneur loses only their time and effort.

This partnership model is not only halal but also promotes fairness and risk-sharing, which are central tenets of Islamic finance. By sharing both the risks and rewards of a business venture, mudarabah ensures that neither party is unfairly burdened or disproportionately enriched. This model stands in stark contrast to conventional loans, where the borrower bears all the risk and must repay the loan with interest, regardless of whether the business succeeds or fails.

Another key principle of halal finance is the concept of musharakah, which is a joint venture where all parties contribute capital and share in the profits and losses according to a predetermined ratio. Like mudarabah, musharakah promotes cooperation and shared responsibility, ensuring that wealth is generated in a way that benefits all parties involved. This model is particularly well-suited to entrepreneurs who wish to grow their businesses without resorting to interest-based financing, as it allows them to attract investment while maintaining their commitment to halal principles.

The beauty of halal finance lies in its inherent justice and balance. In a world where financial systems often create vast inequalities, Islamic finance offers a model that seeks to uplift individuals and communities while ensuring that wealth is distributed fairly. The Quran reminds us, "O you who have believed, do not consume one another's wealth unjustly, but only [in lawful] business by mutual consent" (Quran 4:29). This verse emphasizes the importance of mutual consent and fairness in all financial transactions, a principle that is at the core of halal finance.

For Muslim entrepreneurs, embracing halal finance is not just about avoiding riba; it is about building wealth with integrity and ensuring that their financial dealings are grounded in fairness and transparency. This commitment to ethical finance extends beyond the avoidance of interest-bearing loans to encompass a wide range of financial practices, including investments, partnerships, and charitable giving.

One of the key principles of halal finance is the prohibition of gharar, which refers to excessive uncertainty or ambiguity in financial transactions. In Islam, all parties to a transaction must have full knowledge and understanding of the terms of the agreement, and any form of deceit or exploitation is strictly prohibited. This principle is particularly relevant in today's financial markets, where speculative investments and high-risk ventures often dominate. Halal finance encourages transparency and accountability, ensuring that financial transactions are conducted in a way that is clear, fair, and mutually beneficial.

In addition to promoting fairness and transparency, halal finance also places a strong emphasis on social responsibility. Wealth is not meant to be hoarded or used solely for personal gain; it is a trust from Allah that must be used to benefit others. This is why zakat, the obligatory charity on wealth, is one of the five pillars of Islam. Zakat serves as a means of redistributing wealth within the community, ensuring that the less fortunate are cared for and that wealth does not become concentrated in the hands of a few. The Quran says, "Take from their wealth a charity by which you purify them and cause them increase" (Quran 9:103). This verse highlights the spiritual and societal benefits of zakat, which purifies wealth and brings blessings to both the giver and the receiver.

For Muslim entrepreneurs, zakat is not just a financial obligation; it is a powerful tool for fostering social justice and building a more equitable society. By giving a portion of their wealth to those in need, entrepreneurs not only fulfill their religious duty but also contribute to the well-being of their communities. In this way, halal finance serves as a bridge between personal prosperity and collective welfare, ensuring that wealth is used in ways that benefit society as a whole.

In addition to zakat, the concept of sadaqah, or voluntary charity, plays an important role in halal finance. While zakat is obligatory for those who meet certain financial criteria, sadaqah is encouraged for all Muslims, regardless of their financial situation. The Prophet Muhammad (PBUH) said, "Charity does not decrease wealth" (Muslim), emphasizing the idea that giving to others brings barakah, or blessings, to one's wealth. For Muslim entrepreneurs, sadaqah provides an additional way to give back to society and ensure that their wealth is used in ways that please Allah.

Another important aspect of halal finance is ethical investing. In Islam, wealth must be earned and invested in ways that are halal, or permissible. This means avoiding investments in industries that are considered haram, such as alcohol, gambling, and tobacco, as well as any ventures that involve exploitation or harm to others. The Quran warns against earning wealth through unethical means: "Do not consume one another's wealth unjustly or send it [in bribery] to the rulers in order that [they might aid] you [to] consume a portion of the wealth of the people in sin" (Quran 2:188).

For Muslim entrepreneurs, ethical investing is a way to ensure that their wealth grows in ways that are aligned with Islamic values. By carefully selecting investments that promote social good, environmental sustainability, and ethical business practices, entrepreneurs can build wealth in a way that benefits both themselves and society. In recent years, the rise of Islamic investment funds and halal financial products has made it easier for Muslim entrepreneurs to find investment opportunities that align with their values. These funds operate on the principles of halal finance, ensuring that all investments are free from riba, gharar, and unethical practices.

Ethical investing also includes the concept of *istithmar halal*, or halal entrepreneurship, where the entrepreneur seeks to invest in businesses that contribute positively to society. This means supporting industries that promote health, education, environmental protection, and social welfare. The Quran encourages Muslims to seek out lawful and beneficial endeavors, stating, "And do not desire corruption in the land. Indeed, Allah does not like corrupters" (Quran 28:77). For the Muslim entrepreneur, this verse serves as a reminder that wealth should be earned and invested in ways that benefit the world, rather than contribute to its harm.

The rise of socially responsible investing (SRI) has created new opportunities for Muslim entrepreneurs to align their financial goals with their ethical values. SRI involves selecting investments that prioritize environmental, social, and governance (ESG) criteria, ensuring that companies operate in ways that are sustainable and socially responsible. By incorporating SRI principles into their investment strategies, Muslim entrepreneurs can ensure that their wealth grows in ways that are not only halal but also beneficial to society as a whole.

Another important concept in halal finance is the idea of *qard hasan*, or interest-free loans. In Islam, lending money to those in need is seen as a virtuous act, but it must be done without charging interest. The Quran says, "Who is it that will loan Allah a goodly loan so that He may multiply it for him many times over?" (Quran 2:245). This verse emphasizes the idea that lending money without seeking personal gain is a noble deed that will be rewarded by Allah. For Muslim entrepreneurs, *qard hasan* provides a way to support their fellow Muslims by offering interest-free loans to those in need, whether for personal or business purposes.

The practice of *qard hasan* is particularly relevant in the context of Islamic microfinance, which provides small, interest-free loans to entrepreneurs in developing countries who may not have access to traditional banking services. Islamic microfinance operates on the principles of halal finance, ensuring that all loans are free from riba and that the terms of the loan are fair and transparent. By supporting microfinance initiatives, Muslim entrepreneurs can help create economic opportunities for individuals and communities who are often marginalized by conventional financial systems.

Microfinance is a powerful tool for alleviating poverty and promoting economic development, and it aligns perfectly with the principles of halal finance. The Quran encourages Muslims to support those in need, stating, "The believers are but brothers, so make settlement between your brothers" (Quran 49:10). Through microfinance, Muslim entrepreneurs can help uplift their brothers and sisters by providing them with the financial resources they need to start or grow their own businesses. This not only contributes to individual prosperity but also fosters a sense of solidarity and mutual support within the community.

For Muslim entrepreneurs, engaging in halal finance is not just about personal wealth creation; it is about building a financial system that is just, equitable, and aligned with Islamic values. Whether through ethical investing, profit-sharing partnerships, or charitable giving, halal finance offers a model that prioritizes the well-being of individuals and society over the pursuit of profit at any cost. The Prophet Muhammad (PBUH) said, "The best of people are those who bring the most benefit to others" (Daraqutni). This hadith serves as a guiding principle for Muslim entrepreneurs, reminding them that their financial success should be used as a means to benefit others and contribute to the greater good.

In addition to the financial benefits of adhering to halal principles, Muslim entrepreneurs who embrace halal finance also experience the spiritual rewards of earning halal income. The Prophet Muhammad (PBUH) said, "O people, Allah is good and He accepts only that which is good" (Muslim). This hadith highlights the importance of ensuring that all wealth is earned through lawful means, as only halal income is pleasing to Allah. For the Muslim entrepreneur, this means that every financial decision, from how wealth is earned to how it is invested and distributed, must be guided by the principles of halal finance.

By adhering to these principles, Muslim entrepreneurs can ensure that their businesses are not only profitable but also blessed with barakah. Halal finance offers a path to prosperity that is rooted in justice, fairness, and social responsibility, ensuring that wealth is earned and used in ways that are pleasing to Allah. Through ethical investing, profit-sharing partnerships, charitable giving, and interest-free loans, Muslim entrepreneurs can build wealth with integrity and contribute to the betterment of society.

The ethical landscape of halal finance extends far beyond the mere accumulation of wealth. It calls for a conscious engagement with the world, where the pursuit of profit is tempered by a moral obligation to do good. Wealth in Islam is not viewed as an end in itself but as a tool to achieve higher purposes, fostering both individual well-being and societal welfare. The Prophet Muhammad (PBUH) famously said, "The upper hand is better than the lower hand" (Bukhari), encouraging Muslims to strive to be givers, contributors, and sources of benefit to others. In halal finance, this concept is woven deeply into the fabric of every financial transaction.

One of the remarkable features of halal finance is the emphasis on risk-sharing, which is enshrined in contracts like *mudarabah* and *musharakah*. Unlike conventional financial systems, where interest-bearing loans shift all the risk to the borrower, Islamic finance promotes a more equitable model where both parties share in the risk and reward of the venture. This mutual commitment creates a stronger partnership between the investor and the entrepreneur, fostering a sense of shared responsibility and accountability. The Quran teaches, "Help one another in acts of righteousness and piety, but do not help one another in sin and aggression" (Quran 5:2), reminding Muslim entrepreneurs of the importance of building relationships that are rooted in fairness and justice.

For the Muslim entrepreneur, this principle of risk-sharing not only aligns with Islamic teachings but also enhances the long-term sustainability of their business. In a world where financial instability and inequality have become pressing issues, halal finance offers a model that promotes stability and resilience. By ensuring that wealth is generated in a way that benefits all stakeholders, Muslim entrepreneurs can build businesses that are not only profitable but also enduring. This commitment to fairness and mutual benefit is what sets halal finance apart from conventional models, where profit is often prioritized at the expense of ethical considerations.

In addition to promoting fairness and risk-sharing, halal finance also emphasizes the importance of financial transparency. In Islam, there is no room for deceit, ambiguity, or exploitation in financial dealings. The Quran instructs, "O you who have believed, do not consume one another's wealth unjustly or send it [in bribery] to the rulers in order that [they might aid] you [to] consume a portion of the wealth of the people in sin" (Quran 2:188). For the Muslim entrepreneur, this means ensuring that every financial transaction is conducted with full transparency, that all parties have a clear understanding of the terms, and that there are no hidden costs or unethical practices involved.

Transparency is particularly important when it comes to contracts, partnerships, and investments. In halal finance, all contracts must be clear, unambiguous, and free from any form of deception or uncertainty. This principle, known as *gharar*, prohibits excessive risk or speculation in financial transactions. Islam encourages trade and investment but condemns gambling, speculation, and any activity that involves taking advantage of uncertainty or ignorance. The Prophet Muhammad (PBUH) warned against transactions that involve deception, saying, "He who deceives is not one of us" (Muslim). For the Muslim entrepreneur, this means that every contract must be honest, clear, and fair, ensuring that all parties are fully aware of their rights and obligations.

In today's financial markets, where speculative investments and high-risk ventures often dominate, the principle of *gharar* serves as a powerful reminder of the importance of ethical business practices. Muslim entrepreneurs are encouraged to avoid investments that involve excessive risk or uncertainty, such as day trading, speculative real estate ventures, or high-risk financial derivatives. Instead, they should seek out investments that are stable, productive, and beneficial to society. By adhering to the principle of *gharar*, Muslim entrepreneurs can ensure that their wealth is earned in a way that is ethical, sustainable, and pleasing to Allah.

Another key aspect of halal finance is the concept of wealth redistribution, which is embodied in the practice of *zakat*. Zakat is not simply a charitable act; it is a religious obligation that ensures the fair distribution of wealth within the community. The Quran states, "Take from their wealth a charity by which you purify them and cause them increase, and invoke [Allah's blessings] upon them. Indeed, your invocations are reassurance for them" (Quran 9:103). By giving *zakat*, Muslim entrepreneurs purify their wealth, protect themselves from greed, and contribute to the welfare of society. Zakat ensures that wealth is not hoarded by a few but is shared with those in need, helping to reduce poverty and promote social justice.

For the Muslim entrepreneur, *zakat* represents a powerful tool for fostering economic equality and supporting the most vulnerable members of society. It is a reminder that wealth is a trust from Allah and must be used in ways that benefit others. By giving *zakat*, entrepreneurs not only fulfill their religious obligations but also create a ripple effect of positive change within their communities. The act of giving strengthens social bonds, fosters compassion, and ensures that no one is left behind in the pursuit of economic prosperity.

In addition to *zakat*, the concept of *waqf* (endowment) plays a significant role in Islamic finance and wealth redistribution. A *waqf* is a charitable endowment, typically in the form of property or assets, that is set aside for a specific social or religious purpose. Once established, a *waqf* cannot be sold, inherited, or used for any purpose other than the one for which it was intended. Throughout Islamic history, *waqf* has played a crucial role in supporting education, healthcare, social services, and religious institutions. The Prophet Muhammad (PBUH) said, "When a person dies, his deeds come to an end except for three: ongoing charity, knowledge that is benefited from, or a righteous child who prays for him" (Muslim). A *waqf* represents ongoing charity, as it continues to benefit others long after the donor has passed away.

For Muslim entrepreneurs, establishing a *waqf* is a way to leave a lasting legacy and contribute to the long-term well-being of society. Whether by donating land for a school, setting up a scholarship fund, or supporting a hospital, entrepreneurs can use their wealth to create enduring positive change. In doing so, they not only benefit from the spiritual rewards of ongoing charity but also contribute to the development of their communities in meaningful and lasting ways. The concept of *waqf* aligns perfectly with the principles of halal finance, as it ensures that wealth is used for the greater good and remains a source of benefit for future generations.

Another key principle of halal finance is the prohibition of investing in industries that are considered haram, such as alcohol, gambling, tobacco, and adult entertainment. The Quran explicitly forbids engaging in activities that promote harm, stating, "O you who have believed, indeed, intoxicants, gambling, [sacrificing on] stone alters [to other than Allah], and divining arrows are but defilement from the work of Satan, so avoid it that you may be successful" (Quran 5:90). For Muslim entrepreneurs, this means that their investments and business activities must be aligned with Islamic values, avoiding industries that exploit or harm individuals and society.

Ethical investing, also known as socially responsible investing (SRI), is becoming increasingly popular as more people seek to align their financial goals with their values. For Muslim entrepreneurs, SRI offers a way to grow their wealth in ways that are consistent with halal principles. By investing in industries that promote health, education, environmental sustainability, and social welfare, entrepreneurs can ensure that their wealth is being used to create positive change in the world. This ethical approach to investing is not only beneficial for society but also helps to ensure that wealth is earned in a way that is blessed with barakah.

In the modern world, where financial markets are often driven by short-term gains and speculative investments, halal finance offers a refreshing alternative that prioritizes long-term stability and social good. By focusing on ethical investing, risk-sharing, and wealth redistribution, halal finance creates a financial system that is not only just and equitable but also sustainable and resilient. For Muslim entrepreneurs, this model provides a blueprint for building wealth in ways that are aligned with Islamic teachings and that contribute to the well-being of society.

One of the key benefits of adhering to halal finance principles is the peace of mind that comes from knowing that one's wealth is earned through lawful means. The Prophet Muhammad (PBUH) said, "There will come a time when people will not care how they get their money, whether lawfully or unlawfully" (Bukhari). This hadith serves as a warning about the dangers of unethical financial practices, reminding Muslims of the importance of earning wealth in a way that is halal. For the Muslim entrepreneur, following halal finance principles ensures that their wealth is not tainted by unlawful or unethical practices and that their financial success is pleasing to Allah.

Another important aspect of halal finance is the concept of *qard hasan*, or interest-free loans. As mentioned earlier, Islam strictly prohibits the charging of interest on loans, as it is seen as a form of exploitation. Instead, Muslims are encouraged to offer *qard hasan*—loans that are given without interest and with the intention of helping the borrower. The Quran states, "Who is it that will loan Allah a goodly loan so that He may multiply it for him many times over?" (Quran 2:245). This verse emphasizes the spiritual rewards of offering *qard hasan* and the importance of helping those in need.

For Muslim entrepreneurs, offering *qard hasan* provides a way to support their fellow Muslims and contribute to the economic well-being of their communities. Whether by offering interest-free loans to help others start their own businesses, invest in education, or cover personal expenses, entrepreneurs can play a crucial role in fostering economic empowerment and financial stability. The practice of *qard hasan* not only benefits the borrower but also brings blessings to the lender, as it is seen as an act of charity that is rewarded by Allah.

The concept of *qard hasan* is particularly relevant in the context of Islamic microfinance, which provides small, interest-free loans to entrepreneurs in developing countries. Islamic microfinance has proven to be a powerful tool for poverty alleviation, as it empowers individuals to start their own businesses, generate income, and improve their quality of life. Unlike conventional microfinance, which often charges high interest rates, Islamic microfinance operates on the principles of halal finance, ensuring that all loans are free from riba and that the terms of the loan are fair and transparent.

By supporting Islamic microfinance initiatives, Muslim entrepreneurs can help create economic opportunities for individuals and communities who are often excluded from traditional financial systems. This not only contributes to poverty reduction but also promotes social justice and economic empowerment. The Quran encourages Muslims to support one another in acts of goodness, stating, "The believers are but brothers, so make settlement between your brothers" (Quran 49:10). Through Islamic microfinance, Muslim entrepreneurs can fulfill this obligation by providing their brothers and sisters with the financial resources they need to achieve economic independence and success.

In addition to *qard hasan* and microfinance, the practice of *istithmar halal* (halal entrepreneurship) offers Muslim entrepreneurs a way to invest in businesses that contribute positively to society. This concept emphasizes the importance of supporting industries that promote health, education, environmental protection, and social welfare. By investing in halal businesses, entrepreneurs can ensure that their wealth grows in ways that are not only halal but also beneficial to the world. The Quran instructs, "And do not desire corruption in the land. Indeed, Allah does not like corrupters" (Quran 28:77), reminding Muslim entrepreneurs of their responsibility to avoid industries that harm people or the environment.

As the global economy becomes increasingly interconnected, Muslim entrepreneurs have the opportunity to play a leading role in promoting ethical business practices and halal finance on a global scale. By adhering to the principles of halal finance, entrepreneurs can build businesses that are not only profitable but also serve as models of integrity, fairness, and social responsibility. In doing so, they contribute to the development of a financial system that prioritizes human dignity, social justice, and environmental sustainability, ensuring that wealth is used in ways that benefit all of humanity.

One of the most exciting developments in the field of halal finance is the rise of Islamic fintech (financial technology). Islamic fintech combines the principles of halal finance with cutting-edge technology to create innovative financial products and services that are accessible, transparent, and aligned with Islamic values. From mobile banking apps to peer-to-peer lending platforms, Islamic fintech is revolutionizing the way Muslims manage their finances, offering new opportunities for wealth creation, financial inclusion, and economic empowerment.

For Muslim entrepreneurs, Islamic fintech presents a unique opportunity to leverage technology to promote halal finance and reach a wider audience. Whether by developing their own fintech platforms or partnering with existing fintech companies, entrepreneurs can use technology to provide halal financial services to underserved populations, particularly in developing countries where access to traditional banking services is limited. The Quran encourages Muslims to seek out lawful and beneficial endeavors, stating, "And spend in the way of Allah and do not throw [yourselves] with your [own] hands into destruction [by refraining]. And do good; indeed, Allah loves the doers of good" (Quran 2:195).

Islamic fintech also offers a way to enhance financial transparency and accountability, as many fintech platforms are built on blockchain technology, which provides a secure, decentralized, and tamper-proof record of transactions. This aligns with the principles of halal finance, which emphasize the importance of transparency, fairness, and ethical conduct in all financial dealings. By using blockchain technology, Islamic fintech platforms can ensure that financial transactions are conducted in a way that is fully transparent, reducing the risk of fraud and corruption.

Another key area of innovation in Islamic fintech is the development of digital *waqf* platforms. These platforms allow individuals and businesses to create and manage *waqf* endowments online, making it easier for Muslims to establish charitable endowments and contribute to social and religious causes. By digitizing the *waqf* process, Islamic fintech is helping to revitalize this important institution and ensure that it remains a powerful tool for social welfare in the modern world.

As Islamic fintech continues to evolve, it is opening up new possibilities for how Muslim entrepreneurs engage with the world of finance. By integrating technology with the values of halal finance, it allows for more inclusive and ethical financial solutions. For instance, mobile banking applications powered by Islamic fintech enable individuals in remote areas or those without access to traditional banking services to manage their finances easily and securely. This empowers people from all walks of life to participate in the financial system while adhering to their faith.

In addition to mobile banking, peer-to-peer (P2P) lending platforms built on Islamic finance principles offer an innovative way for Muslims to access interest-free loans. These platforms connect borrowers and lenders directly, eliminating the need for intermediaries like banks, and ensuring that transactions are free from riba. The Quran reminds us, "Whoever fears Allah – He will make for him a way out and will provide for him from where he does not expect" (Quran 65:2-3). This verse serves as a reassurance that when we uphold Islamic values in our dealings, including financial transactions, Allah will provide sustenance in ways that are beyond our expectations.

P2P lending platforms are especially valuable for entrepreneurs and small business owners who may not qualify for traditional financing. By leveraging these platforms, Muslim entrepreneurs can raise funds for their business ventures while avoiding interest-based loans. These platforms also foster a sense of community and mutual support, as individuals come together to help one another succeed financially. In many ways, this mirrors the principles of Islamic microfinance, where wealth is shared, and risks are distributed, promoting social equity and economic empowerment.

Moreover, Islamic fintech is not limited to lending and banking. It also encompasses a wide range of services, including zakat collection platforms, ethical investment portfolios, and digital gold trading platforms. Zakat collection platforms streamline the process of calculating and distributing zakat, ensuring that the obligations of Muslim entrepreneurs and individuals are met efficiently. This not only fulfills the religious duty of zakat but also contributes to the wider economic well-being of the ummah by redistributing wealth to those in need.

Ethical investment portfolios, powered by Islamic fintech, enable Muslim investors to build diversified portfolios that align with halal principles. These platforms filter out investments in haram industries such as alcohol, gambling, and interest-based financial services, allowing Muslims to invest with confidence. By investing in socially responsible industries such as healthcare, education, and renewable energy, Muslim entrepreneurs can grow their wealth while contributing to the betterment of society.

The rise of digital gold trading platforms represents another exciting innovation in Islamic fintech. Gold has always held a special place in Islamic finance due to its intrinsic value and historical significance as a store of wealth. Many Muslims prefer to invest in gold because it is tangible, stable, and free from the volatility often associated with fiat currencies and speculative financial markets. Digital gold trading platforms allow investors to buy, sell, and store gold securely, without the need for physical possession. These platforms ensure that gold transactions comply with Islamic principles by providing full transparency and ensuring that the gold is backed by actual physical reserves.

For Muslim entrepreneurs, digital gold trading offers a valuable opportunity to diversify their investment portfolios while adhering to the principles of halal finance. It also serves as a hedge against inflation and economic instability, providing a reliable store of wealth in uncertain times. The Prophet Muhammad (PBUH) said, "Gold for gold, silver for silver, wheat for wheat, barley for barley, dates for dates, and salt for salt, like for like, equal for equal, hand to hand" (Muslim). This hadith underscores the importance of fairness, equality, and transparency in financial transactions, values that are upheld in digital gold trading platforms.

As the Islamic fintech sector continues to expand, it is important for Muslim entrepreneurs to stay informed about the latest developments and opportunities in this rapidly growing field. By embracing Islamic fintech, entrepreneurs can access new financial tools that enable them to grow their businesses, manage their wealth, and fulfill their religious obligations in ways that were previously unimaginable. The Quran encourages Muslims to seek out knowledge and stay abreast of new developments, stating, "And say: My Lord, increase me in knowledge" (Quran 20:114). This verse reminds us that continuous learning and adaptation are essential to success in both business and spiritual life.

In addition to Islamic fintech, the broader halal economy offers Muslim entrepreneurs a wide range of opportunities for growth and expansion. The global halal economy encompasses industries such as halal food, halal tourism, halal pharmaceuticals, and halal fashion. As consumer demand for halal products and services continues to rise, Muslim entrepreneurs are uniquely positioned to capitalize on this growing market. By adhering to halal principles and offering products that align with Islamic values, entrepreneurs can tap into a vast and loyal customer base that is seeking ethical and faith-aligned solutions.

One of the most prominent sectors of the halal economy is the halal food industry. Halal food is not just about what is permissible to eat; it also encompasses how the food is sourced, prepared, and served. The Quran states, "O you who have believed, eat from the good things which We have provided for you and be grateful to Allah if it is [indeed] Him that you worship" (Quran 2:172). This verse highlights the importance of consuming food that is not only lawful (halal) but also wholesome (tayyib). For Muslim entrepreneurs involved in the halal food industry, this means ensuring that all aspects of their food production and distribution processes adhere to halal standards.

The halal food industry has seen tremendous growth in recent years, with increasing demand from both Muslim and non-Muslim consumers who are seeking ethical, clean, and sustainable food options. For entrepreneurs, this presents a unique opportunity to offer products that cater to a diverse and conscious consumer base. From halal-certified restaurants to organic halal farms, the possibilities within the halal food sector are vast and varied. Entrepreneurs who prioritize quality, transparency, and ethical sourcing can build strong brands that resonate with consumers and stand out in a competitive market.

Another emerging sector within the halal economy is halal tourism. Halal tourism refers to travel services and experiences that cater to the needs of Muslim travelers, offering accommodations, dining options, and recreational activities that align with Islamic principles. With the rise of global travel and the increasing purchasing power of Muslim consumers, halal tourism has become a lucrative industry. Muslim entrepreneurs can tap into this growing market by offering halal-friendly travel packages, halal-certified hotels, and destinations that cater to the needs of Muslim families.

Halal tourism is not only about providing halal food and prayer facilities; it also involves creating experiences that are respectful of Islamic values, such as modesty, privacy, and family-friendly environments. The Quran encourages Muslims to travel and explore the world, stating, "Say, [O Muhammad], travel through the land and observe how He began creation. Then Allah will produce the final creation. Indeed, Allah over all things is competent" (Quran 29:20). By offering halal-compliant travel services, Muslim entrepreneurs can help others fulfill their desire to explore the world while remaining true to their faith.

The halal pharmaceutical and healthcare sector is another area of significant growth within the global halal economy. With increasing awareness of the importance of halal compliance in medicines, supplements, and personal care products, there is a rising demand for halal-certified healthcare solutions. Muslim entrepreneurs can capitalize on this trend by developing and marketing pharmaceutical products that are free from haram ingredients, such as alcohol and gelatin derived from non-halal sources. The Quran emphasizes the importance of seeking treatment and maintaining good health, stating, "And when I am ill, it is He who cures me" (Quran 26:80).

Halal pharmaceuticals not only cater to Muslim consumers but also appeal to health-conscious individuals who are looking for clean and ethically sourced products. By ensuring that their products meet halal standards, entrepreneurs can tap into a growing global market and build brands that are synonymous with trust, quality, and integrity. Moreover, the halal healthcare sector extends beyond pharmaceuticals to include wellness services such as halal-certified spas, fitness centers, and mental health services that respect Islamic values.

The halal fashion industry is another exciting frontier for Muslim entrepreneurs. Halal fashion goes beyond modest clothing; it encompasses the entire production process, ensuring that garments are made from ethically sourced materials and produced under fair labor conditions. The Quran instructs, "O children of Adam, take your adornment at every masjid" (Quran 7:31), reminding Muslims of the importance of dressing modestly and with dignity. For Muslim entrepreneurs, this means creating fashion lines that are not only stylish and modern but also modest and respectful of Islamic guidelines.

Halal fashion has gained immense popularity in recent years, with major fashion brands and designers incorporating modest wear into their collections. However, there is still significant room for growth, particularly for entrepreneurs who focus on sustainable and ethical fashion. By offering clothing that is both fashionable and aligned with Islamic values, Muslim entrepreneurs can cater to a growing market of consumers who seek modest, high-quality fashion that reflects their faith and values.

As Muslim entrepreneurs continue to explore opportunities within the halal economy, it is essential to remember that the pursuit of wealth should always be guided by the principles of halal finance. The Quran provides clear guidance on the importance of earning and using wealth in ways that are lawful and beneficial: "And do not consume one another's wealth unjustly or send it [in bribery] to the rulers in order that [they might aid] you [to] consume a portion of the wealth of the people in sin, while you know [it is unlawful]" (Quran 2:188). This verse serves as a powerful reminder that the pursuit of financial success must always be grounded in ethics, fairness, and justice.

One of the key benefits of participating in the halal economy is the sense of fulfillment that comes from knowing that one's business activities are aligned with both Islamic values and the greater good of society. By adhering to halal principles, Muslim entrepreneurs can build businesses that are not only profitable but also blessed with barakah. Barakah, or divine blessing, is a concept that permeates every aspect of Islamic finance and entrepreneurship. It is the idea that when wealth is earned and used in ways that are pleasing to Allah, it brings both worldly and spiritual success.

The Prophet Muhammad (PBUH) emphasized the importance of earning halal income, stating, "O people, Allah is good and He accepts only that which is good" (Muslim). For the Muslim entrepreneur, this means that every financial decision, from investments to partnerships to business ventures, must be guided by the principles of halal finance. By doing so, entrepreneurs can ensure that their wealth is not only lawful but also a source of blessings for themselves, their families, and their communities.

As the global halal economy continues to grow, Muslim entrepreneurs have the opportunity to play a leading role in shaping the future of ethical business practices. By offering products and services that align with Islamic values, entrepreneurs can build brands that are trusted, respected, and sought after by consumers around the world. Whether through halal food, halal fashion, halal pharmaceuticals, or halal tourism, Muslim entrepreneurs are uniquely positioned to contribute to the development of a global economy that prioritizes ethics, fairness, and social responsibility.

In conclusion, the principles of halal finance provide Muslim entrepreneurs with a comprehensive framework for building wealth with integrity. Whether through profit-sharing partnerships, ethical investing, interest-free loans, or charitable giving, halal finance ensures that wealth is earned and used in ways that are fair, transparent, and beneficial to society. By adhering to these principles, Muslim entrepreneurs can build businesses that are not only successful in a worldly sense but are also blessed with barakah and aligned with their spiritual goals.

The rise of Islamic fintech and the growing demand for halal products and services offer Muslim entrepreneurs unprecedented opportunities to innovate, grow, and expand their businesses. By leveraging technology, embracing ethical business practices, and staying true to the values of halal finance, entrepreneurs can create businesses that stand the test of time and contribute to the well-being of society.

As we look to the future, it is clear that the halal economy will continue to play an increasingly important role in shaping the global economic landscape. Muslim entrepreneurs have the power to lead this transformation, creating businesses that not only generate wealth but also promote social justice, environmental sustainability, and ethical governance. The Prophet Muhammad (PBUH) said, "The best of people are those who bring the most benefit to others" (Daraqutni). By adhering to the principles of halal finance and embracing the opportunities within the halal economy, Muslim entrepreneurs can build businesses that fulfill this noble goal.

As the global halal economy continues to grow, Muslim entrepreneurs are uniquely positioned to become pioneers in their respective industries, leading by example and demonstrating the practical application of halal finance principles. In doing so, they are not merely building profitable enterprises but also contributing to a broader movement that promotes ethical financial practices, social justice, and economic empowerment. Halal finance, when properly understood and applied, provides a blueprint for building a fair and sustainable economy—one that prioritizes human dignity, environmental stewardship, and the equitable distribution of wealth.

An integral aspect of halal finance is the responsibility that comes with wealth. In Islam, wealth is viewed as a trust (amanah) from Allah, and it must be managed with care, integrity, and a sense of accountability. The Quran reminds us, "And spend in the way of Allah and do not throw [yourselves] with your [own] hands into destruction [by refraining]. And do good; indeed, Allah loves the doers of good" (Quran 2:195). This verse highlights the importance of using wealth not only for personal gain but also for the benefit of others. For Muslim entrepreneurs, this means that wealth should be earned through halal means and used to promote the well-being of society.

One of the most important tools for ensuring that wealth is distributed fairly is zakat, the obligatory charity on wealth. Zakat is not merely a tax; it is an essential component of the Islamic financial system, designed to purify wealth and ensure that the needs of the less fortunate are met. The Quran emphasizes the importance of zakat, stating, "And establish prayer and give zakat and bow with those who bow [in worship and obedience]" (Quran 2:43). By giving zakat, Muslim entrepreneurs not only fulfill their religious duty but also contribute to the reduction of poverty and inequality within their communities.

In addition to zakat, sadaqah (voluntary charity) plays a critical role in the redistribution of wealth. While zakat is obligatory, sadaqah is encouraged for all Muslims, regardless of their financial situation. The Prophet Muhammad (PBUH) said, "Charity does not decrease wealth" (Muslim), highlighting the idea that giving to others brings barakah, or blessings, to one's wealth. For Muslim entrepreneurs, giving sadaqah provides an additional way to ensure that their wealth is being used in ways that are pleasing to Allah and beneficial to society. Whether through direct financial contributions, the support of charitable initiatives, or the provision of resources to those in need, sadaqah serves as a means of spiritual growth and social responsibility.

The role of sadaqah in halal finance extends beyond monetary contributions. It can take many forms, including the sharing of knowledge, mentorship, and time. Muslim entrepreneurs, particularly those who have achieved success, are encouraged to give back by offering guidance and support to others who are just beginning their entrepreneurial journeys. By mentoring young entrepreneurs, sharing insights, and offering encouragement, successful entrepreneurs can help cultivate the next generation of Muslim business leaders.

The Quran teaches us, "And cooperate in righteousness and piety, but do not cooperate in sin and aggression" (Quran 5:2). This verse serves as a reminder of the importance of working together for the greater good, and for Muslim entrepreneurs, it underscores the value of supporting one another in the pursuit of halal business ventures. By fostering a sense of community and cooperation, Muslim entrepreneurs can build a strong network of like-minded individuals who are committed to ethical business practices and the promotion of halal finance.

In addition to fostering collaboration within the Muslim business community, halal finance also emphasizes the importance of environmental sustainability. Islam teaches that humans are stewards of the Earth and that we are responsible for its care and preservation. The Quran states, "And do not commit abuse on the earth, spreading corruption" (Quran 2:60). For Muslim entrepreneurs, this means that their business practices should not harm the environment or exploit natural resources in ways that are unsustainable. Instead, they should strive to create businesses that are environmentally responsible, reduce waste, and promote the use of renewable resources.

In recent years, the concept of green finance—financing that supports environmentally sustainable projects—has gained traction in both Islamic and conventional financial markets. For Muslim entrepreneurs, green finance offers an opportunity to invest in projects that align with the principles of halal finance while also contributing to the preservation of the environment. Whether through investments in renewable energy, sustainable agriculture, or eco-friendly technologies, Muslim entrepreneurs can play a vital role in the global effort to combat climate change and promote environmental stewardship.

The integration of environmental sustainability into halal finance is a natural extension of the Islamic principles of fairness, justice, and responsibility. By adopting sustainable business practices and supporting green finance initiatives, Muslim entrepreneurs can ensure that their wealth is used in ways that are not only halal but also beneficial to future generations. The Quran encourages Muslims to leave a positive legacy for those who come after them, stating, "It is He who has made you successors upon the earth" (Quran 35:39). This verse serves as a reminder that we are accountable for the way we use the resources entrusted to us and that we must act with foresight and responsibility.

Beyond environmental sustainability, halal finance also promotes the ethical treatment of workers and the fair distribution of profits. In Islam, workers are entitled to fair wages, safe working conditions, and respectful treatment. The Prophet Muhammad (PBUH) said, "Your employees are your brothers, whom Allah has placed under your command. So whoever has his brother under his command should feed him of what he eats and dress him of what he wears. Do not burden them beyond their capacity, but if you do so, then help them" (Bukhari). This hadith emphasizes the importance of treating employees with kindness and fairness, and it serves as a guiding principle for Muslim entrepreneurs in their business practices.

For Muslim entrepreneurs, ensuring that their businesses adhere to ethical labor practices is not only a religious obligation but also a means of building trust and loyalty with their employees. By providing fair wages, creating safe and supportive work environments, and offering opportunities for growth and development, entrepreneurs can foster a culture of respect and mutual benefit. This approach aligns with the principles of halal finance, which emphasize fairness and transparency in all business dealings.

In addition to treating employees fairly, halal finance also encourages the equitable distribution of profits. In a halal business, wealth should not be concentrated in the hands of a few but should be shared among all stakeholders. This can be achieved through profit-sharing arrangements, where employees and investors are rewarded based on the success of the business. The Quran states, "And do not consume one another's wealth unjustly or send it [in bribery] to the rulers in order that [they might aid] you [to] consume a portion of the wealth of the people in sin, while you know [it is unlawful]" (Quran 2:188). This verse highlights the importance of ensuring that wealth is earned and distributed in ways that are just and lawful.

For Muslim entrepreneurs, profit-sharing arrangements not only align with the principles of halal finance but also create a sense of ownership and accountability among employees. When employees share in the success of the business, they are more likely to be motivated, loyal, and committed to its long-term growth. This collaborative approach to wealth distribution fosters a positive work environment and contributes to the overall success of the business.

In the context of halal finance, profit-sharing also extends to investors and business partners. As mentioned earlier, the concepts of *mudarabah* and *musharakah* provide a framework for equitable risk-sharing in business ventures. In both models, investors and entrepreneurs share in the profits and losses of the business, ensuring that no party is unfairly burdened or enriched. This approach to investment is rooted in the Islamic principles of fairness and mutual benefit, as it ensures that wealth is generated in a way that benefits all stakeholders.

In a *mudarabah* arrangement, the investor provides the capital, while the entrepreneur manages the business. Profits are shared according to a pre-agreed ratio, but if the business incurs a loss, the investor bears the financial loss, while the entrepreneur loses only their time and effort. This risk-sharing model encourages responsible business management and aligns the interests of both the investor and the entrepreneur. It also ensures that wealth is generated through productive enterprise, rather than through the exploitation of interest-bearing loans.

In a *musharakah* arrangement, both the investor and the entrepreneur contribute capital to the business and share in the profits and losses according to a pre-agreed ratio. This model fosters collaboration and shared responsibility, as all parties have a vested interest in the success of the business. By promoting equitable risk-sharing, *musharakah* ensures that wealth is distributed fairly and that no party is disproportionately rewarded or penalized. The Quran encourages Muslims to engage in lawful trade and partnerships, stating, "And let not those of virtue and wealth among you swear not to give [aid] to their relatives and the needy and the emigrants for the cause of Allah, and let them pardon and overlook. Would you not like that Allah should forgive you? And Allah is Forgiving and Merciful" (Quran 24:22).

By adhering to the principles of *mudarabah* and *musharakah*, Muslim entrepreneurs can build businesses that are not only financially successful but also socially responsible. These models provide a framework for generating wealth in a way that promotes fairness, accountability, and mutual benefit, ensuring that the financial success of the business is shared among all stakeholders.

In addition to *mudarabah* and *musharakah*, the concept of *waqf* (endowment) plays a vital role in the redistribution of wealth within Islamic finance. As mentioned earlier, a *waqf* is a charitable endowment that is used to support social, educational, or religious causes. Once established, a *waqf* cannot be sold or inherited, and it continues to benefit the community long after the donor has passed away. The Prophet Muhammad (PBUH) said, "When a person dies, his deeds come to an end except for three: ongoing charity, knowledge that is benefited from, or a righteous child who prays for him" (Muslim). A *waqf* represents ongoing charity, as it continues to provide benefits to others indefinitely.

For Muslim entrepreneurs, establishing a *waqf* is a powerful way to leave a lasting legacy and ensure that their wealth is used to promote the well-being of society. Whether by donating land for a school, supporting a healthcare initiative, or funding scholarships for students, a *waqf* allows entrepreneurs to give back to their communities in meaningful and enduring ways. By incorporating *waqf* into their financial plans, Muslim entrepreneurs can ensure that their wealth continues to serve others long after they are gone.

The concept of *waqf* aligns perfectly with the principles of halal finance, as it ensures that wealth is used for the greater good and that it contributes to the development of society. By supporting social, educational, and religious causes, *waqf* fosters a sense of solidarity and mutual support within the Muslim community. It also helps to create a more equitable society, where resources are shared and opportunities are provided to those who might otherwise be excluded from economic participation.

Another important concept in Islamic finance is the prohibition of *gharar*, which refers to excessive uncertainty or ambiguity in financial transactions. In Islam, all parties to a transaction must have full knowledge and understanding of the terms of the agreement. Any form of deceit, exploitation, or unfair advantage is strictly prohibited. The Prophet Muhammad (PBUH) warned against transactions that involve deception, stating, "He who deceives is not one of us" (Muslim). For Muslim entrepreneurs, this means that every financial transaction must be conducted with honesty, clarity, and transparency.

The prohibition of *gharar* is particularly relevant in today's financial markets, where speculative investments, high-risk ventures, and complex financial derivatives often dominate. In contrast to conventional financial systems, where risk is often shifted onto the weaker party, halal finance promotes transparency and fairness, ensuring that all parties have a clear understanding of the risks and rewards involved. By avoiding transactions that involve excessive risk or uncertainty, Muslim entrepreneurs can ensure that their financial dealings are ethical, responsible, and in line with Islamic teachings.

One of the key benefits of adhering to the prohibition of *gharar* is the peace of mind that comes from knowing that one's wealth is earned through lawful means. The Quran reminds us, "O you who have believed, fear Allah and give up what remains [due to you] of interest, if you should be believers" (Quran 2:278). By avoiding interest-based transactions and speculative investments, Muslim entrepreneurs can ensure that their wealth is earned in a way that is pleasing to Allah and free from the harmful effects of greed and exploitation.

As Muslim entrepreneurs continue to navigate the complexities of the global financial system, the principles of halal finance offer a clear and ethical framework for building wealth with integrity. By adhering to the concepts of *mudarabah*, *musharakah*, *waqf*, and the prohibition of *gharar*, entrepreneurs can ensure that their businesses are built on a foundation of fairness, transparency, and social responsibility. In doing so, they not only contribute to their own financial success but also to the well-being of their communities and the broader global economy.

The future of halal finance is bright, and Muslim entrepreneurs have the opportunity to play a leading role in shaping a more ethical, equitable, and sustainable global financial system. By staying true to the principles of halal finance and embracing the opportunities within the halal economy, entrepreneurs can build businesses that are not only profitable but also blessed with barakah, contributing to the greater good of society and earning the pleasure of Allah.

CHAPTER 4: ETHICAL MARKETING AND BRANDING IN HALAL BUSINESS

In the modern world of business, marketing and branding are essential tools that enable businesses to differentiate themselves in a crowded marketplace. But for Muslim entrepreneurs who adhere to the principles of halal business, marketing and branding must go beyond merely promoting products and services—they must also reflect the values of Islam and ethical conduct. The essence of ethical marketing and branding in a halal business is not only to appeal to customers but also to build trust, respect, and long-term relationships that are rooted in integrity and fairness.

At the heart of ethical marketing lies the concept of honesty. The Quran explicitly warns against deceit and dishonesty, stating, "O you who have believed, do not consume one another's wealth unjustly or send it [in bribery] to the rulers in order that [they might aid] you [to] consume a portion of the wealth of the people in sin, while you know [it is unlawful]" (Quran 2:188). This verse serves as a reminder that the pursuit of profit should never come at the expense of truth and fairness. In marketing, honesty means being transparent about the benefits, features, and limitations of your products and services. Muslim entrepreneurs must ensure that their marketing materials accurately represent what they are offering and refrain from exaggerating or making false claims.

When marketing products or services in a halal business, it is important to remember that customers are not just targets for profit; they are people deserving of respect, fairness, and truth. The Prophet Muhammad (PBUH) said, "He who deceives is not one of us" (Muslim), emphasizing the importance of honesty in all interactions, including business dealings. For the Muslim entrepreneur, this means adopting marketing strategies that are not manipulative, misleading, or exploitative. Instead, marketing should be used as a means of building trust, educating customers, and fostering a long-term relationship that is based on mutual respect and benefit.

One of the most common pitfalls in modern marketing is the temptation to exaggerate the benefits of a product or service in order to attract more customers. However, such practices go against the core principles of halal business. For a marketing strategy to be truly halal, it must be grounded in truthfulness and transparency. The Quran says, "And do not mix the truth with falsehood or conceal the truth while you know [it]" (Quran 2:42). Muslim entrepreneurs must be diligent in ensuring that all claims made in their marketing materials are accurate, verifiable, and consistent with Islamic values.

In addition to honesty, fairness is a key component of ethical marketing in a halal business. The Quran encourages Muslims to be fair in their dealings, stating, "Give full measure and do not be of those who cause loss. And weigh with an even balance" (Quran 26:181-182). This principle extends to how products and services are priced, promoted, and marketed. Muslim entrepreneurs must ensure that their pricing reflects the true value of the product and that customers are not overcharged or misled by hidden fees or deceptive pricing practices.

Fairness also means ensuring that marketing campaigns do not exploit vulnerable populations, such as the elderly, children, or those with limited financial means. Marketing strategies that target such groups with the intent of taking advantage of their vulnerabilities are not only unethical but also haram in Islam. Instead, Muslim entrepreneurs should aim to create marketing campaigns that are inclusive, respectful, and considerate of the diverse needs of their audience. This approach not only builds trust with customers but also aligns with the Islamic values of compassion, fairness, and justice.

Another important aspect of ethical marketing is the avoidance of haram (prohibited) elements. In halal marketing, it is essential to ensure that products and services are free from haram substances and practices, such as alcohol, gambling, and interest-based transactions. The Quran clearly prohibits these activities, stating, "O you who have believed, indeed, intoxicants, gambling, [sacrificing on] stone alters [to other than Allah], and divining arrows are but defilement from the work of Satan, so avoid it that you may be successful" (Quran 5:90). Muslim entrepreneurs must be vigilant in ensuring that their marketing materials do not promote or endorse any haram activities, either directly or indirectly.

In the digital age, social media has become an indispensable tool for marketing and branding. Platforms such as Instagram, Facebook, Twitter, and YouTube allow businesses to reach a global audience with minimal effort and cost. However, the ease of access to these platforms also presents new challenges for Muslim entrepreneurs who wish to maintain ethical standards in their marketing efforts. It is important to remember that the principles of halal business apply to all forms of marketing, including social media. This means avoiding deceptive practices, such as fake reviews, inflated follower counts, or misleading advertisements, which have become common in the world of social media marketing.

> Social media offers an unparalleled opportunity to connect with customers, share the story behind your brand, and promote products in real-time. However, it is also a platform that requires careful management to ensure that Islamic values are upheld. The Quran advises, "Say, 'My Lord, increase me in knowledge'" (Quran 20:114). This verse encourages continuous learning and growth, which is particularly relevant in the fast-paced world of digital marketing. Muslim entrepreneurs must remain vigilant in keeping up with the latest trends in social media marketing while ensuring that their campaigns reflect the ethical standards of halal business.

One effective way to use social media ethically is through storytelling. Storytelling allows businesses to share their values, mission, and vision with their audience in an authentic and engaging way. For Muslim entrepreneurs, storytelling offers a unique opportunity to showcase how their businesses align with the principles of halal, from ethical sourcing to transparent pricing. By sharing the journey of their business, entrepreneurs can build a strong connection with their customers, based on mutual trust and respect. This approach not only differentiates the brand from competitors but also fosters a sense of authenticity that resonates with customers.

Another key aspect of social media marketing is engagement. Engaging with customers in a respectful and meaningful way is essential for building trust and loyalty. The Prophet Muhammad (PBUH) said, "The best of people are those who are most beneficial to others" (Daraqutni). For Muslim entrepreneurs, this means using social media as a platform to offer value to customers, whether through educational content, helpful tips, or thoughtful interactions. By focusing on providing benefit rather than simply promoting products, entrepreneurs can build a loyal following that is based on mutual respect and shared values.

In addition to storytelling and engagement, transparency is crucial in social media marketing. Customers today are increasingly seeking brands that are open and honest about their practices. For Muslim entrepreneurs, this means being transparent about how products are sourced, how they are priced, and how they align with halal principles. Transparency fosters trust and demonstrates a commitment to ethical business practices, which is essential for building a strong and reputable brand. The Quran emphasizes the importance of honesty and transparency, stating, "And do not conceal testimony, for whoever conceals it—his heart is indeed sinful, and Allah is Knowing of what you do" (Quran 2:283).

One of the growing trends in modern marketing is the use of influencers to promote products and services. Influencers, individuals with large followings on social media platforms, have become a powerful force in shaping consumer behavior. For Muslim entrepreneurs, influencer marketing presents both opportunities and challenges. On the one hand, partnering with influencers can significantly increase brand visibility and credibility. On the other hand, it is important to ensure that the influencers chosen align with the values of halal business.

When selecting influencers to represent your brand, it is essential to consider their character, values, and behavior. The Prophet Muhammad (PBUH) said, "A man follows the religion of his friend; so each one should consider whom he makes his friend" (Tirmidhi). This hadith reminds us of the importance of surrounding ourselves with individuals who reflect our values. In the context of influencer marketing, this means partnering with individuals who promote ethical behavior, modesty, and respect. By aligning with influencers who share your values, you can ensure that your brand is represented in a way that is consistent with Islamic principles.

Another consideration in influencer marketing is transparency. It is important to be upfront with customers about the nature of the relationship between the brand and the influencer. Customers should know whether an influencer is being compensated for promoting a product or if they are offering an unbiased opinion. The Quran encourages Muslims to be transparent in their dealings, stating, "O you who have believed, fear Allah and speak words of appropriate justice" (Quran 33:70). By being transparent in your influencer partnerships, you can build trust with your audience and demonstrate a commitment to ethical business practices.

In addition to influencer marketing, content marketing is another powerful tool for building a halal brand. Content marketing involves creating and sharing valuable, relevant content that attracts and engages your target audience. This content can take many forms, including blog posts, videos, social media updates, and educational articles. The goal of content marketing is to provide value to your audience, build trust, and establish your brand as a thought leader in your industry. For Muslim entrepreneurs, content marketing offers a unique opportunity to educate customers about the principles of halal business and how your products or services align with these values.

In creating content for a halal business, it is important to ensure that the content is both valuable and aligned with Islamic teachings. The Prophet Muhammad (PBUH) said, "Speak good or remain silent" (Bukhari). This hadith serves as a reminder that the words we use, whether in person or in writing, should always be meaningful, respectful, and beneficial. For Muslim entrepreneurs, this means that all content, whether in advertisements, social media posts, or blog articles, should be created with the intention of providing value to the audience. Content should be informative, educational, and reflective of the values of halal business.

Another important aspect of content marketing is consistency. Consistency in messaging, tone, and visual elements is essential for building a strong and recognizable brand. The Quran encourages consistency and perseverance, stating, "So remain on a right course as you have been commanded" (Quran 11:112). For Muslim entrepreneurs, this means ensuring that all marketing materials consistently reflect the brand's values, mission, and commitment to ethical business practices. By maintaining consistency in content, entrepreneurs can build a strong brand identity that resonates with their audience and fosters long-term loyalty.

While content marketing is a powerful tool for building a halal brand, it is also important to measure the effectiveness of your marketing efforts. Metrics such as engagement rates, website traffic, and conversion rates can provide valuable insights into how well your content is resonating with your audience. However, it is important to remember that success in halal marketing is not solely measured by numbers. The ultimate goal of halal marketing is to build trust, provide value, and create a positive impact on society. The Quran reminds us, "And whatever good you put forward for yourselves—you will find it with Allah" (Quran 2:110). For Muslim entrepreneurs, this means focusing on the long-term benefits of ethical marketing rather than short-term gains.

In addition to content marketing, email marketing remains one of the most effective ways to connect with customers in a personal and meaningful way. Email marketing allows businesses to communicate directly with their audience, offering personalized messages, product updates, and special promotions. However, as with all forms of marketing, email marketing must be done ethically. Customers should only receive emails if they have given their explicit consent, and the content of the emails should be respectful, honest, and free from manipulation.

The Prophet Muhammad (PBUH) emphasized the importance of kindness and respect in all interactions, stating, "Whoever believes in Allah and the Last Day should speak a good word or remain silent" (Muslim). This hadith applies to all forms of communication, including email marketing. The messages sent to customers should always be polite, clear, and respectful. Additionally, entrepreneurs must provide an easy way for customers to unsubscribe if they no longer wish to receive emails. Forcing customers to remain on an email list or overwhelming them with excessive messages is not only poor business practice but also goes against the principles of respect and fairness in Islam.

One of the benefits of email marketing is the ability to create personalized experiences for customers. By segmenting your email list based on customer preferences, purchase history, or interests, you can send targeted messages that are relevant to each individual. This not only increases the likelihood of a sale but also strengthens the relationship between the customer and the brand. However, personalization should always be done in a way that respects the customer's privacy and autonomy. The Quran teaches us to respect the rights of others, stating, "And do not spy or backbite each other" (Quran 49:12). For Muslim entrepreneurs, this means ensuring that customer data is handled with care and used ethically.

As digital marketing continues to evolve, new technologies such as artificial intelligence (AI) and machine learning are becoming increasingly important in shaping the future of marketing. These technologies offer powerful tools for automating marketing tasks, analyzing customer data, and personalizing marketing efforts. However, it is important to approach these technologies with caution and ensure that their use aligns with the principles of halal business. AI-driven marketing should never be used to manipulate customers or exploit their vulnerabilities. Instead, it should be used as a tool for enhancing the customer experience and providing value.

For Muslim entrepreneurs, the integration of AI into marketing efforts offers an opportunity to stay at the forefront of technological innovation while remaining true to Islamic values. By using AI ethically, businesses can streamline their marketing processes, improve customer engagement, and create more personalized experiences—all while maintaining the trust and respect of their audience.

As Muslim entrepreneurs continue to navigate the world of ethical marketing, one of the most crucial aspects of maintaining a halal brand is upholding the values of modesty and humility. In Islam, modesty is not only a virtue in personal behavior but also extends to how businesses present themselves. The Quran reminds us, "And do not walk upon the earth exultantly. Indeed, you will never tear the earth [apart], and you will never reach the mountains in height" (Quran 17:37). This verse emphasizes the importance of humility and warns against arrogance and extravagance.

For Muslim entrepreneurs, this means that marketing materials, advertisements, and branding strategies should reflect modesty and humility. Flashy, exaggerated, or boastful marketing campaigns may attract attention, but they do not align with the values of halal business. Instead, marketing efforts should focus on the true value of the product or service and the benefit it provides to the customer. By adopting a modest and humble approach to marketing, businesses can build a brand that resonates with customers who value authenticity, sincerity, and ethical behavior.

Another key principle of halal marketing is the concept of *niyyah*—intention. In Islam, intention plays a central role in determining the morality of actions. The Prophet Muhammad (PBUH) said, "Actions are but by intentions, and every man shall have only that which he intended" (Bukhari). This hadith reminds Muslim entrepreneurs that the intention behind their marketing efforts must be pure and in line with Islamic principles. Marketing should not be solely driven by the desire for profit but should aim to provide value, solve problems, and promote ethical behavior.

For example, a halal brand that offers eco-friendly products might highlight its commitment to environmental sustainability in its marketing materials. By doing so, the brand not only promotes its products but also raises awareness about the importance of protecting the environment—a value that is deeply rooted in Islamic teachings. The Quran states, "And do not commit abuse on the earth, spreading corruption" (Quran 2:60). This verse emphasizes the responsibility of Muslims to care for the environment, and by incorporating this message into their marketing efforts, Muslim entrepreneurs can align their business goals with their ethical and spiritual values.

In addition to promoting ethical values, halal marketing also requires businesses to be mindful of how their products are positioned in the marketplace. In a competitive business environment, it is tempting to adopt aggressive marketing tactics that undermine competitors or diminish the value of other businesses. However, Islam teaches that competition should be conducted with fairness and respect. The Prophet Muhammad (PBUH) said, "None of you truly believes until he loves for his brother what he loves for himself" (Bukhari). This hadith encourages Muslim entrepreneurs to treat their competitors with kindness and fairness, avoiding tactics that seek to harm or undermine others.

One of the ethical challenges in modern marketing is the use of comparison advertising, where a business promotes its products by comparing them to those of its competitors. While this may be a common practice in conventional marketing, it raises ethical concerns in halal business. The Quran teaches, "O you who have believed, avoid much [negative] assumption. Indeed, some assumption is sin. And do not spy or backbite each other" (Quran 49:12). For Muslim entrepreneurs, this means refraining from negative or aggressive comparisons that could harm the reputation of other businesses.

Instead of focusing on the weaknesses of competitors, halal marketing should emphasize the strengths and unique benefits of the business's own products and services. By adopting a positive and respectful approach to competition, Muslim entrepreneurs can build a brand that is seen as fair, trustworthy, and ethical. This not only enhances the brand's reputation but also fosters a sense of goodwill and cooperation within the marketplace.

Another important consideration in halal marketing is the representation of gender and modesty in advertisements. In many conventional marketing campaigns, women are often portrayed in ways that do not align with Islamic principles of modesty. The Quran advises both men and women to dress modestly and behave with dignity, stating, "Tell the believing men to lower their gaze and guard their private parts. That is purer for them. Indeed, Allah is Acquainted with what they do. And tell the believing women to lower their gaze and guard their private parts and not expose their adornment" (Quran 24:30-31). For Muslim entrepreneurs, it is important to ensure that their advertisements and marketing materials reflect these values of modesty and respect.

When creating advertisements, Muslim entrepreneurs should avoid using images or language that objectify or exploit individuals, particularly women. Instead, the focus should be on the product or service itself, highlighting its quality, benefits, and alignment with halal principles. By adopting a modest and respectful approach to advertising, businesses can create marketing campaigns that are both effective and ethically sound.

In addition to ethical advertising, halal branding also requires businesses to cultivate a strong and consistent brand identity that reflects their values. A brand is more than just a logo or a tagline; it is the embodiment of the business's mission, values, and identity. For Muslim entrepreneurs, building a halal brand means ensuring that every aspect of the business—its products, services, customer interactions, and marketing materials—aligns with Islamic principles. The Quran emphasizes the importance of consistency and integrity, stating, "So remain on a right course as you have been commanded" (Quran 11:112).

One way to build a strong halal brand is by developing a clear brand narrative that tells the story of the business and its values. A brand narrative is a powerful tool for connecting with customers on a deeper level and differentiating the business from its competitors. For Muslim entrepreneurs, the brand narrative should highlight how the business is rooted in halal principles, from ethical sourcing to fair pricing to social responsibility. By sharing this story with customers, businesses can create an emotional connection that fosters trust and loyalty.

Another important aspect of halal branding is the creation of a consistent visual identity. This includes the design of the business's logo, website, packaging, and marketing materials. The visual identity should reflect the values of the brand and appeal to the target audience while maintaining a sense of modesty and professionalism. For example, a halal brand that focuses on eco-friendly products might use natural colors and imagery in its marketing materials to convey its commitment to sustainability. The visual identity should be simple, clean, and respectful, avoiding any imagery or designs that could be considered offensive or inappropriate.

In addition to developing a strong brand narrative and visual identity, Muslim entrepreneurs should focus on building a reputation for exceptional customer service. The Prophet Muhammad (PBUH) emphasized the importance of treating others with kindness and respect, stating, "The believer is one who is sociable, and there is no good in one who is not sociable" (Tabarani). For halal businesses, this means ensuring that customers are treated with courtesy, professionalism, and respect at every stage of their journey—from the moment they learn about the brand to the post-purchase experience.

Customer service is not just about resolving issues or answering questions; it is about building relationships based on trust and mutual respect. By providing exceptional customer service, businesses can foster long-term loyalty and create a positive brand image. This is especially important in the context of halal business, where customers are likely to place a high value on ethical conduct and integrity. The Quran encourages Muslims to act with kindness and fairness in all dealings, stating, "And do not forget to do good to one another" (Quran 2:237).

Another critical element of halal branding is social responsibility. In Islam, wealth is viewed as a trust from Allah, and it must be used in ways that benefit society. The Quran reminds us, "And whatever you spend of good—it will be fully repaid to you, and you will not be wronged" (Quran 2:272). For Muslim entrepreneurs, this means incorporating social responsibility into the core of their brand. This can take many forms, such as donating a portion of profits to charity, supporting community initiatives, or implementing environmentally sustainable practices.

Social responsibility not only reflects the values of halal business but also resonates with modern consumers who are increasingly seeking out brands that prioritize ethical and sustainable practices. By aligning the brand with social causes that are important to customers, businesses can differentiate themselves in the marketplace and build a strong, loyal customer base.

However, it is important that these efforts are genuine and not simply a marketing ploy. Customers are quick to recognize when a brand's commitment to social responsibility is insincere or superficial. For halal businesses, social responsibility should be a natural extension of the business's values, not a marketing tactic.

In addition to social responsibility, Muslim entrepreneurs should also focus on ethical supply chain management. The Prophet Muhammad (PBUH) said, "Give the worker his wages before his sweat dries" (Ibn Majah), emphasizing the importance of fair treatment of workers. For halal businesses, this means ensuring that all suppliers and partners adhere to ethical labor practices and that workers are treated with dignity and respect. This not only aligns with the principles of halal business but also enhances the brand's reputation for integrity and fairness.

Ethical supply chain management also extends to the sourcing of materials and ingredients. For a business to be truly halal, it must ensure that all products and materials are sourced in accordance with Islamic principles. This means avoiding materials that are derived from haram sources, such as alcohol, pork, or interest-based products. By maintaining a halal supply chain, businesses can ensure that their products are not only lawful but also ethical and beneficial to society.

As the halal business landscape continues to evolve, one of the key challenges facing Muslim entrepreneurs is staying true to their values while navigating the pressures of competition and growth. In a fast-paced and often cutthroat business environment, it can be tempting to compromise on ethics in order to gain a competitive edge. However, the Quran reminds us of the importance of patience and perseverance in the face of challenges: "And be patient, for indeed, Allah does not allow the reward of those who do good to be lost" (Quran 11:115).

For Muslim entrepreneurs, success in business is not just about financial gain; it is about earning halal income that is blessed with barakah. Barakah is a concept that goes beyond material wealth—it refers to the spiritual blessings and contentment that come from conducting business in a way that is pleasing to Allah. The Prophet Muhammad (PBUH) said, "The best of earnings is the work of a man's own hand, and every permissible trade" (Ahmad). By adhering to the principles of halal business, Muslim entrepreneurs can ensure that their wealth is not only lawful but also blessed with barakah, bringing long-term success and fulfillment.

Another key consideration for halal businesses is the importance of continuous improvement and innovation. The Quran encourages Muslims to seek knowledge and strive for excellence, stating, "Indeed, Allah loves those who act justly" (Quran 5:42). For Muslim entrepreneurs, this means staying up to date with industry trends, investing in new technologies, and continually refining their products and services to better serve their customers. However, it is important to ensure that all innovations align with the principles of halal business and that they contribute to the well-being of society.

Innovation in halal business is not just about creating new products; it is about finding new ways to solve problems, improve processes, and deliver value to customers. By adopting a mindset of continuous improvement, Muslim entrepreneurs can stay ahead of the competition while remaining true to their values. Whether through the use of technology, the development of new business models, or the exploration of new markets, innovation offers a powerful tool for growth and success in halal business.

As Muslim entrepreneurs look to the future, one of the most exciting opportunities for growth lies in the expansion of the global halal economy. The halal economy is not limited to food and beverages; it encompasses a wide range of industries, including fashion, pharmaceuticals, cosmetics, travel, and finance. As demand for halal products and services continues to grow, Muslim entrepreneurs have the opportunity to tap into this expanding market and build businesses that cater to the needs of Muslim and non-Muslim consumers alike.

The global halal economy is projected to continue its rapid growth, driven by a rising Muslim population, increasing consumer awareness of halal products, and growing interest in ethical and sustainable business practices. For Muslim entrepreneurs, this presents a unique opportunity to build businesses that are not only profitable but also aligned with Islamic principles. By offering high-quality, halal-certified products and services, businesses can attract a loyal customer base that values integrity, transparency, and social responsibility.

In addition to tapping into the halal economy, Muslim entrepreneurs should also consider the role of partnerships and collaborations in driving growth. The Quran encourages cooperation and mutual support, stating, "Help one another in acts of piety and righteousness" (Quran 5:2). By partnering with like-minded businesses, organizations, and individuals, entrepreneurs can expand their reach, share resources, and achieve common goals. These partnerships can take many forms, from joint ventures to strategic alliances to collaborative marketing efforts.

Partnerships are particularly valuable in the context of the global halal economy, where businesses may face challenges related to certification, distribution, and market access. By working together with other businesses in the halal industry, Muslim entrepreneurs can overcome these challenges and create a more connected and resilient halal ecosystem. Partnerships also provide an opportunity for businesses to learn from one another, share best practices, and contribute to the overall growth and development of the halal economy.

As Muslim entrepreneurs explore the expanding global halal economy, it is crucial to emphasize the importance of quality in every aspect of the business.

High-quality products and services not only reflect the principles of halal but also meet the expectations of discerning consumers who are seeking ethical and reliable offerings. The Quran states, "Indeed, Allah commands you to render trusts to whom they are due" (Quran 4:58). For Muslim entrepreneurs, this command includes delivering products and services that fulfill their promises and uphold the values of fairness, integrity, and excellence.

In the competitive world of business, quality is often a key differentiator that sets successful brands apart. Halal businesses that prioritize quality in their manufacturing processes, customer service, and marketing efforts are more likely to build strong reputations and develop loyal customer bases. By maintaining high standards of quality, Muslim entrepreneurs can ensure that their businesses are not only successful in the short term but also sustainable and respected in the long term.

One of the ways to ensure consistent quality in halal business is through halal certification. Halal certification provides assurance to consumers that the products they are purchasing comply with Islamic dietary laws and ethical guidelines. This certification process involves rigorous testing and verification to ensure that products are free from haram (forbidden) ingredients and are produced in a manner that aligns with Islamic principles. For Muslim entrepreneurs, obtaining halal certification for their products not only enhances the credibility of their brand but also opens up new markets and opportunities for growth.

In addition to halal certification, Muslim entrepreneurs should also consider other certifications that reflect their commitment to quality, such as organic certification, fair trade certification, or eco-friendly certification. These certifications provide further assurance to consumers that the products they are purchasing are not only halal but also produced in ways that are ethical, sustainable, and socially responsible. By offering certified products, businesses can attract a broader customer base that values transparency, integrity, and social impact.

Another important aspect of quality in halal business is the role of innovation in enhancing the customer experience. As technology continues to evolve, Muslim entrepreneurs have the opportunity to leverage new tools and platforms to improve the way they serve their customers. From e-commerce platforms that make it easier for customers to shop online to mobile apps that provide real-time updates on product availability, technology offers endless possibilities for enhancing the customer journey. However, it is important to ensure that these innovations are used in ways that align with the principles of halal business and that they enhance, rather than detract from, the customer experience.

One of the key challenges in modern business is balancing the use of technology with the need for personal, human interaction. While technology can streamline processes and improve efficiency, it can also create a sense of detachment between businesses and their customers. For Muslim entrepreneurs, maintaining a personal connection with customers is essential to building trust and fostering loyalty. The Prophet Muhammad (PBUH) emphasized the importance of human connection, stating, "The best of people are those who are most beneficial to others" (Daraqutni). This hadith reminds us that, at the heart of every successful business, is the desire to serve and benefit others.

Incorporating personal touches into the customer experience can take many forms, from personalized emails and handwritten thank-you notes to offering live customer support that addresses customer inquiries with care and attention. For halal businesses, providing excellent customer service is not just a business strategy; it is a reflection of the Islamic values of kindness, respect, and fairness. By going above and beyond to meet the needs of customers, businesses can create lasting relationships that are built on trust and mutual respect.

Another important consideration in maintaining quality in halal business is the role of ethical leadership. The Prophet Muhammad (PBUH) said, "Each of you is a shepherd, and each of you is responsible for his flock" (Bukhari). This hadith highlights the responsibility that leaders have in ensuring that their businesses operate in a way that is just, ethical, and beneficial to all stakeholders. For Muslim entrepreneurs, ethical leadership means setting an example for employees, suppliers, and partners by adhering to the principles of halal business and making decisions that prioritize fairness, transparency, and social responsibility.

Ethical leadership also involves creating a positive work environment where employees are treated with respect and provided with opportunities for growth and development. The Prophet Muhammad (PBUH) emphasized the importance of treating workers fairly, stating, "Give the worker his wages before his sweat dries" (Ibn Majah). For halal businesses, this means ensuring that employees are paid fairly, given reasonable working conditions, and supported in their personal and professional growth. By fostering a positive and supportive work culture, businesses can create a loyal and motivated workforce that is committed to the success of the company.

In addition to fostering a positive work environment, ethical leadership in halal business also involves making decisions that prioritize the well-being of society and the environment. As stewards of the Earth, Muslim entrepreneurs have a responsibility to ensure that their businesses operate in ways that are sustainable and environmentally friendly. The Quran states, "And do not commit abuse on the earth, spreading corruption" (Quran 2:60). This verse serves as a reminder that businesses should strive to minimize their environmental impact and contribute to the preservation of natural resources.

For halal businesses, sustainability can take many forms, from reducing waste and conserving energy to sourcing materials and ingredients that are environmentally friendly. By adopting sustainable practices, businesses not only fulfill their ethical obligations but also appeal to a growing number of consumers who prioritize environmental responsibility. Sustainability is not just a trend; it is a fundamental aspect of halal business that reflects the Islamic values of stewardship, care for creation, and responsibility for future generations.

In addition to sustainability, halal businesses should also consider their role in promoting social justice. Islam teaches that wealth should be distributed fairly and that the needs of the less fortunate should be prioritized. The Quran emphasizes the importance of charity, stating, "And give the relative his right, and [also] the poor and the traveler, and do not spend wastefully" (Quran 17:26). For Muslim entrepreneurs, this means ensuring that their businesses contribute to the well-being of society by supporting charitable causes, providing fair wages, and promoting economic empowerment.

One way that halal businesses can promote social justice is by implementing profit-sharing models that ensure employees and stakeholders are fairly compensated for their contributions to the company's success. By sharing profits with employees, businesses can create a more equitable work environment where everyone benefits from the company's growth. This approach aligns with the principles of halal finance, which emphasize the importance of fairness, transparency, and mutual benefit in financial transactions. Profit-sharing not only fosters a sense of ownership and responsibility among employees but also enhances the overall success of the business by aligning the interests of all stakeholders.

As Muslim entrepreneurs continue to build their halal businesses, it is important to recognize that success in halal business is not solely measured by financial gain. True success is measured by the positive impact that the business has on its customers, employees, community, and the environment. The Prophet Muhammad (PBUH) said, "The best of people are those who bring the most benefit to others" (Daraqutni). This hadith serves as a guiding principle for halal businesses, reminding entrepreneurs that the ultimate goal of business is to serve others and contribute to the greater good.

For Muslim entrepreneurs, building a successful halal brand means balancing the pursuit of profit with the responsibility to act ethically, treat others with kindness and respect, and use wealth in ways that benefit society. By adhering to the principles of halal business, entrepreneurs can create brands that are trusted, respected, and sought after by consumers who value integrity, transparency, and social responsibility. This approach not only ensures long-term success but also brings barakah—divine blessings—that enrich both the business and the lives of those it touches.

In the dynamic world of halal business, continuous learning and growth are essential for success. Muslim entrepreneurs must stay informed about industry trends, emerging markets, and new technologies while remaining true to their Islamic values. The Quran encourages Muslims to seek knowledge and strive for excellence, stating, "And say: My Lord, increase me in knowledge" (Quran 20:114). By embracing a mindset of continuous improvement, entrepreneurs can innovate, adapt, and thrive in a rapidly changing business environment.

Ultimately, the success of halal business is not determined by the size of the company or the number of customers it serves but by the impact it has on the world. Halal businesses that operate with integrity, treat others with fairness, and contribute to the well-being of society are businesses that will stand the test of time. Muslim entrepreneurs have a unique opportunity to build businesses that not only generate wealth but also promote the values of justice, compassion, and stewardship that are central to Islam.

As the global halal economy continues to grow, Muslim entrepreneurs have the opportunity to play a leading role in shaping the future of ethical business practices. By offering products and services that align with Islamic principles, entrepreneurs can build brands that are trusted and respected by consumers around the world. The demand for halal products and services is not limited to Muslim consumers; increasingly, non-Muslim consumers are seeking out ethical, sustainable, and socially responsible brands. This presents a significant opportunity for halal businesses to expand their reach and attract a diverse customer base.

One of the key drivers of growth in the global halal economy is the increasing awareness of halal certification and its benefits. Consumers are becoming more knowledgeable about the importance of halal certification and are actively seeking out products that are certified as halal. For Muslim entrepreneurs, this presents an opportunity to differentiate their products and services by obtaining halal certification and promoting their commitment to ethical business practices. Halal certification not only provides assurance to consumers but also enhances the credibility and reputation of the brand.

In addition to halal certification, Muslim entrepreneurs should also consider the role of partnerships and collaborations in driving growth. By working together with other businesses, organizations, and individuals who share their values, entrepreneurs can expand their reach, share resources, and achieve common goals. The Quran encourages cooperation and mutual support, stating, "Help one another in acts of piety and righteousness" (Quran 5:2). Partnerships are particularly valuable in the context of the global halal economy, where businesses may face challenges related to certification, distribution, and market access.

Collaborations between halal businesses can take many forms, from joint ventures to co-branded marketing campaigns to collaborative research and development initiatives. These partnerships not only provide practical benefits, such as access to new markets or resources, but also strengthen the halal business community by fostering a sense of solidarity and mutual support. By working together, halal businesses can amplify their impact and contribute to the overall growth and development of the global halal economy.

As Muslim entrepreneurs look to the future, it is important to remain focused on the values and principles that define halal business. In a fast-paced and often competitive business environment, it can be tempting to prioritize short-term gains over long-term ethical considerations. However, the Quran reminds us of the importance of patience and perseverance in the face of challenges, stating, "And be patient, for indeed, Allah does not allow the reward of those who do good to be lost" (Quran 11:115). For halal businesses, success is not just about financial gain; it is about earning halal income that is blessed with barakah and using that wealth to benefit others.

In the ever-evolving landscape of business, Muslim entrepreneurs must remain committed to continuous learning, ethical leadership, and social responsibility. By adhering to the principles of halal business and embracing the opportunities within the global halal economy, entrepreneurs can build businesses that are not only successful but also contribute to the greater good of society. The Prophet Muhammad (PBUH) said, "The best of people are those who bring the most benefit to others" (Daraqutni). By following this guiding principle, Muslim entrepreneurs can create businesses that are truly halal—ethical, just, and beneficial to all.

In the context of building a halal business, one of the most essential components of success is trust. Trust is the cornerstone of every successful relationship, and in the business world, it plays a pivotal role in how brands interact with customers, partners, and even competitors. The Quran reminds us, "And fulfill [every] commitment. Indeed, the commitment is ever [that about which one will be] questioned" (Quran 17:34). For Muslim entrepreneurs, fulfilling commitments and maintaining trust are non-negotiable principles that must guide every business decision and transaction.

Trust is not something that can be built overnight, nor can it be achieved through clever marketing tactics alone. It must be earned through consistent actions, transparency, and integrity in all dealings. Halal businesses that prioritize trust will see long-term benefits, as customers are more likely to remain loyal to brands that they trust. Furthermore, trusted businesses are more likely to receive positive referrals, which are invaluable in a market where word-of-mouth can make or break a brand.

One way to build trust in halal business is through transparent communication. Customers want to know where their products come from, how they are made, and what values the company stands for. For Muslim entrepreneurs, this means providing clear and honest information about the sourcing, production, and certification of halal products. Whether through product labeling, social media updates, or in-store materials, transparency should be a key part of the marketing strategy. The Quran emphasizes the importance of truthfulness, stating, "O you who have believed, fear Allah and be with those who are true" (Quran 9:119). By being open and honest in all communications, halal businesses can build a reputation for integrity and reliability.

In addition to transparency, consistency is another critical factor in building trust. Customers need to feel confident that they can rely on a brand to deliver the same quality and ethical standards every time they make a purchase. Inconsistencies in quality, customer service, or messaging can erode trust and damage a brand's reputation. The Prophet Muhammad (PBUH) said, "The most beloved deed to Allah is the most regular and constant, even if it were little" (Bukhari). This hadith highlights the importance of consistency in actions, and for Muslim entrepreneurs, this means ensuring that their business operations, products, and marketing efforts are consistently aligned with the values of halal business.

One practical way to maintain consistency in halal business is by implementing rigorous quality control processes. Quality control ensures that products meet the highest standards of halal compliance and customer satisfaction. For example, businesses can establish internal checks to verify that ingredients are sourced ethically and that production methods adhere to halal guidelines. By consistently delivering high-quality products, halal businesses can build long-lasting relationships with their customers and enhance their brand reputation.

Another important aspect of trust in halal business is customer feedback and responsiveness. Listening to customers and addressing their concerns is an essential part of maintaining a positive relationship. The Prophet Muhammad (PBUH) said, "The most complete of the believers in faith is the one with the best character" (Tirmidhi). This hadith reminds Muslim entrepreneurs that good character, including humility and a willingness to listen, is key to success in both personal and business life.

For halal businesses, actively seeking feedback from customers provides valuable insights into areas for improvement and innovation. It also demonstrates that the business values its customers' opinions and is committed to continuously improving its offerings. Feedback can be gathered through various channels, such as customer surveys, online reviews, or direct interactions in-store or through social media. However, it is important not only to gather feedback but to act on it. Addressing customer concerns promptly and effectively builds trust and shows that the business genuinely cares about customer satisfaction.

In addition to listening to customer feedback, halal businesses must be responsive to changing market trends and customer needs. The global halal economy is dynamic, and consumer preferences are constantly evolving. By staying attuned to these changes, Muslim entrepreneurs can adapt their products, services, and marketing strategies to meet the needs of their customers. The Quran encourages Muslims to seek knowledge and remain aware of their surroundings, stating, "And say, 'My Lord, increase me in knowledge'" (Quran 20:114). For halal businesses, this means continually learning about new market opportunities, customer preferences, and technological advancements.

One of the key trends in modern business is the growing demand for sustainability and ethical practices. Consumers, both Muslim and non-Muslim, are increasingly concerned about the environmental and social impact of the products they purchase. For halal businesses, this presents a unique opportunity to position themselves as leaders in ethical and sustainable business practices. By promoting environmentally friendly packaging, fair labor practices, and responsible sourcing, businesses can differentiate themselves in the marketplace and appeal to the growing number of conscious consumers.

Sustainability is not only a trend but a responsibility that aligns with the values of halal business. The Quran emphasizes the importance of stewardship over the Earth, stating, "And it is He who has made you successors upon the earth" (Quran 6:165). For Muslim entrepreneurs, this means taking an active role in protecting the environment and ensuring that their business practices are sustainable. By adopting eco-friendly practices, such as reducing waste, conserving energy, and using renewable resources, businesses can contribute to a healthier planet while building a positive brand image.

In addition to promoting sustainability, halal businesses should also focus on promoting inclusivity and diversity in their marketing efforts. The Quran teaches, "O mankind, indeed We have created you from male and female and made you peoples and tribes that you may know one another" (Quran 49:13). This verse emphasizes the importance of diversity and mutual respect among different peoples and cultures. For halal businesses, this means ensuring that their marketing campaigns reflect the diversity of their customers and are inclusive of people from all backgrounds.

In practice, this might involve creating marketing materials that feature diverse models, representing different ethnicities, genders, and age groups. It could also involve offering products and services that cater to the unique needs of different communities, such as modest fashion lines or halal-certified beauty products. By embracing diversity in their marketing efforts, businesses can appeal to a wider customer base and demonstrate their commitment to inclusivity and respect.

Diversity and inclusivity also extend to the workplace. Halal businesses should strive to create an inclusive work environment where employees from all backgrounds feel valued and respected. This includes providing equal opportunities for growth and development, fostering a culture of mutual respect, and promoting diversity in leadership roles. The Prophet Muhammad

(PBUH) said, "The believers, in their mutual kindness, compassion, and sympathy, are just like one body" (Bukhari). For Muslim entrepreneurs, this hadith serves as a reminder that a successful business is one that promotes unity, kindness, and inclusivity both internally and externally.

As businesses grow, the importance of leadership in maintaining a halal brand cannot be overstated. Leaders in halal businesses have a responsibility to set the tone for ethical behavior, transparency, and fairness. Ethical leadership involves making decisions that prioritize the well-being of customers, employees, and society as a whole. The Quran advises, "And do not consume one another's wealth unjustly or send it [in bribery] to the rulers in order that [they might aid] you [to] consume a portion of the wealth of the people in sin, while you know [it is unlawful]" (Quran 2:188). This verse serves as a powerful reminder of the importance of ethical leadership and the need to avoid any form of corruption or exploitation.

For halal businesses, ethical leadership means leading by example and fostering a culture of integrity, fairness, and social responsibility. Leaders must ensure that their business operations align with halal principles and that their employees are treated with respect and dignity. They must also ensure that the business remains focused on its mission to provide value to customers while upholding the values of Islam. By embodying ethical leadership, halal businesses can build strong, resilient brands that stand the test of time.

Another critical component of ethical leadership in halal business is accountability. Leaders must hold themselves and their teams accountable for upholding the principles of halal business. This means setting clear expectations, establishing ethical guidelines, and ensuring that all employees understand and adhere to the company's values. Accountability also involves being transparent with customers and stakeholders about the company's operations, challenges, and successes. The Quran encourages accountability, stating, "And fear a Day when you will be returned to Allah. Then every soul will be compensated for what it earned, and they will not be wronged" (Quran 2:281).

For Muslim entrepreneurs, accountability is not just about meeting financial targets or achieving business goals; it is about fulfilling a higher responsibility to act in accordance with Islamic values. This includes being honest in all dealings, treating others fairly, and ensuring that the business contributes to the well-being of society. By fostering a culture of accountability, halal businesses can build trust with their customers, employees, and partners, ensuring long-term success.

As halal businesses grow and expand, it is important to remain focused on the core values that define the brand. Growth should never come at the expense of ethical principles. The Prophet Muhammad (PBUH) said, "Whoever cheats us is not one of us" (Muslim), underscoring the importance of honesty and integrity in all business dealings. For halal businesses, this means ensuring that growth strategies are aligned with the values of fairness, transparency, and social responsibility.

One common challenge that businesses face as they grow is maintaining the same level of personal connection and customer service that they provided when they were smaller. As a business expands, it becomes more difficult to offer the same personalized attention to each customer. However, Muslim entrepreneurs must strive to maintain their commitment to customer service, even as their business scales. The Prophet Muhammad (PBUH) said, "The most beloved of deeds to Allah are those that are most consistent, even if small" (Bukhari). This hadith emphasizes the importance of consistency, and for halal businesses, this means continuing to provide excellent customer service, regardless of the size of the business.

As businesses grow, technology can play a crucial role in helping maintain personalized customer interactions. Customer relationship management (CRM) systems, for example, can help businesses track customer preferences, purchase history, and feedback, allowing them to offer personalized recommendations and solutions. However, it is important to ensure that the use of technology aligns with the principles of halal business. This means respecting customer privacy, being transparent about how data is collected and used, and ensuring that technology is used to enhance, rather than exploit, the customer experience.

In addition to leveraging technology, halal businesses must also invest in their employees as they grow. A successful business is built on the strength of its workforce, and as the business expands, it is important to ensure that employees are supported in their personal and professional development. This includes providing opportunities for training, mentorship, and career advancement. The Prophet Muhammad (PBUH) emphasized the importance of education, stating, "The seeking of knowledge is obligatory for every Muslim" (Ibn Majah). For halal businesses, this means fostering a culture of learning and growth, where employees are encouraged to develop their skills and contribute to the success of the company.

Employee satisfaction is not only beneficial for the individual employee but also for the overall success of the business. Happy, motivated employees are more likely to be productive, loyal, and committed to the company's mission. For halal businesses, this means creating a positive work environment where employees feel valued, respected, and supported. This aligns with the Islamic principle of treating others with kindness and fairness, as emphasized in the Quran, "And do good; indeed, Allah loves the doers of good" (Quran 2:195).

As businesses continue to grow, another important consideration is maintaining the integrity of the brand. The success of a halal business is not just about financial profitability but about staying true to the values that define the brand. The Quran advises, "And cooperate in righteousness and piety, but do not cooperate in sin and aggression" (Quran 5:2). This verse serves as a reminder that businesses must remain focused on their mission to provide value to customers while upholding the principles of halal business. By maintaining integrity in all operations, halal businesses can build strong, trusted brands that resonate with customers and stand the test of time.

In the global marketplace, halal businesses are uniquely positioned to offer products and services that appeal to a wide range of consumers who value ethical, sustainable, and socially responsible business practices. The global demand for halal products and services is growing, driven by both Muslim and non-Muslim consumers who seek brands that reflect their values. For Muslim entrepreneurs, this presents an opportunity to build businesses that not only generate profit but also promote the values of justice, fairness, and social responsibility.

One of the key drivers of growth in the halal economy is the increasing awareness of halal certification. As consumers become more knowledgeable about halal standards, they are actively seeking out products that are certified as halal. For halal businesses, obtaining halal certification is not just a legal requirement; it is a way to build trust with consumers and demonstrate a commitment to ethical business practices. Halal certification ensures that products meet the highest standards of purity, safety, and ethical sourcing, providing assurance to consumers that they are making informed choices.

In addition to halal certification, Muslim entrepreneurs should also consider the role of corporate social responsibility (CSR) in building a strong halal brand. CSR involves implementing initiatives that contribute to the well-being of society, whether through charitable donations, community development projects, or environmental sustainability efforts. By incorporating CSR into their business strategy, halal businesses can enhance their reputation, build customer loyalty, and contribute to the greater good. The Quran encourages charitable giving, stating, "And spend in the way of Allah and do not throw [yourselves] with your [own] hands into destruction [by refraining]. And do good; indeed, Allah loves the doers of good" (Quran 2:195).

For halal businesses, CSR should not be an afterthought or a marketing gimmick; it should be an integral part of the company's mission and values. By aligning CSR initiatives with the principles of halal business, companies can make a meaningful impact on society while building a positive brand image. Whether through supporting education, providing healthcare, or promoting environmental conservation, halal businesses have the opportunity to use their resources for the betterment of humanity.

As Muslim entrepreneurs continue to grow their businesses, it is important to remember that true success is not measured solely by financial gain. The Prophet Muhammad (PBUH) said, "Richness is not having many possessions, but richness is being content with oneself" (Bukhari). This hadith serves as a reminder that the ultimate goal of halal business is not simply to accumulate wealth but to use that wealth in ways that are pleasing to Allah and beneficial to others.

For Muslim entrepreneurs, building a successful halal brand means staying true to the values of Islam, treating others with kindness and fairness, and using wealth to make a positive impact on the world. By adhering to the principles of halal business and focusing on long-term value rather than short-term gain, entrepreneurs can build businesses that are not only financially successful but also blessed with barakah—divine blessings that enrich both the business and the lives of those it touches.

As the global halal economy continues to grow, Muslim entrepreneurs have a unique opportunity to play a leading role in shaping the future of ethical business practices. By offering products and services that align with Islamic principles, businesses can build trusted brands that resonate with consumers around the world. The Prophet Muhammad (PBUH) said, "The best of people are those who bring the most benefit to others" (Daraqutni). By following this guiding principle, Muslim entrepreneurs can create businesses that are truly halal—ethical, just, and beneficial to all.

CHAPTER 5: THE ROLE OF HALAL COMPLIANCE IN MODERN BUSINESS

In today's rapidly evolving global economy, businesses across all sectors are striving to meet consumer demands for products and services that are both ethical and compliant with diverse cultural and religious values. For Muslim entrepreneurs, the importance of halal compliance extends far beyond simply meeting market demands. Halal compliance is a sacred duty, rooted in the principles of Islam, that governs every aspect of business, from product sourcing and production methods to financial transactions and customer interactions. The Quran reminds us, "O mankind, eat from whatever is on earth [that is] lawful and good and do not follow the footsteps of Satan. Indeed, he is to you a clear enemy" (Quran 2:168). This verse emphasizes the importance of consuming and dealing only in what is lawful (halal) and good (tayyib), and this principle applies equally to all business practices.

For Muslim entrepreneurs, ensuring halal compliance means adhering to strict ethical standards in every part of their business, not just in terms of the products they sell but also in how they run their operations. This involves making decisions that are consistent with Islamic teachings, such as avoiding interest-based financing (riba), conducting fair and transparent trade, and ensuring that workers are treated with dignity and respect. The Prophet Muhammad (PBUH) said, "The truthful and trustworthy merchant is with the prophets, the truthful, and the martyrs" (Tirmidhi). This hadith serves as a reminder that honesty, integrity, and trustworthiness are essential qualities for any businessperson, and these qualities are at the heart of halal compliance.

One of the foundational aspects of halal compliance in business is the prohibition of riba, or interest. The Quran explicitly forbids the practice of riba, stating, "Allah has permitted trade and has forbidden riba" (Quran 2:275). For Muslim entrepreneurs, this means avoiding conventional loans and financial instruments that involve interest. Instead, they are encouraged to seek out halal alternatives, such as profit-sharing arrangements (mudarabah) or partnership models (musharakah), where risks and rewards are shared fairly among all parties. These halal financing methods not only align with Islamic teachings but also promote fairness and mutual benefit, ensuring that no one is exploited in the pursuit of profit.

In addition to avoiding riba, halal compliance also requires businesses to ensure that their products and services are free from any haram (forbidden) elements. This includes not only the ingredients and materials used in manufacturing but also the processes and methods involved in production. The Quran commands, "O you who have believed, eat from the good things which We have provided for you and be grateful to Allah if it is [indeed] Him that you worship" (Quran 2:172). This verse highlights the importance of consuming only what is halal and tayyib (pure), and this principle extends to the goods and services offered by businesses.

For businesses in the food and beverage industry, halal compliance often involves obtaining halal certification from reputable authorities. Halal certification ensures that products meet the stringent requirements of Islamic law, including the proper slaughtering of animals, the avoidance of cross-contamination with haram substances, and the use of permissible ingredients. However, halal compliance goes beyond just food; it applies to a wide range of industries, including pharmaceuticals, cosmetics, fashion, and finance. Muslim entrepreneurs must ensure that all aspects of their business adhere to halal standards, from sourcing raw materials to delivering the final product to the customer.

Halal certification serves as a guarantee to consumers that the products they are purchasing are in full compliance with Islamic teachings. In an increasingly globalized marketplace, where consumers are more conscious than ever about the ethical and religious implications of their purchases, halal certification has become a valuable asset for businesses seeking to build trust and loyalty with Muslim and non-Muslim customers alike. The demand for halal-certified products is on the rise, not only in Muslim-majority countries but also in non-Muslim-majority regions where consumers value ethical and sustainable practices.

One of the key challenges for businesses seeking halal certification is ensuring that their entire supply chain is compliant with halal standards. This requires careful oversight and management, as any lapse in compliance at any stage of the supply chain can render a product haram. For example, a product that is halal in its ingredients may become haram if it is processed or packaged in facilities that also handle non-halal items, particularly those that involve pork or alcohol. To maintain halal compliance, businesses must work closely with their suppliers and partners to ensure that every step of the production process adheres to the highest halal standards.

The Prophet Muhammad (PBUH) said, "Leave that which makes you doubt for that which does not make you doubt" (Tirmidhi). This hadith encourages Muslim entrepreneurs to err on the side of caution when it comes to ensuring halal compliance. If there is any uncertainty about whether a product or practice is halal, it is better to avoid it altogether and seek out a permissible alternative. This cautious approach helps businesses maintain their integrity and ensures that they are operating in full accordance with Islamic principles.

Another important aspect of halal compliance in modern business is the ethical treatment of workers and employees. Islam places a strong emphasis on fairness and justice in all dealings, including labor practices. The Prophet Muhammad (PBUH) said, "Give the worker his wages before his sweat dries" (Ibn Majah), emphasizing the importance of paying workers promptly and fairly for their labor. For Muslim entrepreneurs, this means ensuring that employees are treated with respect, provided with fair wages, and given safe working conditions. Halal compliance is not just about the products a business sells; it is also about how the business treats the people who contribute to its success.

In addition to fair wages and safe working conditions, halal compliance also requires businesses to uphold ethical labor practices, such as avoiding exploitation, forced labor, and child labor. These practices are not only haram but also violate the basic principles of justice and fairness that are central to Islam. Muslim entrepreneurs must be vigilant in ensuring that their businesses operate in a way that upholds the dignity and rights of all workers, regardless of their position or status within the company. This commitment to ethical labor practices not only aligns with Islamic teachings but also enhances the reputation of the business as one that values integrity and social responsibility.

Moreover, halal compliance extends to the way businesses interact with their customers. The Prophet Muhammad (PBUH) said, "Whoever cheats us is not one of us" (Muslim), emphasizing the importance of honesty and transparency in all business dealings. For Muslim entrepreneurs, this means ensuring that marketing materials, product descriptions, and sales practices are truthful and not misleading. Customers should have a clear understanding of the products or services they are purchasing, and businesses should avoid using deceptive practices to boost sales. By maintaining honesty and transparency in their dealings with customers, businesses can build trust and foster long-term relationships based on mutual respect.

In the digital age, where businesses increasingly rely on e-commerce platforms and online marketing, halal compliance also applies to the way businesses conduct their digital transactions. This includes ensuring that online payment systems do not involve riba, avoiding misleading advertisements, and respecting customer privacy. The Quran reminds us, "O you who have believed, fear Allah and speak words of appropriate justice" (Quran 33:70). For Muslim entrepreneurs, this means ensuring that their digital presence reflects the values of honesty, fairness, and transparency that are central to halal business practices.

In addition to ethical labor practices and honest customer interactions, halal compliance also extends to environmental stewardship. The Quran states, "And do not commit abuse on the earth, spreading corruption" (Quran 2:60). For Muslim entrepreneurs, this means taking an active role in protecting the environment and ensuring that their business operations do not cause harm to the planet. Halal compliance involves adopting sustainable practices, such as reducing waste, conserving energy, and sourcing materials in an environmentally responsible manner. By aligning their business practices with the principles of environmental sustainability, Muslim entrepreneurs can contribute to the preservation of the Earth's resources for future generations.

One way that businesses can demonstrate their commitment to environmental sustainability is by obtaining eco-friendly certifications, such as organic or fair trade certifications. These certifications provide assurance to customers that the products they are purchasing have been produced in a way that is both halal and environmentally responsible. By offering eco-friendly products, businesses can appeal to a growing segment of consumers who value sustainability and are willing to support brands that prioritize ethical practices.

Halal compliance also plays a crucial role in financial transparency and ethical investment. In Islam, wealth is viewed as a trust from Allah, and it must be used in ways that are lawful and beneficial to society. The Quran states, "And spend in the way of Allah and do not throw [yourselves] with your [own] hands into destruction [by refraining]. And do good; indeed, Allah loves the doers of good" (Quran 2:195). For Muslim entrepreneurs, this means ensuring that their financial practices are transparent, ethical, and aligned with the principles of halal finance. This includes avoiding interest-based loans, engaging in profit-sharing arrangements, and investing in industries that are beneficial to society.

Ethical investment is a key component of halal compliance, as it ensures that businesses are using their wealth in ways that promote social good and do not contribute to harm. For example, Muslim entrepreneurs should avoid investing in industries that are involved in alcohol, gambling, tobacco, or other haram activities. Instead, they should seek out investment opportunities that align with Islamic values, such as renewable energy, healthcare, education, and social services. By making ethical investment decisions, businesses can ensure that their wealth is being used in ways that benefit both their company and the wider community.

One of the most important aspects of halal compliance is the concept of *niyyah*—the intention behind every action. In Islam, actions are judged by their intentions, and it is the intention to do good and follow the path of righteousness that brings about blessings in one's endeavors. The Prophet Muhammad (PBUH) said, "Actions are but by intentions, and every person will have only that which he intended" (Bukhari). For Muslim entrepreneurs, this means that every business decision, from product development to marketing to customer service, must be guided by the intention to do good, uphold Islamic values, and contribute to the betterment of society.

This focus on *niyyah* is what sets halal businesses apart from their conventional counterparts. While many businesses may prioritize profit above all else, halal businesses are driven by a higher purpose: to please Allah by conducting business in a way that is ethical, fair, and beneficial to others. This does not mean that halal businesses should not seek financial success; rather, it means that success is measured not only in terms of profit but also in terms of the positive impact the business has on its customers, employees, and society as a whole.

The concept of *niyyah* also extends to how businesses handle their profits. In Islam, wealth is not meant to be hoarded or used solely for personal gain; it is a trust from Allah that must be shared with those in need. The Quran emphasizes the importance of charitable giving, stating, "Take from their wealth a charity by which you purify them and cause them increase" (Quran 9:103). For Muslim entrepreneurs, this means giving back to the community through zakat (obligatory charity) and sadaqah (voluntary charity). By incorporating charitable giving into their business practices, Muslim entrepreneurs can ensure that their wealth is being used in ways that are pleasing to Allah and beneficial to society.

Incorporating zakat and sadaqah into business operations also enhances the reputation of the business as one that is socially responsible and committed to the well-being of the community. Customers today are increasingly looking for brands that not only offer high-quality products but also contribute to social causes and make a positive impact on the world. By promoting their charitable initiatives, halal businesses can build stronger connections with customers and foster a sense of loyalty and trust.

As Muslim entrepreneurs strive to build businesses that are fully compliant with halal principles, it is important to remember that halal compliance is not a one-time event; it is an ongoing process that requires constant vigilance and commitment. The Quran reminds us, "So remain on a right course as you have been commanded" (Quran 11:112). This verse serves as a reminder that staying true to the path of halal business requires continuous effort and dedication. Businesses must regularly review their practices, assess their compliance with halal standards, and make any necessary adjustments to ensure that they remain in full alignment with Islamic teachings.

One of the ways businesses can maintain halal compliance is by working with reputable halal certification bodies and scholars who can provide guidance and oversight. These experts can help businesses navigate the complexities of halal compliance, from ensuring that products meet halal standards to providing advice on ethical business practices. By seeking the counsel of knowledgeable scholars and certification bodies, businesses can ensure that they are operating in accordance with Islamic law and maintaining the highest standards of halal compliance.

In addition to seeking guidance from scholars and certification bodies, businesses can also benefit from collaborating with other halal-compliant companies. By building partnerships with like-minded businesses, entrepreneurs can share best practices, resources, and expertise to enhance their halal compliance. The Quran encourages cooperation and mutual support, stating, "Help one another in acts of righteousness and piety, but do not help one another in sin and aggression" (Quran 5:2). For Muslim entrepreneurs, this means fostering a sense of community and collaboration within the halal business sector, where businesses support one another in their efforts to maintain halal standards and promote ethical practices.

Ultimately, halal compliance is not just about following rules and regulations; it is about embodying the values of Islam in every aspect of the business. The Prophet Muhammad (PBUH) said, "The best among you are those who have the best manners and character" (Bukhari). For Muslim entrepreneurs, this means striving to build businesses that reflect the highest standards of integrity, fairness, and social responsibility. By maintaining halal compliance, businesses can not only achieve financial success but also contribute to the greater good of society and earn the pleasure of Allah.

As the demand for halal-certified products and services continues to grow, businesses face the challenge of not only meeting consumer expectations but also ensuring that their practices remain aligned with Islamic principles. Halal compliance, in essence, is about creating a business model that honors both the spiritual and material aspects of commerce. This model prioritizes ethical sourcing, production, and trade while ensuring that the broader social and environmental impact of the business is positive and beneficial.

One area where halal compliance has gained increasing importance is in the realm of sustainable business practices. The Prophet Muhammad (PBUH) emphasized the importance of moderation in all things, including the use of natural resources. He said, "The Earth is green and beautiful, and Allah has appointed you His stewards over it" (Muslim). For Muslim entrepreneurs, this means adopting practices that promote sustainability and reduce the business's ecological footprint. Whether it's implementing energy-efficient processes in manufacturing, reducing waste, or opting for biodegradable packaging, businesses that align their operations with environmental stewardship are not only fulfilling their Islamic obligations but also addressing the growing demand for eco-friendly products.

The intersection of halal compliance and environmental responsibility is especially critical in industries such as food, fashion, and manufacturing, where resource consumption and waste generation are significant. For example, in the food industry, halal certification ensures that ingredients are sourced ethically and processed in a manner that respects Islamic dietary laws. However, businesses that go a step further by adopting sustainable agricultural practices, such as organic farming, crop rotation, or water conservation, demonstrate a deeper commitment to the Islamic principle of *ihsan*—doing things in the best possible way.

In the fashion industry, the rise of modest fashion has created opportunities for Muslim entrepreneurs to blend halal compliance with sustainable fashion. By sourcing ethically produced fabrics, avoiding sweatshops, and offering clothing that adheres to Islamic standards of modesty, businesses can appeal to consumers who are looking for both ethical and fashionable products. The Quran emphasizes modesty, stating, "O children of Adam, take your adornment at every masjid" (Quran 7:31). For Muslim entrepreneurs, this means offering products that reflect Islamic values of modesty and dignity while ensuring that their production processes are fair, transparent, and sustainable.

Another critical aspect of halal compliance is financial integrity. In Islam, wealth is not an end in itself but a means to achieve greater spiritual and social goals. The Quran states, "And those who, when they spend, are neither extravagant nor stingy, but are ever, between that, [justly] moderate" (Quran 25:67). This verse highlights the importance of financial moderation and ethical spending. For Muslim entrepreneurs, maintaining financial integrity means ensuring that their business finances are managed in a way that is transparent, ethical, and free from exploitation.

In practical terms, this involves avoiding interest-based financial instruments, as the prohibition of riba is one of the key principles of Islamic finance. Instead of relying on conventional loans, Muslim entrepreneurs are encouraged to seek out alternative financing options, such as profit-sharing agreements (*mudarabah*) or equity-based partnerships (*musharakah*). These models align with the Islamic emphasis on shared risk and reward, ensuring that all parties involved in a financial transaction are treated fairly and equitably.

Beyond avoiding riba, financial integrity in halal businesses also involves transparency in pricing and sales practices. The Prophet Muhammad (PBUH) said, "He who cheats is not one of us" (Muslim), highlighting the importance of honesty in trade. For businesses, this means being upfront about the true cost of products and services, avoiding deceptive pricing tactics, and ensuring that customers understand exactly what they are paying for. Transparent pricing not only builds trust with customers but also reinforces the business's commitment to ethical conduct.

As the global economy becomes increasingly digitized, halal compliance in financial practices must also extend to e-commerce and online transactions. Businesses that operate online must ensure that their payment systems are Shariah-compliant, avoiding interest-bearing credit facilities and ensuring that transactions are conducted in a fair and transparent manner. Moreover, businesses should take steps to protect customer privacy and data security, as the Quran instructs, "Do not spy or backbite each other" (Quran 49:12). By safeguarding customer information and maintaining ethical standards in digital transactions, businesses can build trust and demonstrate their commitment to both halal principles and modern business ethics.

While financial integrity and environmental responsibility are critical components of halal compliance, another equally important aspect is corporate social responsibility (CSR). Islam places a strong emphasis on social justice and the fair distribution of wealth. The Quran states, "And give the relative his right, and [also] the poor and the traveler, and do not spend wastefully" (Quran 17:26). For Muslim entrepreneurs, this means that their businesses must not only generate profit but also contribute to the well-being of society.

Corporate social responsibility can take many forms, from charitable donations and community outreach programs to ensuring fair labor practices and supporting local economies. Businesses that integrate CSR into their operations demonstrate a commitment to the Islamic values of charity (*sadaqah*) and social equity. For example, a business might dedicate a portion of its profits to fund educational programs, provide healthcare services to underserved communities, or support initiatives that promote economic development.

Incorporating CSR into business operations not only enhances the company's reputation but also fosters a sense of loyalty and trust among customers. Consumers today, particularly millennials and Generation Z, are increasingly looking for brands that align with their values and contribute to the greater good. By actively engaging in CSR initiatives, halal businesses can differentiate themselves from competitors and build strong relationships with socially conscious consumers.

Moreover, CSR in halal businesses should not be limited to charitable donations. It should also encompass ethical labor practices, ensuring that all workers, from entry-level employees to top executives, are treated fairly and with respect. The Prophet Muhammad (PBUH) said, "Your employees are your brothers, whom Allah has placed under your command. So whoever has his brother under his command should feed him of what he eats and dress him of what he wears. Do not burden them beyond their capacity, but if you do so, then help them" (Bukhari). This hadith underscores the importance of treating employees with kindness, fairness, and dignity.

For halal businesses, ensuring that workers are paid fair wages, provided with safe working conditions, and given opportunities for personal and professional growth is not just an ethical obligation but a religious one. Businesses that prioritize the well-being of their employees are more likely to foster a positive work environment, which in turn leads to increased productivity, loyalty, and overall success.

One of the unique aspects of halal compliance is that it encourages businesses to strike a balance between profitability and social responsibility. In the modern world, where profit is often prioritized at the expense of ethical considerations, halal businesses offer a model that emphasizes the importance of doing good while doing well. The Quran teaches, "Do not forget your share of the world, but do good as Allah has done good to you" (Quran 28:77). This verse encourages Muslim entrepreneurs to pursue financial success while maintaining a commitment to ethical conduct and social justice.

In addition to treating employees fairly and engaging in CSR initiatives, halal businesses must also ensure that their supply chains are aligned with Islamic principles. This includes working with suppliers who adhere to halal standards and ensuring that all materials and products used in the business are sourced ethically. For example, in the fashion industry, this might involve sourcing fabrics from manufacturers who do not use child labor or exploit workers. In the food industry, it means ensuring that ingredients are halal-certified and that animals are slaughtered in accordance with Islamic law.

Maintaining a halal supply chain requires diligence and oversight, as any lapse in compliance at any stage of the supply chain can compromise the halal status of the final product. Muslim entrepreneurs must work closely with their suppliers and partners to ensure that all aspects of the production process adhere to halal standards. The Quran advises, "O you who have believed, fulfill [all] contracts" (Quran 5:1). This verse emphasizes the importance of upholding agreements and ensuring that business relationships are based on trust, honesty, and mutual respect.

In addition to maintaining halal supply chains, businesses should also focus on fostering long-term relationships with their suppliers. Building strong, collaborative partnerships not only ensures that the business remains compliant with halal standards but also promotes mutual growth and success. By working together with suppliers who share the same values, halal businesses can create a network of ethical partners that support one another in their pursuit of halal excellence.

As Muslim entrepreneurs continue to expand their businesses and explore new markets, they must remain vigilant in ensuring that their operations align with both halal compliance and the evolving expectations of modern consumers. In a globalized world where business practices are increasingly scrutinized by both governments and consumers, halal businesses have the opportunity to set an example of ethical leadership and integrity.

One of the key challenges that halal businesses face in the modern marketplace is ensuring that their products and services remain relevant and appealing to a diverse and global audience. While the principles of halal compliance are rooted in Islamic law, they also resonate with consumers who are seeking products that are ethical, sustainable, and socially responsible. For example, halal food products are often viewed as healthier and more hygienic, making them attractive to health-conscious consumers regardless of their religious background.

Similarly, halal financial products, such as interest-free loans and profit-sharing investment opportunities, appeal to consumers who are looking for ethical alternatives to conventional banking. By promoting the ethical and inclusive aspects of halal products and services, businesses can expand their reach and attract a wider customer base. The Quran teaches, "Invite to the way of your Lord with wisdom and good instruction, and argue with them in a way that is best" (Quran 16:125). This verse encourages Muslim entrepreneurs to approach their business dealings with wisdom and respect, using ethical practices to attract and engage a diverse audience.

As businesses grow and evolve, it is important to remember that halal compliance is not just about adhering to a set of rules; it is about embodying the values of Islam in every aspect of the business. This includes not only how products are made and sold but also how the business interacts with its customers, employees, and the wider community. By maintaining a focus on ethical conduct, social responsibility, and environmental sustainability, halal businesses can build strong, resilient brands that stand the test of time.

The Prophet Muhammad (PBUH) said, "The best of people are those who bring the most benefit to others" (Daraqutni). This hadith serves as a guiding principle for halal businesses, reminding Muslim entrepreneurs that the true measure of success is not just financial gain but the positive impact their business has on the world. By striving to do good in all aspects of their operations, halal businesses can achieve both spiritual and material success, earning the pleasure of Allah and the trust of their customers.

As the global halal economy continues to grow, Muslim entrepreneurs have the opportunity to play a leading role in shaping the future of ethical business practices. By offering products and services that align with Islamic principles, businesses can build trusted brands that resonate with consumers around the world. The growing demand for halal-certified products and services is not limited to Muslim-majority countries; it is a global trend that reflects the increasing importance of ethical consumerism.

For Muslim entrepreneurs, the key to success in this expanding market lies in maintaining a steadfast commitment to halal compliance while staying attuned to the needs and expectations of modern consumers. This means continuously innovating, adapting to changing market conditions, and finding new ways to integrate halal principles into every aspect of the business. The Quran teaches, "And do not alter the creation of Allah" (Quran 30:30), reminding us of the importance of staying true to the natural and ethical order established by Allah.

One of the ways businesses can stay ahead of the competition while maintaining halal compliance is by leveraging technology and innovation. From e-commerce platforms to blockchain technology for supply chain transparency, modern tools can help businesses enhance their operations, improve customer service, and ensure compliance with halal standards. For example, blockchain technology can be used to provide real-time verification of halal certification, ensuring that consumers can trust the authenticity of the products they are purchasing.

Similarly, advancements in mobile technology have made it easier for consumers to access halal products and services from anywhere in the world. Mobile apps that provide halal restaurant recommendations, prayer times, or Islamic financial services are becoming increasingly popular, offering Muslim consumers greater convenience and accessibility. By embracing these technological innovations, halal businesses can enhance the customer experience and strengthen their position in the global marketplace.

As businesses continue to integrate halal principles into their operations, one of the most exciting areas of growth lies in the development of digital solutions that enhance transparency and trust. Halal compliance in the digital age is not only about adhering to traditional halal standards but also about leveraging technology to ensure that these standards are maintained across global supply chains. The rise of blockchain technology, in particular, has revolutionized the way businesses track and verify the halal status of their products.

Blockchain technology provides an immutable, decentralized record of transactions, making it an ideal tool for ensuring halal compliance across complex supply chains. For example, a food manufacturer can use blockchain to verify the halal status of its ingredients from farm to table. Each step of the supply chain—from the sourcing of halal-certified meat to the packaging of the final product—can be tracked and recorded on a blockchain ledger. This ensures that there is full transparency at every stage of the production process, allowing consumers to trust that the products they are purchasing are genuinely halal.

In addition to enhancing transparency, blockchain technology can also help businesses prevent fraud and counterfeiting, both of which pose significant challenges in the global halal market. The global demand for halal-certified products has led to the emergence of counterfeit goods, which can undermine consumer trust and damage a brand's reputation. By using blockchain to create a tamper-proof record of halal certification, businesses can protect their products from counterfeiting and ensure that consumers are receiving authentic, halal-compliant goods.

Beyond blockchain, other technological innovations are also playing a crucial role in halal compliance. Artificial intelligence (AI) and machine learning, for instance, are being used to enhance quality control and ensure that halal standards are met consistently across production processes. AI-powered systems can monitor production lines, detect potential contamination, and flag any deviations from halal standards in real time. This allows businesses to maintain the highest levels of compliance while minimizing the risk of human error.

For Muslim entrepreneurs, the integration of technology into halal compliance offers new opportunities to innovate while staying true to Islamic principles. By embracing these technological advancements, businesses can improve efficiency, reduce costs, and enhance their ability to serve customers in a global marketplace. The Quran encourages Muslims to seek knowledge and innovation, stating, "Say, 'Are those who know equal to those who do not know?' Only they will remember [who are] people of understanding" (Quran 39:9). This verse serves as a reminder that knowledge and innovation are integral to success in both business and spiritual life.

As businesses continue to innovate and expand their operations, it is essential to remain focused on maintaining ethical practices that are in line with halal principles. One of the key challenges that businesses face as they grow is the temptation to compromise on ethics in the pursuit of profit. However, halal compliance requires businesses to prioritize ethical conduct above all else, ensuring that growth and success are achieved in ways that are lawful and beneficial to society.

The Prophet Muhammad (PBUH) said, "The best of people are those who bring the most benefit to others" (Daraqutni). For Muslim entrepreneurs, this means ensuring that their business practices contribute to the well-being of their employees, customers, and the wider community. Halal businesses are not only responsible for providing products and services that meet Islamic standards but also for creating positive social and environmental impact. This holistic approach to business ensures that halal compliance extends beyond the product itself to encompass every aspect of the business's operations.

In addition to ethical business practices, halal compliance also requires businesses to be vigilant about the marketing and promotion of their products. Marketing plays a crucial role in shaping consumer perceptions and influencing purchasing decisions, but it must be done in a way that aligns with Islamic values. The Quran advises, "O you who have believed, do not consume one another's wealth unjustly or send it [in bribery] to the rulers in order that [they might aid] you [to] consume a portion of the wealth of the people in sin, while you know [it is unlawful]" (Quran 2:188). This verse emphasizes the importance of fairness and honesty in all financial transactions, including marketing.

For Muslim entrepreneurs, this means avoiding deceptive advertising practices, such as making exaggerated claims about the benefits of a product or using manipulative tactics to pressure consumers into making purchases. Instead, marketing should be used as a tool for educating consumers about the value of halal products and services. By providing clear, accurate, and truthful information, businesses can build trust with their customers and foster long-term relationships based on mutual respect and transparency.

One of the most effective ways to promote halal products is through storytelling. By sharing the story behind the brand, including its commitment to halal principles and ethical business practices, businesses can connect with consumers on a deeper level. Storytelling allows businesses to highlight the values that drive their operations, from ethical sourcing to fair labor practices to environmental sustainability. For example, a halal fashion brand might share the story of how its fabrics are sourced from eco-friendly farms or how its garments are produced by workers who are paid fair wages.

In the digital age, social media has become a powerful tool for storytelling and brand building. Platforms like Instagram, Facebook, and YouTube allow businesses to share their message with a global audience in real time, making it easier than ever to reach customers around the world. For halal businesses, social media provides an opportunity to showcase their commitment to halal compliance and ethical practices in a way that resonates with modern consumers.

However, as with all forms of marketing, it is important to approach social media with a focus on integrity and honesty. The Prophet Muhammad (PBUH) said, "Whoever believes in Allah and the Last Day should speak good or remain silent" (Muslim). This hadith reminds us of the importance of using our words—and by extension, our marketing efforts—responsibly. For halal businesses, this means ensuring that all social media content is truthful, respectful, and aligned with Islamic values.

Social media also offers businesses the opportunity to engage directly with their customers, fostering a sense of community and trust. By responding to customer inquiries, addressing concerns, and sharing behind-the-scenes content, businesses can build stronger relationships with their audience. This approach not only enhances customer loyalty but also reinforces the brand's commitment to transparency and halal compliance.

In addition to social media, content marketing is another effective way to educate consumers about the benefits of halal products. Content marketing involves creating and sharing valuable, informative content that helps customers make informed decisions. This can include blog posts, videos, infographics, and more, all designed to provide customers with insights into the halal certification process, the ethical practices behind the business, and the benefits of choosing halal products.

For example, a halal food brand might create a video series that explains the steps involved in obtaining halal certification, from sourcing halal ingredients to ensuring that production methods are in compliance with Islamic law. By providing this kind of educational content, businesses can position themselves as trusted authorities in the halal industry, while also building credibility and trust with their audience.

As businesses continue to grow and expand their presence in the global marketplace, it is essential to maintain a strong focus on customer service. The Prophet Muhammad (PBUH) emphasized the importance of treating others with kindness and respect, stating, "The best among you are those who have the best manners and character" (Bukhari). For halal businesses, this means ensuring that customers are treated with the utmost respect and that their needs are met in a way that aligns with Islamic values.

One of the key components of halal compliance in customer service is the concept of fairness. Businesses must ensure that their pricing, return policies, and customer service practices are fair and transparent. Customers should feel confident that they are being treated fairly, whether they are making a purchase, requesting a refund, or seeking assistance with a product or service. By maintaining fairness in all customer interactions, businesses can build trust and foster long-term loyalty.

In addition to fairness, halal businesses must also prioritize responsiveness in their customer service efforts. The Prophet Muhammad (PBUH) said, "The believer is like a mirror to another believer" (Muslim). This hadith highlights the importance of reflecting the best qualities in our interactions with others, including our customers. For businesses, this means being responsive to customer inquiries, addressing concerns promptly, and going above and beyond to ensure customer satisfaction.

As the global halal economy continues to expand, businesses that prioritize halal compliance in all aspects of their operations—including customer service—are more likely to succeed in the long term. By maintaining a strong focus on ethical conduct, transparency, and customer satisfaction, halal businesses can differentiate themselves in a competitive marketplace and build lasting relationships with customers who value integrity and trust.

The future of halal business is bright, and as more consumers seek out products and services that align with their ethical and spiritual values, the demand for halal-certified offerings will continue to grow. For Muslim entrepreneurs, this presents an exciting opportunity to not only achieve financial success but also contribute to the greater good by upholding the principles of halal compliance in every aspect of their business operations.

As businesses continue to navigate the complexities of the global marketplace, it is important to remain vigilant in ensuring that all aspects of their operations align with halal principles. This requires a commitment to continuous improvement and adaptation, as the market evolves and new challenges arise. The Quran advises, "And say: My Lord, increase me in knowledge" (Quran 20:114), reminding Muslim entrepreneurs of the importance of seeking knowledge and staying informed about the latest developments in their industry.

One of the key areas where businesses can continue to improve is in the area of innovation. The halal economy is dynamic, and businesses that embrace innovation are more likely to stay competitive and meet the changing needs of their customers. For example, in the halal food industry, businesses can explore new product lines that cater to specific dietary needs, such as gluten-free or organic halal products. In the fashion industry, businesses can experiment with sustainable materials and cutting-edge designs that appeal to a modern, global audience.

Innovation should not come at the expense of halal compliance, however. Businesses must ensure that all new products, services, and technologies are developed in a way that aligns with Islamic principles. The Quran reminds us, "And eat of what Allah has provided for you [which is] lawful and good. And fear Allah, in whom you are believers" (Quran 5:88). For businesses, this means ensuring that all innovations are not only lawful (halal) but also good (tayyib)—ethical, beneficial, and in line with the values of Islam.

In addition to product innovation, businesses should also explore new ways to engage with customers and build stronger relationships. One of the most effective ways to do this is through personalized marketing, which allows businesses to tailor their offerings to the specific needs and preferences of individual customers. By using customer data ethically and responsibly, businesses can provide personalized recommendations, special offers, and customized experiences that enhance customer satisfaction and loyalty.

For example, a halal beauty brand might offer personalized skincare recommendations based on a customer's skin type, preferences, and previous purchases. By offering a personalized experience, businesses can differentiate themselves from competitors and build a deeper connection with their customers. However, it is important to ensure that all data collection and personalization efforts are conducted in a way that respects customer privacy and adheres to halal principles.

As businesses continue to explore new opportunities for growth and innovation, they must remain committed to the core values that define halal compliance. The Prophet Muhammad (PBUH) said, "The believer is like a date palm tree—the good you give out always returns to you" (Bukhari). This hadith serves as a reminder that businesses that act with integrity, fairness, and generosity will ultimately be rewarded with success, both in this world and the hereafter.

For halal businesses, this means staying true to the principles of ethical conduct, transparency, and social responsibility, even as they grow and evolve. By maintaining a strong focus on halal compliance, businesses can build trusted brands that resonate with consumers around the world and contribute to the greater good of society. The future of halal business is not just about financial success—it is about creating positive impact, fostering ethical leadership, and upholding the values of Islam in every aspect of business.

As the global halal economy continues to expand, Muslim entrepreneurs have the opportunity to play a leading role in shaping the future of ethical business practices. By offering products and services that align with Islamic principles, businesses can build trusted brands that resonate with consumers around the world. The Prophet Muhammad (PBUH) said, "The best of people are those who bring the most benefit to others" (Daraqutni). By following this guiding principle, Muslim entrepreneurs can create businesses that are truly halal—ethical, just, and beneficial to all.

As Muslim entrepreneurs navigate the growing global halal economy, one of the greatest challenges is maintaining the balance between traditional values and modern business practices. Halal compliance requires a constant effort to uphold Islamic principles while adapting to the demands of a rapidly evolving market. The Prophet Muhammad (PBUH) said, "Allah loves that whenever any of you does something, he should excel in it" (Tabarani). This hadith serves as a reminder that Muslim entrepreneurs are called to strive for excellence in all aspects of their business, ensuring that halal standards are not compromised, even as the business scales and grows.

For businesses to excel in maintaining halal compliance, there must be an ongoing commitment to training and education. This applies not only to business owners and leaders but also to employees and partners throughout the supply chain. Ensuring that every individual involved in the production, marketing, and sales process understands the importance of halal compliance is critical to maintaining the integrity of the business. Training programs can focus on the ethical dimensions of halal compliance, such as sourcing materials in accordance with Islamic law, ensuring that all production processes meet halal standards, and understanding the spiritual significance of adhering to halal principles.

For example, a business in the food industry might conduct regular training sessions for its employees to ensure that they understand the halal certification process, including how to handle halal ingredients, avoid cross-contamination with haram substances, and ensure that all products are properly labeled as halal. By providing this type of education, businesses can empower their employees to take ownership of the halal compliance process, creating a culture of integrity and accountability that extends throughout the entire organization.

In addition to internal training programs, businesses can also benefit from collaborating with external experts, such as halal certification bodies and Islamic scholars. These experts can provide valuable guidance on how to navigate the complexities of halal compliance, helping businesses to identify potential challenges and find solutions that are in line with Islamic teachings. The Quran advises, "So ask the people of knowledge if you do not know" (Quran 16:43). For Muslim entrepreneurs, seeking guidance from knowledgeable sources is essential to ensuring that their business remains compliant with halal standards, even as they expand into new markets and industries.

One of the key areas where businesses can seek guidance from experts is in the realm of halal certification. As the global demand for halal-certified products continues to rise, obtaining and maintaining halal certification has become a critical component of business success. Halal certification provides consumers with the assurance that the products they are purchasing meet the strict requirements of Islamic law, and it serves as a valuable marketing tool for businesses looking to build trust with their customers.

However, obtaining halal certification is not always a straightforward process, especially for businesses that operate in multiple countries or industries. Each country may have its own halal certification bodies, each with its own set of standards and requirements. For example, the requirements for halal certification in the food industry may differ significantly from those in the cosmetics or pharmaceuticals industries. To navigate these complexities, businesses must work closely with reputable halal certification bodies that are recognized both locally and internationally.

In addition to meeting the technical requirements of halal certification, businesses must also ensure that their products are free from haram substances, such as alcohol, pork, or other forbidden ingredients. This requires diligent oversight of the entire supply chain, from the sourcing of raw materials to the final packaging of the product. The Quran states, "And eat of what Allah has provided for you [which is] lawful and good" (Quran 5:88). For Muslim entrepreneurs, this verse serves as a reminder of the importance of ensuring that all products are both halal (lawful) and tayyib (pure).

Halal certification not only benefits Muslim consumers but also appeals to a growing segment of non-Muslim consumers who are seeking products that align with their ethical and dietary preferences. Many consumers today view halal-certified products as being healthier, cleaner, and more humane, making them an attractive option for those who prioritize ethical consumption. For businesses, this presents an opportunity to expand their customer base and appeal to a wider audience, while still adhering to the principles of halal compliance.

In addition to halal certification, another important aspect of maintaining halal compliance in modern business is the development of strong relationships with suppliers and partners. A business's ability to maintain halal standards depends largely on the integrity of its supply chain. If any part of the supply chain fails to meet halal standards, the entire product may be compromised. For this reason, businesses must work closely with their suppliers and partners to ensure that they share the same commitment to halal compliance.

The Prophet Muhammad (PBUH) said, "The one who does not have mercy on people, Allah will not have mercy on him" (Tirmidhi). This hadith highlights the importance of compassion and fairness in all dealings, including business partnerships. For Muslim entrepreneurs, this means ensuring that all suppliers and partners are treated with respect, paid fairly, and held accountable to the same high standards of integrity and halal compliance. By fostering strong, collaborative relationships with their supply chain partners, businesses can ensure that their products remain compliant with halal standards while promoting fairness and justice throughout the supply chain.

One way to ensure that suppliers meet halal standards is by conducting regular audits and inspections. These audits can help businesses identify any potential issues in the supply chain and ensure that all materials, ingredients, and processes comply with halal standards. In addition to formal audits, businesses can also encourage open communication with their suppliers, creating a culture of transparency and collaboration. By working together with suppliers, businesses can address any challenges that arise and find solutions that are in line with both halal principles and business objectives.

Another important consideration in maintaining halal compliance is the issue of cross-contamination. In industries such as food and cosmetics, where halal and non-halal products may be produced in the same facilities, there is a risk of cross-contamination between halal and haram substances. To mitigate this risk, businesses must implement strict protocols to ensure that halal products are kept separate from non-halal products at every stage of the production process. This may involve using dedicated equipment, implementing thorough cleaning procedures, and providing specialized training for employees.

In addition to ensuring compliance within the supply chain, businesses must also focus on maintaining halal standards in their marketing and advertising practices. The way a business presents its products and services to the public plays a significant role in building trust with consumers, and it is essential that all marketing efforts align with Islamic values. The Quran advises, "And speak to people good words" (Quran 2:83). For Muslim entrepreneurs, this means ensuring that all marketing materials are truthful, respectful, and free from any form of deception or manipulation.

One of the key challenges in modern marketing is the use of exaggeration or false claims to boost sales. In a competitive marketplace, businesses may be tempted to overstate the benefits of their products or use misleading advertising techniques to attract customers. However, halal compliance requires businesses to prioritize honesty and transparency in all communications. The Prophet Muhammad (PBUH) said, "He who cheats us is not one of us" (Muslim). This hadith serves as a powerful reminder that honesty is a cornerstone of halal business practices, and businesses must ensure that all marketing efforts reflect the true value of their products.

In addition to honesty, businesses must also be mindful of the images and messages they use in their advertising. Islamic values place a strong emphasis on modesty and dignity, and businesses must ensure that their marketing materials reflect these values. This means avoiding advertisements that objectify individuals, promote haram products, or appeal to base desires. Instead, businesses should focus on promoting the ethical, health, and spiritual benefits of their products, highlighting the ways in which they align with halal principles and contribute to the well-being of society.

Social media presents both opportunities and challenges for halal businesses. On one hand, social media platforms provide businesses with an unprecedented ability to reach a global audience, share their message, and engage with customers in real-time. On the other hand, the fast-paced, often superficial nature of social media can sometimes lead to marketing tactics that are inconsistent with Islamic values. For Muslim entrepreneurs, it is essential to approach social media marketing with the same level of care and responsibility that they apply to other aspects of their business. This includes ensuring that all content is respectful, truthful, and aligned with the values of halal compliance.

In addition to maintaining halal standards in marketing and advertising, businesses must also ensure that their customer service practices are in line with Islamic values. The way a business treats its customers is a reflection of its commitment to halal principles, and businesses must strive to provide exceptional service that reflects the values of fairness, kindness, and respect. The Prophet Muhammad (PBUH) said, "The best of people are those who are most beneficial to others" (Daraqutni). For Muslim entrepreneurs, this means going above and beyond to ensure that customers are satisfied with their products and services and that any issues are resolved quickly and fairly.

One of the key aspects of providing excellent customer service is responsiveness. Customers today expect businesses to respond to their inquiries and concerns in a timely manner, and businesses that fail to meet these expectations risk losing customer trust and loyalty. For halal businesses, responsiveness is not just a matter of good business practice—it is a reflection of the Islamic value of mutual respect. Businesses should make it a priority to respond to customer inquiries promptly, provide clear and accurate information, and address any concerns with empathy and professionalism.

In addition to responsiveness, businesses must also ensure that their customer service practices are transparent and fair. This includes providing clear information about pricing, shipping, return policies, and warranties, as well as offering customers easy access to support if they need assistance. The Quran advises, "And give full measure when you measure, and weigh with an even balance" (Quran 17:35), emphasizing the importance of fairness in all transactions. By ensuring that their customer service practices are fair and transparent, businesses can build trust with their customers and foster long-term loyalty.

As businesses continue to grow and expand their operations, it is important to remember that halal compliance is not a static goal but an ongoing process. The Quran reminds us, "Indeed, Allah is with those who fear Him and those who are doers of good" (Quran 16:128). For Muslim entrepreneurs, this means that maintaining halal compliance requires continuous effort, vigilance, and a commitment to upholding Islamic principles in every aspect of the business. By staying true to these values, businesses can achieve both spiritual and material success, building trusted brands that contribute to the well-being of society.

The role of halal compliance in modern business extends beyond individual companies and products—it has the potential to shape the future of global business practices. As more consumers and businesses recognize the value of ethical, sustainable, and halal-certified products, the principles of halal compliance are becoming increasingly relevant to a broader audience. The global halal economy is growing rapidly, and Muslim entrepreneurs have the opportunity to lead the way in promoting ethical business practices that align with both Islamic teachings and the demands of modern consumers.

One of the key drivers of this growth is the increasing awareness of halal certification among non-Muslim consumers. Halal-certified products are often seen as synonymous with quality, cleanliness, and ethical sourcing, making them appealing to consumers who value transparency and sustainability. For businesses, this presents an opportunity to expand their customer base by promoting the universal benefits of halal compliance. By highlighting the ethical and health-related aspects of halal products, businesses can attract a diverse range of customers who are seeking products that align with their personal values.

In addition to expanding their customer base, businesses that prioritize halal compliance also have the opportunity to contribute to the greater good by promoting social justice, environmental sustainability, and ethical labor practices. The Quran teaches, "And cooperate in righteousness and piety, but do not cooperate in sin and aggression" (Quran 5:2). For Muslim entrepreneurs, this means working together with other businesses, organizations, and communities to promote ethical practices that benefit both individuals and society as a whole.

As the global halal economy continues to grow, businesses that prioritize halal compliance will play a leading role in shaping the future of ethical business practices. By staying true to Islamic principles, embracing innovation, and maintaining a strong commitment to transparency and fairness, Muslim entrepreneurs can build successful businesses that contribute to the well-being of society and earn the trust of consumers around the world.

As we reflect on the role of halal compliance in modern business, it is clear that halal is not just a certification or a set of rules—it is a way of life. For Muslim entrepreneurs, halal compliance is about conducting business in a way that is pleasing to Allah, beneficial to society, and aligned with the values of Islam. The Prophet Muhammad (PBUH) said, "Whoever seeks the Hereafter through lawful means of living in this world, Allah will bless him" (Tabarani). This hadith reminds us that when we pursue success in a lawful and ethical manner, we are rewarded both in this life and the next.

For Muslim entrepreneurs, building a halal business is an opportunity to make a positive impact on the world while earning a halal income that is blessed with barakah (divine blessings). By upholding the principles of halal compliance in every aspect of their operations—from sourcing and production to marketing and customer service—businesses can build strong, trusted brands that contribute to the greater good of society. In doing so, they not only achieve material success but also fulfill their spiritual obligations and earn the pleasure of Allah.

The future of halal business is bright, and as more consumers seek out products and services that align with their ethical and spiritual values, the demand for halal-certified offerings will continue to grow. For Muslim entrepreneurs, this presents an exciting opportunity to not only achieve financial success but also contribute to the greater good by upholding the principles of halal compliance in every aspect of their business operations.

CHAPTER 6: BUILDING TRUST AND LOYALTY IN HALAL BUSINESS

In the ever-evolving landscape of global business, trust and loyalty stand as pillars of success. For a business rooted in halal principles, trust goes beyond customer relationships—it is a commitment to upholding Islamic values, ensuring ethical conduct, and delivering on promises consistently. The Quran speaks of this deep sense of responsibility, "And fulfill [every] commitment. Indeed, the commitment is ever [that about which one will be] questioned" (Quran 17:34). This verse highlights the essential nature of trust and accountability in all human endeavors, particularly business.

Trust in halal business is multifaceted. It is earned through honest dealings, transparency in communication, and a steadfast adherence to the principles of halal compliance. For Muslim entrepreneurs, the journey to building trust begins with ensuring that all products and services meet the highest halal standards—products that are lawful, ethical, and pure (tayyib). This extends beyond just certification; it encompasses the integrity of every transaction, the ethical treatment of workers, and the moral values embedded in every aspect of the business.

The halal market is not just about catering to a religious requirement; it is about fulfilling a moral obligation to provide products and services that are genuinely beneficial to society. Consumers today are more conscious than ever of the ethical implications of their purchases. They seek out brands that are transparent, responsible, and trustworthy. For halal businesses, this presents an opportunity to stand out by building strong foundations of trust through transparent operations, ethical sourcing, and the promotion of products that align with both Islamic values and universal ethical standards.

Moreover, trust is built through consistency. Customers expect to receive the same level of quality and service every time they interact with a brand. Whether it is the consistency of product quality, the reliability of customer service, or the transparency in business practices, halal businesses must ensure that they are meeting these expectations at every point of contact. The Prophet Muhammad (PBUH) said, "The honest and trustworthy businessman will be in the company of the Prophets, the truthful, and the martyrs" (Tirmidhi). For Muslim entrepreneurs, this hadith serves as a reminder that trustworthiness is not just a business strategy; it is a pathway to spiritual success.

In halal business, trust is further deepened through a strong commitment to ethical sourcing and fair trade. Customers are increasingly looking for products that are not only halal but also produced in a way that respects human rights, promotes fair wages, and protects the environment. The Quran advises, "And weigh with an even balance" (Quran 26:182), a principle that encourages fairness and justice in all dealings, including business transactions. For Muslim entrepreneurs, this means working closely with suppliers and partners to ensure that all materials are sourced ethically, workers are treated with dignity, and environmental impacts are minimized.

In industries such as fashion and food, where exploitation and environmental degradation are all too common, halal businesses have the opportunity to set themselves apart by promoting ethical practices. For example, a halal clothing brand might source fabrics from fair-trade-certified farms or employ artisans who are paid fair wages and provided with safe working conditions. By embedding these values into their supply chains, businesses not only uphold halal standards but also build trust with consumers who are looking for brands that reflect their own values of fairness, sustainability, and responsibility.

Another aspect of building trust in halal business is transparency. Customers want to know where their products come from, how they are made, and what values the brand stands for. For halal businesses, transparency means providing clear and honest information about every stage of the production process, from sourcing to manufacturing to packaging. The Prophet Muhammad (PBUH) said, "He who deceives is not one of us" (Muslim). This powerful statement underscores the importance of honesty in all dealings, and for halal businesses, it means ensuring that customers can trust the information they receive about the products they are buying.

One practical way to enhance transparency is through the use of digital tools that allow customers to trace the origin of their products. For example, a halal food company might offer a QR code on its packaging that allows customers to see the journey of the product from farm to table. This type of transparency not only builds trust but also reinforces the brand's commitment to halal compliance and ethical practices.

In addition to transparency, loyalty is fostered through personalized experiences that cater to the unique needs and preferences of customers. While the halal market serves a diverse global audience, from devout Muslims to ethical consumers, personalization can help businesses build stronger relationships with individual customers. The Quran advises, "And cooperate in righteousness and piety, but do not cooperate in sin and aggression" (Quran 5:2). This principle of cooperation encourages businesses to engage with their customers in a meaningful way, ensuring that their products and services meet the specific needs of their target audience.

One of the most effective ways to personalize the customer experience is through the use of data analytics. By analyzing customer preferences, purchase histories, and feedback, halal businesses can offer personalized product recommendations, special promotions, and tailored content that resonates with their customers. For example, a halal beauty brand might recommend specific skincare products based on a customer's skin type and previous purchases, creating a personalized shopping experience that enhances customer satisfaction and fosters loyalty.

However, personalization must be approached with care and respect for customer privacy. The Quran teaches, "Do not spy on one another, and do not backbite each other" (Quran 49:12). For halal businesses, this means ensuring that all customer data is collected and used in a way that respects privacy and adheres to ethical standards. Businesses should be transparent about how they collect, store, and use customer data, giving customers control over their information and ensuring that their privacy is protected at all times.

Another important element of building customer loyalty is providing exceptional customer service. The Prophet Muhammad (PBUH) said, "The most beloved of people to Allah are those who are most beneficial to others" (Tabarani). For halal businesses, this hadith serves as a guiding principle in the way they interact with their customers. Providing helpful, responsive, and compassionate customer service not only enhances customer loyalty but also reflects the core values of Islam—kindness, respect, and generosity.

Customer loyalty in halal business is not just about repeat purchases; it is about creating a sense of community and belonging. Halal businesses have the opportunity to build strong, lasting relationships with their customers by fostering a sense of shared values and purpose. This can be achieved through community engagement initiatives, social media interactions, and loyalty programs that reward customers for their support.

One way to build a community around a halal brand is by creating content that educates and inspires customers. For example, a halal food brand might share recipes, cooking tips, and nutritional information that help customers make informed choices about their meals. By providing valuable content that aligns with the principles of halal living, businesses can position themselves as trusted sources of information and build deeper connections with their audience.

In addition to content marketing, social media plays a crucial role in building community and fostering loyalty. Platforms like Instagram, Facebook, and YouTube allow halal businesses to engage directly with their customers, share behind-the-scenes content, and showcase their commitment to halal principles. By using social media to create a two-way dialogue with their audience, businesses can build trust, foster loyalty, and create a sense of belonging among their customers.

For example, a halal fashion brand might use Instagram to showcase its latest collection, share stories about the artisans who create the garments, and engage with customers through live Q&A sessions. By involving customers in the brand's journey and highlighting the ethical values behind the products, the business can create a loyal community of customers who feel connected to the brand's mission.

In addition to social media, loyalty programs are another powerful tool for building long-term customer relationships. Loyalty programs allow businesses to reward their customers for their continued support, fostering a sense of appreciation and reciprocity. The Quran encourages generosity, stating, "And whatever good you put forward for yourselves—you will find it with Allah. It is better and greater in reward" (Quran 73:20). For halal businesses, this verse serves as a reminder that acts of generosity, whether through discounts, exclusive offers, or special rewards, are not only good business practices but also align with the values of Islam.

A well-designed loyalty program can go beyond simple discounts and offer customers meaningful rewards that enhance their experience with the brand. For example, a halal travel company might offer loyal customers access to exclusive travel experiences, such as guided tours of historical Islamic sites or personalized halal meal plans for their trips. By offering rewards that align with the values and interests of their customers, businesses can deepen their relationships and create a sense of loyalty that goes beyond transactional benefits.

In addition to traditional loyalty programs, businesses can also foster loyalty through acts of kindness and generosity that reflect the core values of Islam. The Prophet Muhammad (PBUH) said, "None of you truly believes until he loves for his brother what he loves for himself" (Bukhari). For halal businesses, this hadith serves as a reminder that loyalty is not just about what the customer gives to the business—it is about what the business gives back to the customer and the community.

One practical way to embody this principle is by engaging in charitable initiatives that resonate with the brand's mission and values. For example, a halal food brand might donate a portion of its profits to support food security initiatives in underserved communities. By aligning their charitable efforts with their business objectives, halal businesses can demonstrate their commitment to making a positive impact on society, while also building loyalty and trust among their customers.

As Muslim entrepreneurs continue to build trust and loyalty in halal business, it is important to remember that these qualities are not built overnight—they are earned through consistent, ethical actions over time. The Quran advises, "Indeed, Allah is with those who fear Him and those who are doers of good" (Quran 16:128). For halal businesses, this means that building trust and loyalty requires a long-term commitment to doing good, both in business practices and in interactions with customers.

One of the most important ways to build long-term trust is by maintaining a strong focus on quality. Customers expect halal products to meet the highest standards of quality, and any deviation from these standards can quickly erode trust. Whether it is the quality of the ingredients used in a halal food product or the craftsmanship of a halal fashion item, businesses must ensure that every product they offer meets the expectations of their customers. By consistently delivering high-quality products, businesses can build a reputation for reliability and trustworthiness.

In addition to product quality, businesses must also ensure that their operations are transparent and accountable. The Quran reminds us, "And do not consume one another's wealth unjustly or send it [in bribery] to the rulers in order that [they might aid] you [to] consume a portion of the wealth of the people in sin, while you know [it is unlawful]" (Quran 2:188). For halal businesses, this means maintaining the highest standards of transparency in all financial and operational dealings, ensuring that customers can trust the integrity of the business.

Accountability is another key component of building trust in halal business. Customers want to know that businesses are willing to take responsibility for their actions, whether it is addressing a product defect, resolving a customer complaint, or correcting an error in communication. By demonstrating accountability, businesses can show that they are committed to doing the right thing, even when mistakes are made. This not only builds trust but also fosters a sense of loyalty among customers who appreciate the business's integrity.

As halal businesses strive to build and maintain trust, one of the most powerful tools at their disposal is communication. Clear, honest, and open communication is essential for fostering strong relationships with customers, suppliers, and partners. The Quran emphasizes the importance of truthful speech, stating, "O you who have believed, fear Allah and speak words of appropriate justice" (Quran 33:70). For Muslim entrepreneurs, this means ensuring that all communications, whether in marketing materials, customer service interactions, or public statements, reflect honesty, fairness, and respect.

In today's digital age, businesses have an unprecedented ability to communicate directly with their customers through social media, email, and other online platforms. While these tools offer great opportunities for engagement, they also come with the responsibility to communicate in a way that is ethical and transparent. For halal businesses, this means avoiding any form of manipulation, false promises, or exaggerated claims in their marketing efforts. Instead, businesses should focus on sharing authentic stories, promoting the genuine benefits of their products, and providing clear, accurate information about the value they offer.

For example, a halal beauty brand might share real stories of how their products have positively impacted customers' lives, while also providing detailed information about the halal certification process and the ethical sourcing of ingredients. By being transparent about the journey behind their products, businesses can build deeper connections with their audience and foster trust in their brand. This type of authentic communication not only enhances customer loyalty but also reinforces the business's commitment to halal principles.

Moreover, communication is not just about what a business says—it is also about how it listens. Halal businesses must be attentive to the needs, concerns, and feedback of their customers, ensuring that they feel heard and valued. The Prophet Muhammad (PBUH) said, "The believer is not one who eats his fill while his neighbor goes hungry" (Bukhari). This hadith reminds us of the importance of empathy and consideration for others, and for halal businesses, this means actively listening to their customers and responding to their needs with care and compassion.

One way to enhance communication with customers is through regular feedback loops, where businesses seek input from their customers about their products, services, and overall experience. By gathering feedback through surveys, reviews, and direct interactions, businesses can gain valuable insights into what their customers value most and identify areas for improvement. In addition, acting on this feedback shows customers that the business truly values their opinions and is committed to making changes that enhance their experience.

Building trust and loyalty in halal business is not just about meeting immediate needs—it is about creating a long-term vision that aligns with Islamic values and serves the greater good. The Quran teaches, "And whatever good you put forward for yourselves—you will find it with Allah. It is better and greater in reward" (Quran 73:20). For halal businesses, this means looking beyond short-term profits and focusing on long-term success that is rooted in ethical conduct, social responsibility, and a commitment to the well-being of society.

One of the ways businesses can achieve long-term success is by adopting a holistic approach to their operations that integrates halal compliance with sustainability, social justice, and community engagement. For example, a halal food company might focus not only on providing halal-certified products but also on sourcing ingredients from sustainable farms, supporting fair labor practices, and reducing its environmental footprint. By aligning their business practices with the values of halal and sustainability, businesses can build trust with a broader audience of consumers who value ethical and environmentally responsible products.

Similarly, halal businesses can build long-term loyalty by supporting social justice initiatives that resonate with their customers. The Quran emphasizes the importance of justice, stating, "O you who have believed, be persistently standing firm in justice, witnesses for Allah, even if it be against yourselves or parents and relatives" (Quran 4:135). For businesses, this means taking a stand on issues that matter, such as promoting fair wages, supporting marginalized communities, or advocating for environmental protection.

By aligning their brand with causes that reflect the values of justice and fairness, halal businesses can create a deeper connection with their customers, who are increasingly looking to support brands that are socially responsible. This alignment not only strengthens customer loyalty but also reinforces the business's commitment to making a positive impact on society. When customers see that a brand is dedicated to making a difference, they are more likely to feel loyal to that brand and support it over the long term.

Another important aspect of building long-term loyalty is creating a sense of shared purpose between the business and its customers. Customers who feel that they are part of a larger mission or community are more likely to remain loyal to the brand, even in the face of competition. Halal businesses can foster this sense of shared purpose by involving their customers in their journey, whether through community engagement initiatives, customer-driven product innovations, or collaborative charity efforts.

One practical way to build a sense of community and shared purpose is through partnerships and collaborations with like-minded businesses, organizations, and community groups. The Quran encourages cooperation and mutual support, stating, "Help one another in acts of righteousness and piety" (Quran 5:2). For halal businesses, this means forming partnerships that align with their values and allow them to amplify their positive impact.

For example, a halal cosmetics company might partner with an environmental organization to promote sustainable beauty practices, or a halal restaurant might collaborate with a local charity to provide meals to those in need. These partnerships not only strengthen the brand's reputation but also create opportunities for customers to engage with the brand in meaningful ways. By inviting customers to participate in these initiatives, businesses can build a loyal community of supporters who share the same values and are invested in the brand's success.

Partnerships can also extend to collaborations with influencers, thought leaders, and content creators who share the brand's values. In the digital age, influencers play a significant role in shaping consumer perceptions and building brand loyalty. For halal businesses, working with influencers who are committed to promoting ethical, halal, and sustainable products can help amplify their message and reach a wider audience. However, it is important to ensure that these partnerships are authentic and aligned with the business's values, as customers can quickly detect insincerity or misalignment.

Influencers who genuinely believe in the brand's mission can serve as powerful advocates, helping to build trust with their followers and encourage loyalty to the brand. For example, a halal fashion brand might collaborate with modest fashion influencers to showcase its ethical clothing line, highlighting the brand's commitment to sustainability, modesty, and fair trade. By aligning with influencers who share their values, businesses can create authentic connections with their audience and build a loyal following.

In addition to partnerships and collaborations, businesses can foster long-term loyalty by creating memorable experiences that go beyond the products or services they offer. The Prophet Muhammad (PBUH) said, "Verily, Allah has prescribed excellence in everything" (Muslim). For halal businesses, this means striving for excellence not only in the quality of their products but also in the experiences they provide to their customers.

One way to create memorable experiences is by offering exceptional customer service that reflects the values of kindness, generosity, and respect. Whether it is through personalized interactions, thoughtful gestures, or going the extra mile to meet customer needs, businesses that prioritize excellent service can leave a lasting impression on their customers. For example, a halal travel agency might offer personalized travel itineraries that cater to the specific halal needs of their clients, such as arranging for halal meals, prayer facilities, and visits to Islamic historical sites. By providing a seamless and personalized experience, businesses can create a loyal customer base that returns again and again.

Memorable experiences can also be created through unique and meaningful events that engage the community. For example, a halal brand might host an event that celebrates Islamic culture, educates the public about halal practices, or showcases the artisans behind its products. By inviting customers to participate in these experiences, businesses can create lasting memories that strengthen the emotional connection between the brand and its audience.

Another way to enhance the customer experience is by offering exclusive perks or rewards to loyal customers. Whether through VIP access to new products, special discounts, or invitations to private events, these exclusive benefits can make customers feel valued and appreciated. The Quran teaches, "And whoever does a good deed, We will increase for him good therein" (Quran 42:23). For halal businesses, this verse serves as a reminder that acts of generosity and appreciation can lead to increased blessings, both in business and in life.

While loyalty programs and exclusive rewards can help build a sense of appreciation, it is also important to ensure that these initiatives align with the broader values of the brand. Halal businesses should design their loyalty programs in a way that reflects Islamic values of fairness, generosity, and responsibility. For example, instead of offering discounts that encourage excessive consumption, a halal brand might offer rewards that promote sustainability or support charitable causes.

For instance, a halal skincare company might reward loyal customers by planting a tree for every purchase or donating a portion of their profits to environmental conservation efforts. By aligning their loyalty programs with ethical and sustainable practices, businesses can reinforce their commitment to making a positive impact on the world while building long-term loyalty among customers who share these values.

In addition to offering rewards that reflect Islamic values, halal businesses can foster loyalty by engaging customers in meaningful ways that allow them to contribute to the brand's mission. This might include inviting customers to participate in product development, offering opportunities for customer feedback, or involving them in charitable initiatives. For example, a halal food brand might invite customers to vote on new product flavors or contribute recipes that align with halal principles. By involving customers in the decision-making process, businesses can create a sense of ownership and investment in the brand's success.

Ultimately, building trust and loyalty in halal business is about creating relationships that are rooted in shared values, mutual respect, and a commitment to doing good. The Prophet Muhammad (PBUH) said, "The believer is like a mirror to his brother" (Bukhari). For halal businesses, this hadith serves as a reminder that the relationships they build with their customers should reflect the best of their values—honesty, kindness, fairness, and compassion.

As businesses continue to grow and expand their operations, it is essential to remain focused on these core values, ensuring that trust and loyalty are nurtured at every stage of the customer journey. The future of halal business is bright, and as more consumers seek out products and services that align with their ethical and spiritual values, the demand for halal-certified offerings will continue to grow. For Muslim entrepreneurs, this presents an exciting opportunity to not only achieve financial success but also contribute to the greater good by upholding the principles of halal compliance in every aspect of their business operations.

By staying true to these values, halal businesses can build strong, trusted brands that resonate with consumers around the world and foster long-term loyalty. As the Quran advises, "O you who have believed, fear Allah and speak words of appropriate justice" (Quran 33:70). For Muslim entrepreneurs, this verse serves as a guiding principle in their quest to build businesses that are not only successful but also rooted in trust, loyalty, and the values of Islam.

Trust is not merely a business transaction; it is a commitment to upholding promises, delivering value, and safeguarding relationships. In the halal business world, trust is deeply intertwined with the concept of *amanah*—a responsibility or trust given to us by Allah. When Muslim entrepreneurs engage in business, they are not just working for themselves; they are fulfilling an obligation to do good for society, serve their customers ethically, and act as responsible stewards of the resources Allah has provided. The Quran states, "Indeed, Allah commands you to render trusts to whom they are due and when you judge between people to judge with justice" (Quran 4:58). This verse serves as a reminder that trust, in all its forms, must be upheld with justice and fairness.

For halal businesses, building trust means ensuring that every aspect of the business—from sourcing materials to delivering the final product—is done with integrity. Trust is not a one-time achievement; it is an ongoing process that must be nurtured over time through consistent, ethical actions. For example, a halal food brand must not only ensure that its products are halal-certified, but it must also maintain transparency about where the ingredients come from, how they are processed, and what measures are taken to ensure halal compliance throughout the supply chain. Customers trust businesses that are open and honest about their practices, and in the halal industry, this transparency is even more critical.

A key aspect of building trust in halal business is ensuring that promises are consistently met. Whether it's delivering products on time, offering reliable customer service, or maintaining consistent product quality, businesses must ensure that they live up to the expectations they set. The Prophet Muhammad (PBUH) said, "The signs of a hypocrite are three: when he speaks, he lies; when he makes a promise, he breaks it; and when he is entrusted with something, he betrays that trust" (Bukhari). This hadith serves as a stern warning against breaking promises and betraying trust—actions that can quickly erode customer confidence in a brand.

Consistency is key in the halal business environment. Whether dealing with food, fashion, cosmetics, or finance, customers expect that the products and services they receive are always compliant with halal standards. If a customer has doubts about the halal status of a product or feels that the business is not transparent about its practices, their trust in the brand will be compromised. To avoid this, businesses must not only comply with halal standards but must also communicate this compliance clearly and confidently to their customers.

In addition to transparency and consistency, trust in halal business is also built through a deep respect for customer relationships. The Prophet Muhammad (PBUH) said, "Whoever is kind, Allah will be kind to him; therefore, be kind to man on the earth. He who is in heaven will show mercy on you" (Tirmidhi). Kindness is a cornerstone of trust, and in halal business, this means treating customers with respect, dignity, and empathy. Businesses that prioritize kindness in their dealings with customers—whether through responsive customer service, thoughtful interactions, or generous policies—create lasting bonds of trust.

For example, a halal beauty brand that prioritizes customer care might offer a flexible return policy that allows customers to try products risk-free, knowing that their satisfaction is the brand's top priority. By offering personalized recommendations and ensuring that customers feel valued, businesses can foster a sense of loyalty that goes beyond mere transactions. This kind of trust-building is essential in the halal business world, where the relationship between business and customer is not just about profit but about mutual benefit and ethical engagement.

Another important aspect of building trust is accountability. Customers are more likely to trust businesses that are willing to take responsibility for their actions, particularly when things go wrong. Whether it's a delayed shipment, a product defect, or a service that didn't meet expectations, businesses that own up to their mistakes and work quickly to resolve them demonstrate integrity and commitment to customer satisfaction. The Quran advises, "But if you pardon and overlook and forgive—then indeed, Allah is Forgiving and Merciful" (Quran 64:14). For halal businesses, this means adopting a culture of forgiveness and accountability, where mistakes are acknowledged and efforts are made to make amends.

For instance, if a halal food brand accidentally mislabels a product, they must immediately inform their customers, issue a recall if necessary, and ensure that all future products are correctly labeled. By being transparent about mistakes and taking swift action to correct them, businesses can prevent a loss of trust and maintain their reputation for honesty and reliability.

Another powerful element of building trust in halal business is corporate social responsibility (CSR). Today's consumers are increasingly looking for brands that not only offer quality products but also contribute to the greater good. For halal businesses, CSR presents an opportunity to build trust by demonstrating a commitment to social justice, environmental sustainability, and ethical labor practices. The Quran emphasizes the importance of giving back to society, stating, "And spend in the way of Allah and do not throw [yourselves] with your [own] hands into destruction [by refraining]. And do good; indeed, Allah loves the doers of good" (Quran 2:195).

By incorporating CSR initiatives into their business model, halal businesses can build a reputation for ethical leadership and strengthen the trust of their customers. For example, a halal fashion brand might donate a portion of its profits to support educational programs in underserved communities, or a halal restaurant might commit to reducing food waste and partnering with local charities to provide meals to those in need. These initiatives not only reflect the values of halal business but also resonate with customers who want to support brands that are making a positive impact on the world.

In addition to supporting charitable causes, halal businesses can also build trust by adopting environmentally sustainable practices. With growing concerns about climate change and environmental degradation, consumers are increasingly seeking out brands that prioritize sustainability. For halal businesses, this means ensuring that their products are produced in a way that minimizes environmental impact, whether through sustainable sourcing, reducing waste, or using eco-friendly packaging. By aligning their business practices with environmental stewardship, halal businesses can demonstrate their commitment to ethical values that resonate with both Muslim and non-Muslim consumers alike.

A halal skincare brand, for instance, might source its ingredients from organic, pesticide-free farms and use recyclable or biodegradable packaging for its products. By promoting these practices, the brand can attract environmentally conscious consumers and build trust with those who are looking for products that align with their ethical values.

In halal business, trust is further strengthened by maintaining strong relationships with suppliers and partners who share the same values. The Quran advises, "O you who have believed, fulfill [all] contracts" (Quran 5:1). For Muslim entrepreneurs, this means ensuring that all business relationships—whether with suppliers, manufacturers, or distributors—are based on mutual trust, transparency, and ethical conduct. A halal business is only as strong as its supply chain, and if any part of the supply chain fails to meet halal standards, the entire product or service can be compromised.

To build trust within the supply chain, halal businesses must work closely with their suppliers to ensure that all materials and ingredients are sourced ethically and in compliance with halal standards. Regular audits, inspections, and open communication can help businesses verify that their suppliers are meeting these standards. By fostering strong, collaborative relationships with their suppliers, businesses can ensure that their products maintain the highest levels of halal compliance, from sourcing to final delivery.

Moreover, businesses that maintain ethical supply chains not only build trust with their customers but also strengthen their reputation within the halal industry. By partnering with suppliers who prioritize ethical labor practices, fair wages, and environmental sustainability, halal businesses can position themselves as leaders in the ethical business movement. These values are becoming increasingly important to consumers, and businesses that align with them will be better positioned to build lasting trust and loyalty.

For example, a halal food company might work with farmers who practice sustainable agriculture, ensuring that the ingredients used in their products are both halal and environmentally friendly. By promoting these partnerships and sharing the stories behind their supply chain, businesses can build a stronger connection with their customers and reinforce their commitment to halal values.

As halal businesses continue to grow and expand their operations, they must remain focused on the principles that have earned them the trust of their customers. The Prophet Muhammad (PBUH) said, "Whoever believes in Allah and the Last Day, let him speak good or remain silent" (Muslim). For halal businesses, this means ensuring that every action, every decision, and every communication reflects the values of integrity, honesty, and kindness. Trust is fragile, and businesses must work continuously to preserve it by staying true to their values and upholding their promises.

One way to maintain trust is by fostering a culture of continuous improvement. The halal industry is constantly evolving, and businesses must stay ahead of the curve by investing in new technologies, improving their processes, and responding to changing consumer needs. By demonstrating a commitment to innovation and excellence, businesses can show their customers that they are dedicated to providing the best possible products and services, while still adhering to the values of halal compliance.

For example, a halal fashion brand might invest in new, sustainable fabrics that offer greater comfort and durability, while also aligning with Islamic values of modesty and ethical production. By continuously improving their products and services, businesses can maintain the trust of their customers and build a reputation for excellence.

At the same time, businesses must also be mindful of maintaining a balance between innovation and tradition. While innovation is important, it should never come at the expense of halal compliance or ethical values. The Quran teaches, "And eat of what Allah has provided for you [which is] lawful and good. And fear Allah, in whom you are believers" (Quran 5:88). This verse reminds us that halal is not just about following rules—it is about maintaining a commitment to goodness, ethics, and responsibility in every aspect of business.

As businesses continue to grow and adapt to new market trends, they must also stay connected to the communities they serve. Trust is built not just through transactions but through relationships, and halal businesses that engage with their communities on a deeper level are more likely to foster loyalty and long-term success. The Prophet Muhammad (PBUH) said, "The best of people are those who are most beneficial to others" (Daraqutni). For halal businesses, this means finding ways to give back to the community, whether through charitable initiatives, educational programs, or simply providing products and services that improve people's lives.

One practical way for businesses to engage with their communities is by supporting local causes that align with their values. For example, a halal restaurant might partner with local food banks to provide meals for those in need or sponsor events that promote healthy, halal eating habits. By showing that they care about the well-being of their community, businesses can strengthen their relationships with their customers and build trust based on shared values.

Community engagement also extends to listening to and acting on customer feedback. Halal businesses that are open to receiving feedback and making improvements based on that feedback demonstrate a willingness to serve their customers better. This not only enhances the customer experience but also reinforces the business's commitment to continuous improvement and ethical conduct. By actively involving customers in the decision-making process, businesses can create a sense of partnership and trust that goes beyond the typical customer-brand relationship.

For instance, a halal cosmetics company might invite its customers to provide input on new product formulations or participate in surveys that help shape the company's future offerings. By involving customers in these processes, the business not only fosters loyalty but also ensures that its products meet the needs and preferences of its target audience.

Trust in halal business is not just about transactions—it's about building relationships rooted in respect, empathy, and shared values. As Muslim entrepreneurs, the responsibility to uphold these values extends beyond the business itself; it impacts the lives of the customers, employees, and communities that the business serves. The Quran reminds us, "O mankind, indeed We have created you from male and female and made you peoples and tribes that you may know one another" (Quran 49:13). This verse encourages mutual understanding and cooperation, emphasizing that human relationships—especially in business—should be built on a foundation of respect and shared purpose.

One of the key elements of building long-term loyalty in halal business is creating a sense of belonging. Customers who feel that they are part of a community, united by shared values, are more likely to remain loyal to a brand. For halal businesses, this means fostering a sense of inclusion and connection that goes beyond simply selling products. It's about creating an experience, a mission, and a relationship that resonates with the hearts of customers.

To create this sense of belonging, halal businesses can focus on creating meaningful experiences that engage customers on a deeper level. This might involve hosting events, launching campaigns that promote ethical living, or creating platforms for dialogue and community engagement. For example, a halal food company might host cooking workshops that teach customers how to prepare healthy, halal meals, or a halal fashion brand might organize fashion shows that celebrate modest fashion and empower women to feel confident in their faith and style.

Another way to create a sense of belonging is by aligning the brand's mission with the values of its customers. In today's marketplace, consumers are increasingly drawn to brands that stand for something beyond profit. They want to support companies that are making a positive impact on society, whether through charitable initiatives, environmental sustainability, or social justice causes. For halal businesses, this means aligning their values with the broader ethical and social concerns of their customers.

For instance, a halal cosmetics brand that promotes cruelty-free beauty products can create a loyal customer base of ethically conscious consumers who appreciate the brand's commitment to animal welfare. By aligning their mission with the ethical concerns of their customers, halal businesses can create a sense of loyalty that is rooted in shared values and a common purpose.

Loyalty is not only fostered through shared values, but also through the act of giving back. The Prophet Muhammad (PBUH) said, "He is not a believer whose stomach is filled while his neighbor goes hungry" (Muslim). This hadith emphasizes the importance of giving and sharing with others, and for halal businesses, this principle can be applied by creating a culture of generosity. Businesses that give back to their communities, support charitable causes, and demonstrate a commitment to social responsibility are more likely to build lasting loyalty with their customers.

One practical way for halal businesses to give back is by establishing charity partnerships or creating dedicated social responsibility programs. For example, a halal food brand might partner with local charities to provide meals for underserved communities during Ramadan, or a halal clothing company might donate a portion of its proceeds to organizations that support women's empowerment. By incorporating these initiatives into their business model, halal businesses not only fulfill their Islamic obligation to give back but also create a deeper connection with their customers, who appreciate brands that align with their own values of charity and compassion.

In addition to charitable giving, businesses can foster loyalty by showing appreciation for their customers in tangible ways. Whether it's offering personalized discounts, sending handwritten thank-you notes, or recognizing loyal customers through special rewards programs, businesses that demonstrate genuine appreciation for their customers are more likely to build long-lasting relationships. These small acts of kindness can make a significant impact on customer loyalty, showing customers that they are valued and appreciated.

For example, a halal skincare brand might offer exclusive discounts to customers who have supported the brand since its inception or send a special gift to customers during Eid as a token of appreciation. By going the extra mile to show customers that they are more than just transactions, businesses can create a sense of loyalty that is built on trust and genuine human connection.

One of the most powerful tools in building trust and loyalty is storytelling. Stories have the ability to connect people, convey values, and create emotional bonds. For halal businesses, storytelling is not just about promoting products—it's about sharing the journey, the mission, and the purpose behind the brand. The Quran tells us, "So relate the stories that perhaps they will give thought" (Quran 7:176), reminding us of the importance of stories in conveying wisdom and values.

Through storytelling, halal businesses can share their commitment to ethical sourcing, sustainable practices, and the spiritual values that guide their operations. For example, a halal fashion brand might tell the story of the artisans who create its garments, highlighting the fair wages and ethical labor practices that ensure the dignity and well-being of the workers. By sharing these stories, businesses can build a deeper connection with their audience, allowing customers to feel that they are part of something larger than themselves.

In addition to telling the brand's story, businesses can also engage customers by sharing the stories of their customers themselves. Customer testimonials, user-generated content, and customer success stories can be powerful tools for building trust and loyalty. When customers see others like them who have benefited from the brand's products and services, they are more likely to trust the brand and feel a sense of connection with it.

For example, a halal health and wellness brand might feature testimonials from customers who have experienced positive health changes after using the brand's products. By sharing these stories, the brand can inspire trust in potential customers while reinforcing its commitment to providing products that genuinely benefit the health and well-being of its audience.

Moreover, storytelling can be used to educate and inspire customers about the broader principles of halal living. A halal food company, for example, might create a series of videos or blog posts that explore the spiritual and ethical dimensions of halal eating, teaching customers how to make mindful food choices that align with their faith. By providing this type of educational content, businesses can position themselves as trusted sources of knowledge and build deeper relationships with their customers.

Another critical component of building loyalty in halal business is delivering consistently high-quality products and services. The Quran advises,

"And do not mix the truth with falsehood or conceal the truth while you know [it]" (Quran 2:42). For halal businesses, this means being honest about the quality and integrity of their products, ensuring that they meet the highest standards of halal compliance, and delivering on the promises they make to their customers.

Quality is one of the most important factors in earning and maintaining customer trust. When customers know they can rely on a brand to consistently deliver products that meet their expectations, they are more likely to remain loyal to that brand. This is especially true in the halal market, where customers often place a high value on the ethical and spiritual integrity of the products they purchase.

To ensure consistent quality, halal businesses must implement rigorous quality control measures at every stage of the production process, from sourcing raw materials to manufacturing, packaging, and distribution. Regular audits, halal certification, and compliance with international quality standards can help businesses maintain the trust of their customers by demonstrating their commitment to providing safe, ethical, and high-quality products.

For example, a halal food company might work closely with halal certification bodies to ensure that all ingredients are sourced from halal-approved suppliers and that production processes meet the strictest standards of halal compliance. By consistently delivering high-quality products that customers can trust, businesses can build a reputation for reliability and excellence, fostering long-term loyalty.

In addition to maintaining product quality, businesses must also ensure that their customer service reflects the same high standards. Excellent customer service is not just about resolving issues—it's about creating positive, memorable experiences that leave customers feeling valued and appreciated. Whether it's through quick response times, personalized support, or going above and beyond to meet customer needs, businesses that prioritize customer service are more likely to build loyalty and trust.

For example, a halal travel agency might offer 24/7 customer support to help travelers navigate any challenges they encounter while on a trip, providing peace of mind and reassurance. By offering exceptional customer service, businesses can create positive experiences that keep customers coming back.

Loyalty is not only about retaining existing customers but also about inspiring them to become advocates for the brand. When customers have a positive experience with a halal business—whether it's through the quality of the products, the values of the brand, or the level of customer care—they are more likely to recommend the brand to their friends and family. Word-of-mouth referrals are one of the most powerful forms of marketing, and businesses that prioritize trust and loyalty can turn their customers into brand ambassadors who spread the word about their products and services.

For halal businesses, creating a community of loyal advocates can be achieved by engaging with customers in meaningful ways and rewarding them for their loyalty. This might include creating referral programs that incentivize customers to refer new customers, offering exclusive access to new products or services, or hosting events that allow customers to connect with the brand and with each other.

For example, a halal beauty brand might launch a referral program that rewards customers with discounts or free products when they refer their friends to the brand. By creating a system that encourages and rewards customer advocacy, businesses can build a network of loyal supporters who actively promote the brand to others.

Another way to turn customers into advocates is by involving them in the brand's journey. Businesses that involve their customers in decision-making processes, such as voting on new product launches or providing feedback on product development, create a sense of ownership and investment in the brand's success. When customers feel that their voices are heard and that they are part of the brand's growth, they are more likely to become advocates who promote the brand to their networks.

As businesses continue to grow and expand, it is important to remain focused on the values that have helped them build trust and loyalty in the first place. The Prophet Muhammad (PBUH) said, "The best of people are those who bring the most benefit to others" (Daraqutni). For halal businesses, this hadith serves as a guiding principle, reminding them that the true measure of success is not just financial profit but the positive impact they have on their customers, their communities, and society as a whole.

Loyalty in halal business is not just about customer retention—it's about creating relationships that are rooted in mutual respect, shared values, and a commitment to doing good. By staying true to the principles of halal compliance, ethical business practices, and social responsibility, businesses can build lasting trust with their customers and create a loyal community that supports them for the long term.

The future of halal business is bright, and as more consumers seek out products and services that align with their ethical and spiritual values, the demand for halal-certified offerings will continue to grow. For Muslim entrepreneurs, this presents an exciting opportunity to not only achieve financial success but also contribute to the greater good by upholding the principles of halal compliance in every aspect of their business operations.

The journey to building trust and loyalty in halal business is ongoing, and it requires a continuous commitment to excellence, integrity, and compassion. The Prophet Muhammad (PBUH) said, "Verily, Allah has prescribed excellence in everything" (Muslim). For halal businesses, this means striving for excellence not only in the quality of their products but also in the way they treat their customers, the way they engage with their communities, and the way they uphold the values of halal compliance.

By consistently delivering high-quality products, maintaining transparency in their operations, and fostering meaningful relationships with their customers, halal businesses can build a legacy of trust and loyalty that stands the test of time. As they continue to grow and evolve, Muslim entrepreneurs have the opportunity to lead by example, showing the world that halal business is not just about following rules—it's about creating a better, more ethical, and more compassionate world for everyone.

CHAPTER 7: LEADERSHIP AND ETHICAL GOVERNANCE IN HALAL BUSINESS

In the realm of halal business, leadership is more than a position of power—it is a sacred trust, a responsibility to uphold the values of justice, fairness, and integrity in every decision made. The Quran speaks of the importance of leadership and responsibility, reminding us, "And those who have believed and done righteous deeds—we charge no soul except [with that within] its capacity. Those are the companions of Paradise; they will abide therein eternally" (Quran 7:42). Leadership in halal business, therefore, is not just about managing operations or increasing profitability; it is about being a role model of ethical governance and leading by example.

Ethical governance begins with the intention (*niyyah*) behind every action. A leader in a halal business must be driven by a sincere intention to create value, benefit society, and act in accordance with Islamic principles. The Prophet Muhammad (PBUH) said, "Verily, deeds are only with intentions, and every person will have what they intended" (Bukhari). For Muslim entrepreneurs, this means that their success is not measured solely by material gains but by their commitment to conducting business in a way that is pleasing to Allah and beneficial to others.

The role of leadership in halal business is to ensure that all aspects of the business, from production to marketing to customer service, adhere to the highest standards of halal compliance and ethical behavior. This requires a deep understanding of both Islamic teachings and modern business practices. A successful halal business leader is one who can navigate the complexities of the global marketplace while remaining firmly grounded in the values of Islam. This balance between faith and commerce is what sets halal businesses apart and allows them to thrive in a competitive environment.

Moreover, leadership in halal business is not just about the individual at the top; it is about creating a culture of ethical governance that permeates every level of the organization. The Quran teaches, "And hold firmly to the rope of Allah all together and do not become divided" (Quran 3:103). For Muslim entrepreneurs, this means fostering a sense of unity and shared purpose within their teams, ensuring that every employee understands and embraces the values of halal compliance and ethical conduct. By building a culture of integrity and accountability, leaders can create an environment where ethical behavior is the norm, not the exception.

One of the key responsibilities of a leader in a halal business is to establish and enforce policies that promote transparency and accountability. The Prophet Muhammad (PBUH) said, "Each of you is a shepherd, and each of you is responsible for his flock" (Bukhari). For business leaders, this hadith serves as a reminder that they are accountable not only for their own actions but also for the actions of those under their leadership. It is the leader's duty to ensure that the entire organization operates in accordance with Islamic principles, from the way employees are treated to the way products are sourced and marketed.

Transparency is a critical component of ethical governance. Customers, employees, and partners must be able to trust that the business is operating in a fair and honest manner. For halal businesses, this means being open about the halal certification process, providing clear information about the sourcing and production of products, and ensuring that all financial transactions are conducted in a lawful and transparent manner. The Quran advises, "O you who have believed, fear Allah and be with those who are true" (Quran 9:119). For business leaders, this means ensuring that their actions are guided by truth and honesty in every aspect of their operations.

In addition to promoting transparency, leaders must also ensure that their businesses are accountable to both their customers and their employees. This involves setting clear expectations, establishing ethical guidelines, and holding everyone in the organization accountable for upholding these standards. Accountability is not just about identifying and correcting mistakes; it is about creating a culture of continuous improvement, where everyone is encouraged to strive for excellence in all that they do.

For example, a halal food company might implement regular audits of its supply chain to ensure that all ingredients are sourced in compliance with halal standards. By holding suppliers accountable and maintaining strict oversight of the production process, the business can ensure that its products meet the highest standards of quality and integrity. This level of accountability builds trust with customers, who can be confident that the products they purchase are genuinely halal and produced in an ethical manner.

In addition to transparency and accountability, ethical governance in halal business also requires a commitment to social justice. The Quran teaches, "O you who have believed, be persistently standing firm in justice, witnesses for Allah, even if it be against yourselves or parents and relatives" (Quran 4:135). For business leaders, this means ensuring that their operations promote fairness and justice at every level, from the treatment of employees to the way they interact with customers and suppliers.

One of the key areas where social justice must be prioritized is in the treatment of workers. The Prophet Muhammad (PBUH) said, "Give the worker his wages before his sweat dries" (Ibn Majah), emphasizing the importance of fair and timely compensation for labor. For halal businesses, this means ensuring that all employees are paid fair wages, provided with safe working conditions, and treated with dignity and respect. Ethical governance requires business leaders to go beyond the minimum legal requirements and ensure that their operations reflect the values of compassion and fairness that are central to Islam.

In industries where labor exploitation is common, such as fashion and agriculture, halal businesses have a unique opportunity to set themselves apart by promoting ethical labor practices. For example, a halal clothing company might choose to partner with fair-trade-certified suppliers, ensuring that the workers who produce their garments are paid fair wages and provided with safe working conditions. By promoting ethical labor practices, halal businesses not only uphold Islamic values but also build trust with consumers who are increasingly concerned about the social impact of the products they purchase.

Another important aspect of social justice in halal business is the promotion of gender equality. The Quran teaches, "And for women are rights over men similar to those of men over women" (Quran 2:228), emphasizing the importance of fairness and equality between men and women. For business leaders, this means ensuring that women are provided with equal opportunities for advancement, fair wages, and a safe and supportive work environment. By promoting gender equality and supporting the advancement of women in the workplace, halal businesses can set an example of ethical leadership that aligns with both Islamic principles and modern values.

In addition to promoting social justice, leadership in halal business also involves a commitment to environmental stewardship. The Quran reminds us, "And do not commit abuse on the earth, spreading corruption" (Quran 2:60), urging believers to care for the environment and avoid actions that harm the planet. For Muslim entrepreneurs, this means adopting sustainable business practices that minimize environmental impact and contribute to the preservation of natural resources.

Environmental stewardship is becoming increasingly important in the global marketplace, as consumers are more conscious of the environmental impact of their purchases. For halal businesses, this presents an opportunity to differentiate themselves by promoting environmentally friendly products and practices. For example, a halal cosmetics company might use sustainable packaging made from recyclable materials or source ingredients from organic farms that practice environmentally responsible agriculture. By aligning their business practices with the values of environmental sustainability, halal businesses can build trust with consumers who value ethical and eco-friendly products.

Leadership in environmental stewardship also extends to the way businesses manage their energy consumption, waste, and water usage. For example, a halal food processing company might implement energy-efficient technologies in its production facilities to reduce its carbon footprint, or a halal fashion brand might adopt zero-waste production methods to minimize fabric waste. By taking proactive steps to reduce their environmental impact, halal businesses can demonstrate their commitment to ethical governance and inspire other businesses to follow suit.

Moreover, promoting environmental sustainability aligns with the broader principles of halal, which emphasize cleanliness, purity, and the preservation of natural resources. By incorporating sustainability into their business practices, halal businesses can strengthen their reputation as ethical leaders in their industry while also contributing to the greater good of society.

Another key element of leadership in halal business is fostering a culture of continuous learning and innovation. The Quran encourages the pursuit of knowledge, stating, "And say, 'My Lord, increase me in knowledge'" (Quran 20:114). For business leaders, this means staying informed about the latest developments in their industry, exploring new technologies and business models, and continuously seeking ways to improve their operations.

Innovation is critical for staying competitive in the modern business world, but for halal businesses, it is important to ensure that innovation aligns with Islamic principles. For example, a halal financial institution might explore new fintech solutions to offer Shariah-compliant financial products that meet the needs of modern consumers. By embracing innovation while staying true to the values of halal compliance, businesses can create products and services that are both cutting-edge and ethically sound.

Continuous learning also extends to the development of employees. Ethical leadership involves investing in the personal and professional growth of employees, providing them with opportunities for training, mentorship, and advancement. The Prophet Muhammad (PBUH) said, "The best of people are those who bring the most benefit to others" (Daraqutni). For business leaders, this means fostering an environment where employees are encouraged to grow, contribute, and thrive.

By creating a culture of continuous learning and development, halal businesses can build a strong, motivated workforce that is committed to the company's mission and values. This not only enhances the overall performance of the business but also helps to attract and retain top talent, as employees are more likely to stay with companies that invest in their growth and well-being.

In halal business, leadership is not just about making decisions for the present; it is about planning for the future and ensuring that the business remains sustainable and ethical in the long term. The Quran teaches, "And whatever good you put forward for yourselves—you will find it with Allah. It is better and greater in reward" (Quran 73:20). For Muslim entrepreneurs, this means that the decisions they make today will have lasting consequences, both in this world and the hereafter.

Long-term planning in halal business involves setting clear goals, creating strategies for growth, and ensuring that the business remains true to its values as it expands. This requires careful consideration of both the financial and ethical implications of every decision. For example, a halal business looking to expand into new markets must ensure that its products remain compliant with local halal certification standards and that its operations continue to reflect the values of fairness, transparency, and social responsibility.

Leadership in halal business also involves being adaptable and responsive to changing market conditions. The business world is constantly evolving, and successful leaders must be able to navigate challenges, seize opportunities, and adjust their strategies as needed. However, adaptability must never come at the expense of ethical governance. The Quran advises, "And establish weight in justice and do not make deficient the balance" (Quran 55:9). For business leaders, this means ensuring that their actions are always guided by justice and fairness, even in the face of change.

By maintaining a focus on ethical governance, continuous learning, and long-term sustainability, leaders in halal business can build organizations that not only succeed in the marketplace but also make a positive impact on society. These businesses become a reflection of the values of Islam, demonstrating that it is possible to achieve both financial success and spiritual fulfillment through ethical and responsible leadership.

Leadership in halal business is deeply rooted in the principles of fairness, accountability, and moral responsibility. The Quran speaks to these values by advising, "O you who have believed, fear Allah and speak words of appropriate justice" (Quran 33:70). For a leader, this command entails more than just ensuring financial prosperity. It calls for the guidance of their teams and business operations with a moral compass, upholding honesty and fairness as the foundation of all dealings. The role of a leader in a halal business is thus to act as a model of ethical integrity, influencing others to adopt these values.

In halal business, leaders must not only ensure that their practices are in line with Islamic principles, but they must also promote a sense of accountability and responsibility within their organizations. This involves setting clear expectations for ethical behavior, implementing policies that reinforce accountability, and ensuring that every member of the organization is aware of the role they play in upholding halal standards. Accountability means that leaders are transparent about the decisions they make and are prepared to explain the rationale behind these decisions, particularly when they impact the wider community or society as a whole.

One way to build accountability in halal business is by creating a system of checks and balances that ensures all actions align with the values of fairness, justice, and transparency. For example, a halal food company might implement internal audits to ensure that all products meet halal certification standards, or a halal finance company might establish a Shariah supervisory board to oversee its operations and ensure compliance with Islamic law. These structures not only promote transparency but also provide an additional layer of trust for customers and stakeholders.

Moreover, in businesses where the supply chain involves multiple partners, a leader's role in maintaining ethical governance becomes even more significant. The Prophet Muhammad (PBUH) said, "The best of you are those who are best in fulfilling their trusts" (Tirmidhi). This hadith highlights the importance of trust in business partnerships. Leaders must work diligently to ensure that their suppliers, distributors, and other business partners adhere to the same high standards of halal compliance and ethical behavior. This involves regular communication, audits, and a willingness to terminate partnerships that do not align with the values of the business.

Effective leadership in halal business also involves empowering others within the organization to uphold these values. A true leader does not act in isolation but rather cultivates a sense of ownership and responsibility among their team members. The Quran advises, "And consult them in the matter. And when you have decided, then rely upon Allah" (Quran 3:159). This verse highlights the importance of consultation and collaboration in decision-making. For halal business leaders, this means creating a culture where employees feel valued and involved in the decisions that shape the direction of the company.

Consultative leadership is especially important in halal businesses, where ethical considerations often intersect with complex market dynamics. By involving employees in discussions about ethical practices, halal certification processes, and social responsibility initiatives, leaders can create a sense of shared purpose that motivates the entire team to uphold the values of the organization. For example, a halal fashion brand might hold regular meetings with its design and production teams to ensure that all materials used in its garments are ethically sourced and compliant with halal standards. By involving employees in these conversations, leaders not only promote accountability but also foster a culture of continuous learning and improvement.

In addition to empowering employees through consultation, effective leaders also provide opportunities for professional development and growth. The Prophet Muhammad (PBUH) said, "The most beloved people to Allah are those who are most beneficial to the people" (Daraqutni). For halal business leaders, this means investing in the development of their employees, providing them with the tools and resources they need to grow both personally and professionally. This might involve offering training programs on halal compliance, ethical business practices, or leadership development. By supporting the growth of their employees, leaders can build a strong, motivated workforce that is committed to the values of the organization.

For instance, a halal financial institution might offer training programs on Islamic finance principles for its employees, ensuring that they are well-equipped to provide customers with Shariah-compliant financial solutions. This not only enhances the knowledge and skills of the employees but also strengthens the reputation of the institution as a trusted provider of ethical financial services.

Another important aspect of leadership in halal business is the ability to adapt to changing market conditions while staying true to Islamic principles. The business landscape is constantly evolving, and leaders must be able to navigate these changes while maintaining the ethical foundations of their organization. The Quran encourages adaptability and resilience, stating, "Indeed, Allah will not change the condition of a people until they change what is in themselves" (Quran 13:11). For halal business leaders, this means being open to innovation and change while ensuring that all decisions align with the values of halal compliance and ethical governance.

One of the ways leaders can embrace innovation while maintaining halal compliance is by leveraging new technologies to improve their operations. For example, a halal food company might use blockchain technology to track the sourcing and production of its ingredients, ensuring transparency and traceability throughout the supply chain. By adopting innovative solutions that enhance transparency and efficiency, halal businesses can remain competitive in the global marketplace while upholding their commitment to ethical practices.

Innovation in halal business is not limited to technology; it also extends to the development of new products and services that meet the evolving needs of consumers. For example, a halal beauty brand might introduce a line of eco-friendly, cruelty-free products that appeal to both Muslim and non-Muslim consumers who are looking for ethical alternatives. By staying attuned to market trends and consumer preferences, halal businesses can innovate in ways that align with both Islamic principles and modern values.

However, it is important for leaders to ensure that innovation never comes at the expense of halal compliance or ethical governance. The Quran advises, "And do not mix the truth with falsehood or conceal the truth while you know [it]" (Quran 2:42). For halal business leaders, this means ensuring that any new products, services, or technologies introduced by the company are fully compliant with Islamic law and do not compromise the ethical values of the organization.

In addition to embracing innovation, effective leaders in halal business must also be prepared to make difficult decisions that uphold the values of fairness and justice. The Quran teaches, "O you who have believed, be persistently standing firm in justice, witnesses for Allah, even if it be against yourselves or parents and relatives" (Quran 4:135). For business leaders, this means making decisions that are not always easy but are necessary to maintain the ethical integrity of the organization.

For example, a halal business leader might face pressure to cut costs by sourcing materials from suppliers who do not adhere to halal standards. While this decision might offer short-term financial benefits, it would ultimately compromise the ethical foundation of the business and erode the trust of its customers. A strong leader must have the courage to stand firm in their commitment to halal compliance, even when it means making difficult choices that may impact the company's bottom line in the short term.

In addition to standing firm in their commitment to halal principles, leaders must also ensure that their decisions promote social justice and contribute to the greater good of society. The Prophet Muhammad (PBUH) said, "The best of people are those who bring the most benefit to others" (Daraqutni). For halal business leaders, this means considering the broader impact of their decisions on the community and society at large. Ethical governance requires leaders to think beyond profit and consider how their business can contribute to positive social change.

For example, a halal business might choose to invest in community development programs that provide education and job opportunities for underserved populations. By aligning their business decisions with the values of social justice and fairness, leaders can create a lasting positive impact on society while building a reputation for ethical leadership.

Ethical governance in halal business also extends to financial transparency and accountability. The Quran advises, "And give full measure and weight in justice. We do not charge any soul except [with that within] its capacity" (Quran 6:152). For business leaders, this means ensuring that all financial transactions are conducted in a transparent and lawful manner, free from any form of deception or exploitation.

One of the ways leaders can promote financial transparency is by implementing clear and ethical financial policies that ensure all transactions are in compliance with Islamic principles. For example, a halal finance company might offer interest-free loans or profit-sharing arrangements that align with the principles of Shariah-compliant finance. By providing ethical financial solutions, halal businesses can build trust with their customers and stakeholders while upholding their commitment to halal compliance.

In addition to promoting ethical financial practices, leaders must also ensure that their businesses are financially accountable to their customers, employees, and shareholders. This involves maintaining accurate financial records, providing regular reports on the company's financial performance, and ensuring that all financial dealings are conducted with integrity. By promoting financial transparency and accountability, leaders can build a culture of trust and reliability within their organization.

Leadership in halal business is ultimately about embodying the values of Islam in every aspect of the business. The Prophet Muhammad (PBUH) said, "The best among you are those with the best manners and character" (Bukhari). For halal business leaders, this means leading by example, demonstrating kindness, fairness, and integrity in all their dealings. It is through their actions that leaders can inspire others to uphold the values of halal compliance and ethical governance.

By fostering a culture of ethical leadership, transparency, and accountability, leaders in halal business can build organizations that not only succeed in the marketplace but also make a positive impact on society. These businesses serve as a testament to the power of ethical governance, showing that it is possible to achieve financial success while staying true to the values of fairness, justice, and integrity.

As halal businesses continue to grow and evolve, their leaders have the opportunity to set a new standard for ethical leadership, one that reflects the values of Islam and serves as a model for businesses around the world. The future of halal business is bright, and with strong leadership, these businesses can continue to thrive while making a meaningful difference in the world.

Leadership in halal business is a journey that encompasses spiritual, ethical, and social responsibilities. It is not only about setting the vision for the company but about ensuring that the vision aligns with the values and principles of Islam. The Quran guides leaders by stating, "So fear Allah as much as you are able and listen and obey and spend [in the way of Allah]; it is better for your souls" (Quran 64:16). This highlights that true leadership in Islam involves responsibility, a sense of justice, and a commitment to doing good. For Muslim entrepreneurs, this is an important reminder that their leadership role is not only an opportunity for business success but also a means of achieving spiritual reward.

In the context of halal business, this sense of responsibility means leading with humility and being aware that every decision can have far-reaching effects—on employees, customers, communities, and the environment. A leader's responsibility is to weigh these decisions carefully, ensuring that the outcome promotes fairness, justice, and goodness. For instance, a halal business leader might face the temptation to cut corners in the supply chain to reduce costs. However, a true leader will recognize that such actions could compromise the integrity of the business and the trust of its customers, and will instead choose to maintain high standards of halal compliance and ethical governance.

One of the key aspects of ethical leadership is fairness in the treatment of employees. The Prophet Muhammad (PBUH) said, "Your employees are your brothers, whom Allah has placed under your authority. So whoever has his brother under his command should feed him of what he eats and dress him of what he wears. Do not burden them beyond their capacity, and if you do so, then help them" (Bukhari). This hadith underscores the importance of treating employees with kindness, fairness, and respect, ensuring that they are provided with fair wages, safe working conditions, and opportunities for growth.

In halal business, leadership also involves fostering a positive and inclusive work culture that promotes the well-being of employees. This can be achieved by providing opportunities for professional development, ensuring that employees are treated with dignity, and promoting a healthy work-life balance. For example, a halal business leader might offer flexible working hours or ensure that employees have time and space to perform their prayers. By supporting the spiritual and personal needs of their employees, halal businesses can create a work environment that is both productive and fulfilling, contributing to the overall success of the organization.

Moreover, a halal business leader should encourage collaboration and teamwork, recognizing that the success of the organization depends on the collective efforts of all its members. The Quran advises, "And cooperate in righteousness and piety, but do not cooperate in sin and aggression" (Quran 5:2). This verse emphasizes the importance of working together for the common good and avoiding actions that harm others. For leaders, this means promoting a culture of cooperation and teamwork, where employees are encouraged to support one another, share ideas, and work toward common goals.

Leaders in halal business must also be mindful of how they handle conflict and disagreements within the organization. The Quran teaches, "And if you disagree over anything, refer it to Allah and the Messenger, if you should believe in Allah and the Last Day. That is the best [way] and best in result" (Quran 4:59). For Muslim entrepreneurs, this means approaching conflicts with patience, wisdom, and fairness, seeking solutions that are in line with Islamic principles. By promoting a culture of open communication and resolving disputes in a just and ethical manner, leaders can maintain harmony within their organization and ensure that it continues to operate in accordance with halal values.

In addition to fostering internal harmony, leaders in halal business must also focus on building strong relationships with external stakeholders, including customers, suppliers, and partners. The Prophet Muhammad (PBUH) said, "None of you truly believes until he loves for his brother what he loves for himself" (Bukhari). For business leaders, this hadith serves as a reminder that ethical governance extends beyond the walls of the organization; it involves treating all stakeholders with fairness, honesty, and respect.

One way to build strong relationships with external stakeholders is by maintaining transparency in all business dealings. For example, a halal food company might provide detailed information about the sourcing and production of its ingredients, ensuring that customers can trust that the products they purchase are genuinely halal and produced ethically. By being open and honest with customers and partners, leaders can build trust and foster long-term relationships that benefit both the business and the community.

In halal business, trust is the cornerstone of all relationships. The Prophet Muhammad (PBUH) said, "The honest and trustworthy merchant will be with the prophets, the truthful, and the martyrs" (Tirmidhi). For Muslim entrepreneurs, this hadith highlights the spiritual reward that comes with conducting business in an honest and trustworthy manner. Leaders must ensure that their business practices reflect these values, from the way products are marketed to the way customer complaints are handled.

Marketing, in particular, is an area where ethical governance is crucial. In a competitive marketplace, businesses may be tempted to use deceptive marketing tactics to attract customers, but halal businesses must avoid such practices at all costs. The Quran advises, "And do not mix the truth with falsehood or conceal the truth while you know [it]" (Quran 2:42). For halal businesses, this means ensuring that all marketing materials are truthful, transparent, and aligned with Islamic values. This might involve providing clear information about the halal certification process, being upfront about the ingredients used in products, and avoiding exaggerated claims about the benefits of the product.

In addition to ensuring honesty in marketing, leaders must also focus on building trust through excellent customer service. The Prophet Muhammad (PBUH) said, "The best of people are those who bring the most benefit to others" (Daraqutni). For halal business leaders, this means prioritizing customer satisfaction, addressing customer concerns promptly and fairly, and going above and beyond to ensure that customers feel valued and appreciated. By offering excellent customer service, businesses can build lasting relationships with their customers and foster loyalty that extends beyond the initial purchase.

One practical way to demonstrate a commitment to customer satisfaction is by offering flexible return policies or providing customers with personalized support. For example, a halal fashion brand might offer free exchanges or returns for customers who are not satisfied with their purchase, or a halal financial institution might provide personalized financial advice to help customers make informed decisions. By showing that they care about their customers' needs, halal businesses can build trust and strengthen their reputation as ethical and responsible organizations.

In addition to building trust with customers, halal business leaders must also focus on fostering strong relationships with suppliers and partners. The Quran emphasizes the importance of fulfilling contracts and agreements, stating, "O you who have believed, fulfill [all] contracts" (Quran 5:1). For halal businesses, this means ensuring that all agreements with suppliers and partners are honored, and that all parties are treated with fairness and respect.

One way to promote ethical governance in supplier relationships is by conducting regular audits of the supply chain to ensure that all materials and products meet halal standards. For example, a halal food company might conduct audits of its suppliers to ensure that all ingredients are sourced from halal-certified farms and that the production process adheres to Islamic principles. By maintaining strict oversight of the supply chain, businesses can ensure that their products are genuinely halal and build trust with their customers.

Leaders must also be mindful of the social and environmental impact of their supply chains. The Quran advises, "And do not commit abuse on the earth, spreading corruption" (Quran 2:60). For business leaders, this means ensuring that their supply chains are sustainable and that their business practices do not harm the environment or exploit workers. For example, a halal cosmetics company might choose to work with suppliers who use sustainable farming practices and pay their workers fair wages. By aligning their supply chains with the values of ethical governance, halal businesses can promote social justice and environmental stewardship while building a strong reputation for responsibility and integrity.

In halal business, leadership is not just about financial success—it is about creating a positive impact on society and the environment. The Prophet Muhammad (PBUH) said, "The best among you are those who have the best manners and character" (Bukhari). For halal business leaders, this means leading by example, demonstrating kindness, fairness, and ethical behavior in all their dealings. By fostering a culture of ethical governance, transparency, and social responsibility, leaders can create businesses that not only succeed in the marketplace but also contribute to the greater good of society.

Leaders in halal business must also ensure that their organizations are compliant with legal and regulatory requirements, both in the countries where they operate and within the framework of Islamic law. The Quran states, "And do not consume one another's wealth unjustly or send it [in bribery] to the rulers in order that [they might aid] you [to] consume a portion of the wealth of the people in sin, while you know [it is unlawful]" (Quran 2:188). This verse emphasizes the importance of conducting business in a lawful and ethical manner, free from corruption or exploitation.

For halal business leaders, this means ensuring that all financial dealings are transparent and in compliance with both local laws and Shariah principles. This might involve working with Islamic finance experts to ensure that all financial products and transactions are Shariah-compliant, or conducting regular audits to ensure that the business is in full compliance with local regulations. By promoting financial transparency and accountability, leaders can build trust with their customers, employees, and shareholders, ensuring that the business operates in an ethical and responsible manner.

In addition to ensuring legal and financial compliance, leaders must also promote ethical governance in their decision-making processes. The Quran advises, "And establish weight in justice and do not make deficient the balance" (Quran 55:9). For business leaders, this means ensuring that all decisions are guided by justice and fairness, even when faced with difficult choices. Whether it's deciding how to allocate resources, managing employee relations, or navigating market challenges, leaders must prioritize fairness and ethical behavior in every decision they make.

For example, a halal business leader might face a situation where the company is forced to downsize due to economic challenges. In such a case, the leader must ensure that the process is handled with fairness and transparency, providing employees with adequate notice, severance packages, and support in finding new employment opportunities. By demonstrating compassion and fairness in difficult decisions, leaders can maintain the trust and loyalty of their employees, even in challenging times.

Leadership in halal business is not solely about making decisions in the boardroom; it's about fostering a culture of ethical integrity that permeates every aspect of the organization. The Quran instructs, "O you who have believed, why do you say what you do not do? Great is hatred in the sight of Allah that you say what you do not do" (Quran 61:2-3). This powerful verse reminds leaders of the importance of aligning words with actions, particularly in business. True leadership is demonstrated not just by what is said, but by the consistency of actions that align with ethical principles.

In the context of halal business, this means ensuring that the entire organization operates with transparency and accountability, from top management to the most junior employees. Leaders must lead by example, demonstrating a commitment to ethical conduct in every aspect of their role—from decision-making and strategic planning to employee relations and customer service. By embodying the values of fairness, justice, and honesty, leaders can inspire their teams to do the same, creating a culture of ethical governance that strengthens the organization from within.

A leader's example is perhaps most visible in times of difficulty or crisis. Whether the challenge is financial, operational, or related to market changes, the way a leader handles adversity can set the tone for the entire organization. The Prophet Muhammad (PBUH) said, "He who is not merciful to people, Allah will not be merciful to him" (Muslim). For halal business leaders, this means approaching difficult situations with compassion, patience, and wisdom, always considering the impact of their decisions on others.

For example, during an economic downturn, a halal business leader may face the difficult decision of reducing the workforce to keep the company viable. In such cases, the leader must handle the situation with care, ensuring that employees are treated with respect and fairness, offering severance packages, and providing support to those affected. By acting with kindness and responsibility in such situations, the leader can preserve the trust and loyalty of the remaining workforce and maintain the organization's reputation for ethical governance.

In addition to leading through example, halal business leaders must also focus on building a culture of accountability within their organization. The Quran states, "And those who avoid the major sins and immoralities, and when they are angry, they forgive" (Quran 42:37). This verse emphasizes the importance of self-control and forgiveness, but also suggests that leaders must establish systems that encourage accountability and personal responsibility.

Creating a culture of accountability begins with setting clear ethical standards and expectations for behavior within the organization. Leaders must communicate these standards to all employees, ensuring that they understand their responsibilities and the importance of upholding the values of halal compliance. This can be achieved through regular training programs, workshops, and clear policies that outline the ethical standards expected from every employee. Additionally, leaders must ensure that there are consequences for unethical behavior, but these consequences should be fair, measured, and in alignment with Islamic principles of justice and compassion.

For example, a halal food company might implement strict quality control measures to ensure that all products meet halal certification standards. If a supplier or employee fails to adhere to these standards, the leader must take swift action to rectify the situation, whether by conducting a product recall or terminating the relationship with the supplier. However, in line with the principles of forgiveness and fairness, leaders should also provide opportunities for employees to learn from their mistakes and improve, offering guidance and support to help them align with the organization's ethical values.

In addition to fostering accountability within the organization, leaders must also ensure that they themselves are accountable to their stakeholders, including customers, employees, shareholders, and the wider community. The Prophet Muhammad (PBUH) said, "Each of you is a shepherd, and each of you is responsible for his flock" (Bukhari). For business leaders, this hadith serves as a reminder that they are ultimately responsible for the well-being of their organization and the people it impacts.

One practical way to promote accountability is through regular communication with stakeholders, providing updates on the organization's performance, goals, and challenges. For example, a halal finance company might hold quarterly meetings with shareholders to discuss the company's financial performance and ensure that all business decisions align with Shariah-compliant principles. By being open and transparent with stakeholders, leaders can build trust and ensure that the organization remains accountable for its actions.

Leadership in halal business also requires a deep commitment to social responsibility. The Quran teaches, "And spend in the way of Allah and do not throw [yourselves] with your [own] hands into destruction [by refraining]. And do good; indeed, Allah loves the doers of good" (Quran 2:195). For business leaders, this means ensuring that their organization contributes to the greater good of society, both through charitable giving and through business practices that promote social justice and environmental sustainability.

One way for halal businesses to demonstrate their commitment to social responsibility is by supporting charitable causes that align with the values of Islam. For example, a halal food brand might donate a portion of its profits to provide meals for underserved communities during Ramadan, or a halal clothing company might support initiatives that promote education and empowerment for women in disadvantaged areas. These charitable efforts not only reflect the values of halal business but also resonate with customers who appreciate brands that prioritize giving back to society.

In addition to charitable giving, social responsibility in halal business involves promoting fair and ethical labor practices. The Prophet Muhammad (PBUH) said, "Give the worker his wages before his sweat dries" (Ibn Majah), emphasizing the importance of fair compensation and the ethical treatment of workers. For halal businesses, this means ensuring that all employees are paid fair wages, provided with safe working conditions, and treated with dignity and respect. Moreover, ethical governance requires that leaders ensure their supply chains are free from exploitation, promoting fair labor practices not just within their own organization but throughout the entire supply chain.

For example, a halal cosmetics company might choose to work with suppliers that pay fair wages to their workers and avoid using harmful chemicals that can negatively impact the health of employees or the environment. By promoting ethical labor practices and environmental sustainability, halal businesses can position themselves as leaders in social responsibility while building trust with consumers who value ethical products.

In addition to social responsibility, leadership in halal business also involves a commitment to environmental stewardship. The Quran advises, "And do not commit abuse on the earth, spreading corruption" (Quran 2:60). For business leaders, this means ensuring that their organization operates in a way that protects the environment and promotes sustainability. Environmental stewardship is becoming increasingly important as consumers seek out products and services that align with their ethical values, including a commitment to preserving the planet for future generations.

One practical way for halal businesses to promote environmental sustainability is by adopting eco-friendly practices in their operations. For example, a halal food company might use sustainable packaging made from recyclable materials or source ingredients from organic farms that avoid harmful pesticides and promote biodiversity. Similarly, a halal fashion brand might use environmentally friendly fabrics and adopt a zero-waste production model that minimizes textile waste. By aligning their business practices with environmental sustainability, halal businesses can demonstrate their commitment to ethical governance and build trust with consumers who are looking for eco-friendly products.

In addition to promoting sustainability within their own operations, halal business leaders can also encourage their suppliers and partners to adopt environmentally friendly practices. For example, a halal cosmetics company might work with suppliers who use sustainable farming methods or prioritize water conservation in their production processes. By promoting sustainability throughout the supply chain, businesses can contribute to a broader movement toward environmental responsibility and demonstrate their commitment to protecting the earth.

Leadership in environmental stewardship is not just about meeting consumer demand for sustainable products—it is about fulfilling a moral obligation to care for the planet that Allah has entrusted to us. The Quran teaches, "It is He who has made you successors upon the earth" (Quran 35:39), reminding us that we are responsible for the stewardship of the environment. For halal business leaders, this means taking proactive steps to reduce their environmental impact, promote sustainability, and contribute to the preservation of natural resources for future generations.

As halal business leaders continue to navigate the complexities of the modern marketplace, they must remain steadfast in their commitment to ethical governance and halal compliance. The Prophet Muhammad (PBUH) said, "Verily, Allah has prescribed excellence in everything" (Muslim). This hadith serves as a guiding principle for leaders, reminding them that excellence is not just about achieving financial success but about striving for excellence in character, integrity, and responsibility.

One of the key ways leaders can promote excellence in their organization is by fostering a culture of continuous improvement. This involves regularly reviewing business practices, identifying areas for improvement, and implementing new strategies to enhance the company's operations and ethical governance. For example, a halal financial institution might invest in new technology to improve the transparency and efficiency of its Shariah-compliant services, or a halal food company might develop new halal-certified products that meet the evolving needs of consumers.

Continuous improvement also extends to the development of employees. Leaders must ensure that their teams are equipped with the knowledge, skills, and resources they need to succeed. This might involve offering training programs on halal compliance, leadership development, or ethical business practices. By investing in the growth and development of their employees, leaders can build a strong, motivated workforce that is committed to the success of the organization and its values.

Another important aspect of promoting excellence in halal business is ensuring that the organization remains adaptable and resilient in the face of change. The Quran advises, "Indeed, Allah will not change the condition of a people until they change what is in themselves" (Quran 13:11). For business leaders, this means being open to innovation, responding to market trends, and adapting to new challenges while staying true to the values of halal compliance and ethical governance.

For example, a halal beauty brand might introduce a new line of eco-friendly, cruelty-free products to meet the growing demand for ethical and sustainable cosmetics. By embracing innovation while maintaining halal standards, the business can remain competitive and relevant in the global marketplace while upholding its commitment to Islamic principles.

Leadership in halal business requires an unwavering commitment to both ethical excellence and adaptability. The Quran teaches, "So whoever does an atom's weight of good will see it" (Quran 99:7). This verse emphasizes that even the smallest acts of goodness and righteousness will be rewarded, reminding business leaders that every decision, no matter how small, must align with ethical and moral principles. For Muslim entrepreneurs, this means that integrity should guide every aspect of their leadership, ensuring that their business practices reflect the highest standards of halal compliance and ethical governance.

To lead with integrity, business leaders must ensure that they consistently prioritize long-term ethical goals over short-term financial gains. For example, a halal business leader may be faced with opportunities to cut costs through unethical sourcing practices or exploitative labor conditions. However, the true measure of leadership lies in resisting these temptations and making decisions that honor the principles of justice, fairness, and compassion. Leaders who maintain this level of ethical integrity not only earn the trust and loyalty of their customers but also contribute to the greater good of society by upholding the values of Islam.

At the same time, adaptability is essential for leaders who wish to succeed in the dynamic world of halal business. Markets are continuously evolving, consumer preferences are shifting, and technological advancements are reshaping the business landscape. The Quran advises, "And prepare against them whatever you are able of power and of steeds of war" (Quran 8:60), highlighting the importance of preparedness and readiness to face challenges. In halal business, this means that leaders must remain open to change, constantly seeking ways to improve and evolve while staying true to their ethical commitments.

For instance, as halal businesses expand globally, leaders may need to adapt their products and services to meet the preferences of different markets while maintaining halal certification and compliance. A halal food company might explore plant-based alternatives to traditional halal meat products, catering to the growing demand for sustainable and health-conscious food options. By embracing innovation and staying attuned to consumer trends, halal businesses can continue to thrive and meet the needs of a diverse, global audience.

Adaptability also extends to the way leaders manage their teams and foster an environment of inclusivity and collaboration. The Quran teaches, "And their affairs are [determined by] consultation among themselves" (Quran 42:38), emphasizing the importance of consultation and collective decision-making. For halal business leaders, this means creating a culture where employees feel empowered to share their ideas, contribute to discussions, and play an active role in the decision-making process.

By fostering a collaborative environment, leaders can harness the creativity and expertise of their teams to drive innovation and ethical excellence. For example, a halal fashion brand might involve its design team in discussions about how to source more sustainable fabrics or create new designs that reflect both modesty and modern fashion trends. By encouraging input from employees at all levels of the organization, leaders can make more informed decisions and build a stronger, more cohesive team.

In addition to promoting collaboration, effective leadership also involves providing opportunities for employee development. The Prophet Muhammad (PBUH) said, "The best of people are those who are most beneficial to others" (Daraqutni). For business leaders, this hadith serves as a reminder that one of the most important aspects of leadership is helping others grow and succeed. In halal business, this means offering training programs, mentorship opportunities, and career development resources that enable employees to reach their full potential.

For instance, a halal financial institution might offer its employees training on Shariah-compliant finance, ensuring that they have a deep understanding of the ethical principles that underpin Islamic banking. By investing in the professional development of their employees, leaders can build a knowledgeable and motivated workforce that is committed to the success of the organization and the values of halal compliance.

As leaders in halal business continue to guide their organizations, they must remain focused on the core values of fairness, justice, and responsibility. The Quran advises, "O you who have believed, be persistently standing firm in justice, witnesses for Allah, even if it be against yourselves or parents and relatives" (Quran 4:135). This verse serves as a powerful reminder that leaders must uphold justice, even when it is difficult or when it goes against their personal interests. For Muslim entrepreneurs, this means ensuring that their business decisions are guided by a commitment to fairness and ethical governance, regardless of the challenges they may face.

One practical way for leaders to uphold justice in their organizations is by ensuring that all employees are treated with respect and given equal opportunities to succeed. This includes promoting diversity and inclusion within the workforce, ensuring that employees of all backgrounds feel valued and supported. For example, a halal business might implement policies that promote gender equality, offering leadership opportunities to women and ensuring that the workplace is free from discrimination.

In addition to promoting fairness within the organization, leaders must also ensure that their business practices reflect a commitment to social justice in the wider community. The Prophet Muhammad (PBUH) said, "None of you truly believes until he loves for his brother what he loves for himself" (Bukhari). For halal business leaders, this means ensuring that their products and services contribute to the well-being of society and do not harm others. Whether it's through fair trade practices, charitable giving, or promoting environmental sustainability, leaders must ensure that their business contributes to the greater good.

For example, a halal beauty brand might commit to using cruelty-free ingredients, ensuring that its products are not tested on animals, while also donating a portion of its profits to support environmental conservation efforts. By aligning their business practices with the principles of social justice and environmental responsibility, halal business leaders can create positive change in the world while building a strong, ethical brand that resonates with consumers.

As halal businesses continue to grow and expand, their leaders have the opportunity to set a new standard for ethical governance, one that reflects the values of Islam and promotes fairness, justice, and compassion in every aspect of the organization. By staying true to these principles, halal business leaders can build successful, sustainable organizations that make a positive impact on both their customers and the world at large.

CHAPTER 8: BUILDING A RESILIENT AND SUSTAINABLE HALAL BUSINESS

In the world of commerce, resilience and sustainability have become paramount for businesses seeking long-term success, especially for those operating within the framework of halal principles. The Quran teaches, "And Allah has made for you from your homes a place of rest and made for you from the hides of the animals tents which you find light on the day of travel and when you stop for rest" (Quran 16:80). This verse emphasizes that the provision of necessities is a gift from Allah, and it is our duty to ensure that these resources are used responsibly, providing lasting benefit to ourselves and others.

In halal business, resilience refers to the ability to navigate challenges, overcome obstacles, and sustain growth in the face of external pressures. Whether these challenges come in the form of economic downturns, shifting market trends, or changes in consumer behavior, a resilient halal business must be adaptable and resourceful, ensuring that its core principles remain intact regardless of the external environment. However, building a resilient business is not only about surviving hardships; it is about thriving in a way that reflects the values of Islam, promoting ethical practices and fostering trust with customers and stakeholders alike.

For a halal business to be sustainable, it must go beyond mere financial success. Sustainability involves a commitment to social responsibility, environmental stewardship, and long-term value creation. The Quran advises, "Indeed, Allah will not change the condition of a people until they change what is in themselves" (Quran 13:11), a reminder that positive change begins from within. In this context, sustainable business practices must be rooted in the intention to serve society, preserve the environment, and provide products and services that are beneficial and tayyib (pure) in every sense.

Building a resilient and sustainable halal business requires a holistic approach, one that integrates the principles of ethical governance, social justice, and environmental responsibility with innovation and strategic foresight. By doing so, businesses can not only weather the storms of change but also create a lasting legacy of trust, integrity, and positive impact.

A key component of building resilience in halal business is adaptability. Markets evolve rapidly, and businesses must be prepared to respond to changes in consumer preferences, technological advancements, and regulatory environments. The Quran reminds us, "So take what I have given you and be among the grateful" (Quran 7:144), encouraging gratitude for the opportunities and resources at hand. For business leaders, this means recognizing that change is an opportunity for growth and innovation rather than a threat.

Adaptability begins with understanding the needs and preferences of consumers. For example, in recent years, there has been a growing demand for halal-certified products that also meet environmental and health-conscious standards. Businesses that can pivot to meet these demands while maintaining their commitment to halal principles will be better positioned to succeed in the long term. A halal food company, for instance, might explore plant-based alternatives to traditional meat products, catering to a growing market of environmentally conscious consumers who seek halal options that align with their ethical and dietary preferences.

In addition to consumer demands, technological advancements are reshaping the way businesses operate. From e-commerce platforms to supply chain management systems, technology offers halal businesses the tools they need to streamline operations, reduce costs, and enhance transparency. For example, blockchain technology can be used to track the entire supply chain of halal products, ensuring that every step of the process adheres to halal certification standards. This level of transparency not only builds trust with consumers but also strengthens the business's resilience by reducing the risk of errors or miscommunication.

However, adaptability must never come at the expense of ethical governance or halal compliance. While businesses may need to embrace new technologies or adjust their product offerings to remain competitive, they must always ensure that their core values of fairness, transparency, and social responsibility are upheld. The Prophet Muhammad (PBUH) said, "The best of people are those who bring the most benefit to others" (Daraqutni). For halal businesses, this means ensuring that all innovations and adaptations are in service of providing genuine value to consumers and society at large.

Another essential aspect of building resilience in halal business is financial sustainability. A resilient business must have a solid financial foundation that allows it to weather economic downturns, market fluctuations, and other challenges. The Quran advises, "And give full measure when you measure, and weigh with an even balance. That is the best [way] and best in result" (Quran 17:35). For business leaders, this means ensuring that financial decisions are made with fairness, accuracy, and responsibility, both in terms of managing expenses and generating revenue.

One way to build financial sustainability is through diversification. A halal business that relies too heavily on a single product or market may be vulnerable to disruptions if demand shifts or competition increases. By diversifying its product offerings or expanding into new markets, a business can create multiple revenue streams and reduce its overall risk. For example, a halal skincare company might diversify by offering both skincare products and halal-certified wellness supplements, appealing to a broader customer base while maintaining its commitment to halal compliance.

Another important aspect of financial sustainability is cost management. Businesses must ensure that they are operating efficiently, minimizing unnecessary expenses while maintaining the quality and integrity of their products. This might involve implementing cost-saving measures such as automating certain processes, renegotiating supplier contracts, or adopting more sustainable practices that reduce waste and improve resource efficiency. However, cost-cutting must never compromise the ethical standards of the business. The Quran teaches, "And do not consume one another's wealth unjustly or send it [in bribery] to the rulers in order that [they might aid] you [to] consume a portion of the wealth of the people in sin, while you know [it is unlawful]" (Quran 2:188). For halal businesses, this means ensuring that all financial decisions are made with integrity and respect for the rights of others.

In addition to internal financial management, businesses must also ensure that they are compliant with external financial regulations, both locally and internationally. This includes adhering to Islamic finance principles, which prohibit interest-based transactions (riba) and encourage profit-sharing arrangements that are fair and transparent. By aligning their financial practices with Islamic principles, halal businesses can build trust with their customers and stakeholders, reinforcing their commitment to ethical governance and long-term sustainability.

Sustainability in halal business also extends to environmental responsibility. The Quran advises, "And do not commit abuse on the earth, spreading corruption" (Quran 2:60). For business leaders, this means ensuring that their operations have a minimal impact on the environment and that they actively contribute to the preservation of natural resources. In today's marketplace, consumers are increasingly seeking out products that align with their ethical values, including a commitment to environmental sustainability. For halal businesses, this presents an opportunity to differentiate themselves by promoting environmentally responsible practices that align with both Islamic principles and modern consumer expectations.

One practical way for businesses to promote environmental sustainability is by adopting eco-friendly production methods. For example, a halal food company might source ingredients from organic farms that avoid the use of harmful pesticides and prioritize sustainable farming practices. Similarly, a halal fashion brand might use eco-friendly fabrics and adopt a zero-waste production model that minimizes textile waste. By aligning their production processes with sustainable practices, halal businesses can demonstrate their commitment to environmental stewardship and build trust with consumers who are looking for ethical products.

In addition to promoting sustainability within their own operations, halal businesses can also encourage their suppliers and partners to adopt environmentally friendly practices. For instance, a halal beauty brand might work with suppliers who use sustainable farming methods or prioritize water conservation in their production processes. By promoting sustainability throughout the supply chain, businesses can contribute to a broader movement toward environmental responsibility while building a strong reputation for ethical governance.

Moreover, halal businesses can also explore opportunities to reduce their carbon footprint through energy efficiency and waste reduction. This might involve adopting renewable energy sources, implementing energy-efficient technologies in production facilities, or developing packaging solutions that are biodegradable or recyclable. By taking proactive steps to minimize their environmental impact, businesses can align their operations with the principles of halal, which emphasize cleanliness, purity, and the preservation of natural resources.

Sustainability in halal business is not limited to environmental practices—it also involves fostering social responsibility and ethical governance. The Prophet Muhammad (PBUH) said, "The best of people are those who are most beneficial to others" (Daraqutni). For halal businesses, this means ensuring that their operations contribute to the well-being of society, both through the products and services they offer and through their broader social impact.

One way businesses can promote social responsibility is by supporting fair labor practices throughout their supply chain. The Quran advises, "Give full measure and do not be of those who cause loss" (Quran 26:181). For halal businesses, this means ensuring that all workers involved in the production and distribution of their products are treated fairly, paid a living wage, and provided with safe and healthy working conditions. Ethical governance requires that businesses hold themselves and their suppliers accountable for upholding these standards, creating a supply chain that is free from exploitation and aligned with the values of social justice.

In addition to promoting fair labor practices, halal businesses can also contribute to social responsibility by supporting charitable causes that align with their values. The Quran advises, "And establish prayer and give zakat, and whatever good you put forward for yourselves—you will find it with Allah" (Quran 2:110). For halal businesses, this might involve donating a portion of their profits to support community development initiatives, providing scholarships for disadvantaged students, or partnering with charitable organizations that provide essential services to those in need.

For example, a halal clothing brand might donate unsold inventory to refugees or low-income communities, ensuring that those in need have access to clean, modest clothing. By aligning their charitable efforts with their business values, halal businesses demonstrate their commitment to social responsibility and build a positive reputation that resonates with consumers who value ethical products.

Another important aspect of sustainability in halal business is fostering resilience through strong relationships with customers, employees, and stakeholders. The Quran teaches, "And cooperate in righteousness and piety, but do not cooperate in sin and aggression" (Quran 5:2). For business leaders, this means building relationships that are rooted in trust, respect, and mutual benefit, ensuring that all interactions are guided by the principles of fairness and ethical governance.

One of the most important relationships a business can cultivate is with its customers. Trust is the foundation of any successful business, and for halal businesses, trust is built through transparency, consistency, and a commitment to halal compliance. The Prophet Muhammad (PBUH) said, "The honest and trustworthy businessman will be with the prophets, the truthful, and the martyrs" (Tirmidhi). For halal businesses, this means ensuring that all products and services are genuinely halal, clearly labeled, and marketed in an honest and ethical manner. By maintaining high standards of quality and transparency, businesses can build lasting relationships with their customers, fostering loyalty and trust that will sustain them through challenges.

In addition to building trust with customers, halal businesses must also focus on cultivating strong relationships with their employees. The Prophet Muhammad (PBUH) said, "Your employees are your brothers, whom Allah has placed under your authority. So whoever has his brother under his command should feed him of what he eats and dress him of what he wears" (Bukhari). For business leaders, this means ensuring that employees are treated with fairness, respect, and dignity, providing them with opportunities for professional development and creating a work environment that is both supportive and fulfilling.

A halal business that invests in its employees will not only build a strong, motivated workforce but also foster resilience within the organization. Employees who feel valued and supported are more likely to remain loyal to the company, contribute to its success, and help navigate challenges when they arise. This is particularly important in times of crisis, when a strong, unified workforce can make the difference between survival and failure.

Resilience in halal business is not only about overcoming challenges but also about creating systems that ensure long-term sustainability. The Quran advises, "And spend in the way of Allah and do not throw [yourselves] with your [own] hands into destruction [by refraining]. And do good; indeed, Allah loves the doers of good" (Quran 2:195). This verse serves as a reminder that businesses must not only focus on immediate profits but also consider the broader impact of their actions on society and the environment. For a business to be truly resilient, it must adopt practices that promote sustainability in all its forms—economic, social, and environmental.

One key aspect of building long-term resilience is ensuring that the business is financially sound, with enough reserves to withstand economic fluctuations. Financial stability requires prudent financial management, including maintaining an emergency fund, minimizing debt, and carefully managing cash flow. A resilient business anticipates potential risks and plans accordingly, ensuring that it has the resources to navigate difficult periods without compromising its halal principles or the quality of its products.

In addition to prudent financial management, businesses must also focus on creating sustainable revenue streams. This might involve expanding into new markets or diversifying product offerings to appeal to a broader customer base. For example, a halal travel company might expand its services by offering halal-friendly vacation packages that cater to Muslim travelers looking for ethical and halal-certified experiences. By diversifying its offerings, the business can create additional revenue streams and reduce its dependence on any single product or market, making it more resilient to changes in consumer demand.

Another important factor in building financial resilience is fostering strong relationships with suppliers and partners. The Quran reminds us, "And fulfill [every] commitment. Indeed, the commitment is ever [that about which one will be] questioned" (Quran 17:34). For halal businesses, this means ensuring that all relationships with suppliers and partners are built on trust, transparency, and mutual benefit. Strong, reliable partnerships are essential for ensuring that the supply chain remains intact, even in times of crisis. By working closely with suppliers to ensure that all materials are sourced ethically and sustainably, businesses can maintain the integrity of their products while strengthening their resilience.

In addition to financial sustainability, building resilience in halal business also involves fostering a culture of innovation. The Prophet Muhammad (PBUH) said, "Seek knowledge from the cradle to the grave" (Bukhari). This hadith highlights the importance of continuous learning and innovation in every aspect of life, including business. For halal businesses, this means staying informed about industry trends, technological advancements, and changes in consumer behavior, and using this knowledge to drive innovation.

Innovation in halal business can take many forms, from product development to process improvement. For example, a halal food company might invest in research and development to create new halal-certified products that meet the evolving needs of consumers. Similarly, a halal financial institution might explore new technologies, such as blockchain, to enhance the transparency and security of its transactions. By fostering a culture of innovation, businesses can stay ahead of the competition and remain resilient in the face of changing market conditions.

However, innovation must always be guided by the principles of halal compliance and ethical governance. The Quran advises, "And do not mix the truth with falsehood or conceal the truth while you know [it]" (Quran 2:42). For halal businesses, this means ensuring that all innovations are aligned with

Islamic values, providing genuine value to customers and upholding the integrity of the business. Whether it's developing new products, improving operational efficiency, or exploring new business models, businesses must ensure that their innovations are ethical, sustainable, and compliant with halal standards.

One practical way to foster innovation within a halal business is by encouraging collaboration and open communication among employees. By creating an environment where employees feel empowered to share their ideas and contribute to the development of new products and services, leaders can tap into the collective creativity and expertise of their workforce. This might involve holding regular brainstorming sessions, creating cross-functional teams, or offering incentives for employees who come up with innovative solutions to business challenges.

Resilience in halal business is not just about internal processes—it's also about maintaining strong, trusting relationships with customers. The Prophet Muhammad (PBUH) said, "The best of people are those who are most beneficial to others" (Daraqutni). For halal businesses, this means ensuring that their products and services meet the needs of their customers in a way that aligns with Islamic values. Trust is the foundation of any successful business, and for halal businesses, this trust is built through transparency, honesty, and a commitment to halal compliance.

One way to build trust with customers is by being transparent about the halal certification process. Customers who purchase halal products want to know that they are genuinely halal, produced in accordance with Islamic principles and free from any haram ingredients or practices. By providing clear information about the certification process and the steps taken to ensure halal compliance, businesses can build trust with their customers and foster long-term loyalty.

For example, a halal beauty brand might provide detailed information about the sourcing of its ingredients, the certification process, and the ethical standards it adheres to in its production methods. By being transparent about these practices, the brand can build a loyal customer base that values its commitment to both halal compliance and ethical governance.

In addition to transparency, businesses must also focus on delivering consistent quality. Customers who trust a halal brand expect the same level of quality every time they purchase a product. Whether it's the taste of a halal-certified food product, the performance of a halal skincare product, or the reliability of a halal financial service, consistency is key to maintaining trust. Businesses that consistently deliver high-quality products and services are more likely to build long-term relationships with their customers, fostering resilience through customer loyalty.

Another important aspect of resilience in halal business is customer engagement. In today's digital age, businesses have more opportunities than ever to connect with their customers, gather feedback, and build meaningful relationships. The Quran teaches, "And speak to people good [words]" (Quran 2:83), reminding us of the importance of positive communication and building relationships based on kindness and respect.

For halal businesses, this means actively engaging with customers through social media, customer service channels, and other digital platforms. By responding to customer inquiries, addressing concerns, and offering personalized support, businesses can demonstrate their commitment to customer satisfaction and build stronger relationships with their audience. For example, a halal food brand might use social media to share recipes, offer cooking tips, and engage with customers who have questions about the halal certification process. By fostering a sense of community and offering valuable content, the brand can strengthen its relationship with customers and build loyalty.

Customer feedback is another valuable tool for building resilience. By actively seeking feedback from customers and using it to improve products and services, businesses can ensure that they are meeting the needs of their audience and staying competitive in the market. For example, a halal financial institution might conduct regular customer surveys to gather feedback on its services and identify areas for improvement. By listening to its customers and acting on their feedback, the institution can enhance its offerings and build a more resilient business.

In addition to engaging with customers, businesses must also focus on building strong relationships with their employees. A resilient business is one that has a motivated, engaged workforce that is committed to the success of the organization. The Prophet Muhammad (PBUH) said, "The believer is not one who eats his fill while his neighbor is hungry" (Bukhari). For business leaders, this hadith serves as a reminder of the importance of taking care of employees and ensuring that they have the support they need to thrive.

One practical way to build a resilient workforce is by offering opportunities for professional development and career growth. For example, a halal company might provide training programs on halal compliance, ethical business practices, or leadership development. By investing in the growth and development of their employees, leaders can build a strong, knowledgeable team that is committed to the values of the organization and capable of navigating challenges.

In halal business, resilience also means being prepared for unexpected challenges, whether they come in the form of economic downturns, supply chain disruptions, or changes in consumer behavior. The Quran teaches, "And whoever fears Allah—He will make for him a way out. And will provide for him from where he does not expect" (Quran 65:2-3). For business leaders, this means planning for the future and being prepared to adapt to changing circumstances while trusting in Allah's guidance.

One way to prepare for challenges is by developing a contingency plan that outlines how the business will respond to various scenarios, such as a drop in sales, a disruption in the supply chain, or changes in regulatory requirements. By identifying potential risks and creating strategies to mitigate them, businesses can ensure that they are well-prepared to navigate challenges and continue to operate smoothly, even in times of uncertainty.

For example, a halal fashion brand might create a contingency plan that includes alternative suppliers in case its primary supplier is unable to deliver materials on time. By having backup options in place, the business can minimize disruptions and ensure that it continues to meet the needs of its customers. Similarly, a halal financial institution might develop a plan for managing liquidity in the event of an economic downturn, ensuring that it has the resources needed to continue operating and serving its clients.

In addition to contingency planning, resilience also involves maintaining a positive mindset and focusing on opportunities for growth. The Quran teaches, "With every hardship comes ease" (Quran 94:6), reminding us that challenges are often accompanied by opportunities. For halal businesses, this means viewing challenges as opportunities for growth, innovation, and improvement. Whether it's developing new products, exploring new markets, or improving operational efficiency, businesses that remain positive and proactive in the face of challenges are more likely to succeed in the long term.

Resilience in halal business also involves a focus on continuous improvement. The Quran states, "Indeed, Allah does not change the condition of a people until they change what is in themselves" (Quran 13:11). For business leaders, this is a call to constantly seek ways to improve their operations, products, and services. A business that remains stagnant is at risk of being overtaken by competitors or losing relevance in a fast-paced market. Continuous improvement, driven by a commitment to excellence, allows a business to not only survive but thrive.

One of the key areas where halal businesses can focus on continuous improvement is in quality control. Consistency in the quality of products and services is essential for maintaining customer trust and loyalty. For example, a halal food business must ensure that its products consistently meet the highest standards of taste, safety, and halal compliance. This may involve implementing rigorous quality control processes throughout the production and distribution stages, conducting regular audits, and working closely with halal certification bodies to ensure that all products meet halal standards.

In addition to improving product quality, businesses can also enhance their operational efficiency by streamlining processes and reducing waste. This might involve adopting new technologies that improve productivity, such as automation in manufacturing or digital inventory management systems that reduce the risk of stock shortages or overproduction. For example, a halal cosmetics company might implement a digital system to track ingredient sourcing, production timelines, and quality control, ensuring that all products meet both halal and ethical standards. By improving operational efficiency, businesses can reduce costs while maintaining high standards of quality and ethical governance.

Continuous improvement also extends to customer service. Businesses that invest in improving their customer service processes are more likely to build lasting relationships with their customers. For example, a halal fashion brand might implement a customer feedback system that allows shoppers to share their experiences and suggest improvements. By acting on this feedback, the brand can improve its offerings and enhance customer satisfaction, fostering loyalty and repeat business.

In addition to focusing on internal improvements, halal businesses must also remain attuned to changes in the external market environment. The Quran advises, "And take provision, but indeed, the best provision is fear of Allah. And fear Me, O you of understanding" (Quran 2:197). This verse serves as a reminder to be prepared and to anticipate future challenges and opportunities. For business leaders, this means staying informed about industry trends, consumer preferences, and regulatory changes that may impact their business.

One way businesses can stay ahead of market trends is by conducting regular market research and analysis. For example, a halal food company might conduct consumer surveys to understand changing dietary preferences, such as the growing demand for plant-based or gluten-free halal options. By staying informed about these trends, the business can adapt its product offerings to meet the evolving needs of its customers. Similarly, a halal financial institution might stay abreast of changes in regulatory requirements related to Islamic finance, ensuring that its products remain compliant with Shariah law and relevant local regulations.

Another important aspect of market awareness is staying informed about technological advancements that can enhance business operations. As technology continues to evolve, businesses that embrace digital transformation are better positioned to succeed in the long term. For example, a halal travel agency might invest in a digital booking platform that makes it easier for customers to find halal-friendly accommodations and travel packages. By incorporating technology into its operations, the agency can improve customer convenience, reduce costs, and streamline its processes.

However, it is important to ensure that technological advancements do not compromise the ethical integrity of the business. The Quran warns, "Do not consume one another's wealth unjustly or send it [in bribery] to the rulers in order that [they might aid] you [to] consume a portion of the wealth of the people in sin, while you know [it is unlawful]" (Quran 2:188). For halal businesses, this means ensuring that all technological innovations align with Islamic principles and do not involve any form of exploitation or deception.

Another essential aspect of building resilience in halal business is fostering a strong organizational culture that aligns with Islamic values. The Prophet Muhammad (PBUH) said, "The believers are like a single body; if one part of the body feels pain, the whole body suffers" (Bukhari). For business leaders, this hadith serves as a reminder that their organization is a community, and every member plays an important role in its success. A resilient business is one that fosters a sense of unity, collaboration, and mutual support among its employees.

One way to build a strong organizational culture is by promoting a shared sense of purpose. When employees feel that their work contributes to a larger mission that aligns with their values, they are more likely to be motivated, engaged, and committed to the success of the business. For halal businesses, this sense of purpose is rooted in the principles of halal compliance, ethical governance, and social responsibility. By communicating these values to employees and providing opportunities for them to contribute to the company's mission, leaders can create a cohesive and resilient team.

For example, a halal business might involve employees in its social responsibility initiatives, such as charitable giving or environmental sustainability efforts. By allowing employees to actively participate in these initiatives, the business fosters a sense of pride and ownership in its mission, strengthening the bonds between employees and the organization.

In addition to promoting a shared sense of purpose, leaders must also focus on creating an inclusive and supportive work environment. The Prophet Muhammad (PBUH) said, "Your employees are your brothers, whom Allah has placed under your authority. So whoever has his brother under his command should feed him of what he eats and dress him of what he wears" (Bukhari). For business leaders, this means treating employees with kindness, fairness, and respect, ensuring that they are provided with the resources and support they need to succeed.

One practical way to create a supportive work environment is by offering professional development opportunities that allow employees to grow both personally and professionally. For example, a halal financial institution might provide its employees with training on Shariah-compliant finance, leadership development, or ethical business practices. By investing in the development of its workforce, the business not only enhances the skills and knowledge of its employees but also strengthens the organization's overall resilience.

Building resilience in halal business also involves fostering strong relationships with external stakeholders, including suppliers, partners, and the broader community. The Quran advises, "O you who have believed, fulfill [all] contracts" (Quran 5:1). For business leaders, this means ensuring that all relationships with external stakeholders are built on trust, transparency, and mutual benefit.

One way to foster strong relationships with suppliers and partners is by maintaining open lines of communication and working closely to ensure that all materials and services meet halal standards. For example, a halal food company might regularly audit its suppliers to ensure that all ingredients are sourced in compliance with halal certification requirements. By maintaining strong relationships with suppliers, businesses can ensure that their products are of the highest quality and that their supply chain remains reliable and resilient.

In addition to maintaining strong supplier relationships, halal businesses must also focus on building positive relationships with the communities they serve. The Prophet Muhammad (PBUH) said, "None of you truly believes until he loves for his brother what he loves for himself" (Bukhari). For halal businesses, this means ensuring that their operations contribute positively to the well-being of the community and that they are actively involved in addressing social challenges.

One way businesses can contribute to the community is by supporting local initiatives that align with their values. For example, a halal fashion brand might partner with local charities to donate clothing to those in need or to provide job training programs for disadvantaged individuals. By aligning their community involvement with their business values, halal businesses can build a strong reputation for social responsibility and foster positive relationships with the communities they serve.

Furthermore, halal businesses should actively engage with their customers and seek opportunities to collaborate with them in meaningful ways. By creating a platform where customers feel valued and heard, businesses can build lasting relationships that foster loyalty and trust. For example, a halal cosmetics company might involve its customers in the product development process by seeking their feedback on new product formulations or offering them the opportunity to vote on future product launches. By engaging customers in this way, the company not only strengthens its relationship with its audience but also ensures that its products align with customer preferences and expectations.

Resilience in halal business is ultimately about creating a lasting legacy that reflects the values of Islam and contributes to the greater good of society. The Quran teaches, "And whatever good you put forward for yourselves—you will find it with Allah" (Quran 73:20). For halal business leaders, this means ensuring that their business practices, products, and services leave a positive, lasting impact on the world, benefiting both the present and future generations.

One practical way for businesses to create a lasting legacy is by incorporating sustainability into every aspect of their operations. Sustainability is not just about environmental responsibility—it's about ensuring that the business continues to provide value to society for years to come. For example, a halal financial institution might develop long-term strategies for sustainable growth, such as offering Islamic savings plans that help customers build wealth over time in a Shariah-compliant manner. By offering products and services that promote financial well-being, the institution not only meets the needs of its customers but also contributes to the long-term prosperity of the community.

In addition to financial sustainability, businesses must also focus on creating products that are both ethical and beneficial. The Prophet Muhammad (PBUH) said, "The best among you are those who bring the most benefit to people" (Daraqutni). For halal businesses, this means ensuring that their products and services are genuinely beneficial to their customers, promoting health, well-being, and ethical consumption.

For example, a halal skincare brand might develop products that are free from harmful chemicals and made with natural, ethically sourced ingredients. By offering products that are both safe and effective, the brand can build trust with its customers and create a lasting positive impact on their health and well-being.

Resilience and sustainability in halal business go beyond immediate success; they are about ensuring that the business thrives for future generations. The Quran teaches, "And whatever you spend of good – it will be fully repaid to you, and you will not be wronged" (Quran 2:272). This verse highlights that the rewards of ethical and sustainable practices are long-lasting, even if they are not immediately apparent. For halal businesses, this means adopting strategies that prioritize long-term benefits over short-term gains, ensuring that the business remains viable, ethical, and impactful in the years to come.

One key aspect of building a sustainable business is succession planning. The Prophet Muhammad (PBUH) emphasized the importance of preparing for the future, saying, "Tie your camel, and trust in Allah" (Tirmidhi). This hadith serves as a reminder that while faith in Allah is essential, businesses must also take practical steps to ensure their long-term survival. For business leaders, this means identifying and grooming future leaders who can continue the business's mission and uphold its values.

Succession planning involves identifying individuals within the organization who have the potential to take on leadership roles in the future. These individuals should be mentored, trained, and given opportunities to develop the skills and knowledge needed to lead the business. By preparing future leaders in this way, businesses can ensure that their values, vision, and ethical principles are preserved even after the current leadership steps down.

For example, a halal business might implement a leadership development program that provides employees with training in areas such as halal compliance, ethical governance, and strategic decision-making. By investing in the growth and development of future leaders, the business can create a pipeline of talent that is ready to take on leadership roles when needed. This not only strengthens the resilience of the business but also ensures that its mission and values continue to be upheld for generations to come.

In addition to succession planning, businesses must also focus on building a resilient organizational structure. The Quran advises, "And consult them in the matter. And when you have decided, then rely upon Allah" (Quran 3:159), emphasizing the importance of consultation and collaborative decision-making. For halal businesses, this means creating an organizational structure that promotes open communication, collaboration, and shared responsibility. A resilient organization is one where employees at all levels are empowered to contribute to the decision-making process, ensuring that the business is adaptable and responsive to challenges.

One way to build a resilient organizational structure is by decentralizing decision-making authority. This involves empowering managers and team leaders to make decisions within their areas of responsibility, rather than relying solely on top-down directives. By distributing decision-making authority, businesses can respond more quickly to challenges and opportunities, as decisions can be made at the level where the relevant information and expertise are most readily available.

For example, a halal food company might give its regional managers the authority to make decisions about local sourcing and distribution, ensuring that the business remains responsive to the needs of each market. By decentralizing decision-making in this way, the business can operate more efficiently and adapt more quickly to changing conditions.

Another important aspect of a resilient organizational structure is promoting a culture of continuous learning. The Prophet Muhammad (PBUH) said, "The seeking of knowledge is obligatory for every Muslim" (Ibn Majah). For halal businesses, this means creating an environment where employees are encouraged to seek knowledge, develop new skills, and stay informed about industry trends and best practices.

Continuous learning can be fostered through training programs, workshops, and mentorship opportunities. For example, a halal financial institution might offer its employees ongoing training in areas such as Islamic finance principles, ethical investing, and customer service excellence. By promoting a culture of learning and development, businesses can ensure that their workforce remains skilled, knowledgeable, and capable of navigating the challenges of a rapidly changing market.

Resilience in halal business is also about creating value that extends beyond the immediate needs of the business. The Quran teaches, "And do good; indeed, Allah loves the doers of good" (Quran 2:195). For business leaders, this means ensuring that their business creates value not only for shareholders but also for employees, customers, suppliers, and the broader community. By adopting a stakeholder-focused approach, businesses can build stronger relationships, enhance their reputation, and create a lasting positive impact on society.

One way businesses can create value for their stakeholders is by adopting fair and transparent pricing practices. The Quran advises, "And give full measure when you measure, and weigh with an even balance. That is the best [way] and best in result" (Quran 17:35). For halal businesses, this means ensuring that prices are set fairly, reflecting the true value of the products or services being offered while maintaining transparency in how prices are determined. Fair pricing not only builds trust with customers but also ensures that the business remains competitive in the marketplace.

In addition to fair pricing, businesses can create value by focusing on customer education. Many consumers are becoming more interested in understanding the ethical and environmental impact of the products they purchase. By providing customers with clear, accurate information about the halal certification process, ethical sourcing practices, and the sustainability of the products, businesses can empower their customers to make informed decisions that align with their values.

For example, a halal cosmetics brand might create an educational campaign that explains how its products are made, where the ingredients are sourced, and how the production process aligns with halal principles. By being transparent and providing valuable information, the brand not only builds trust with its customers but also enhances its reputation as a responsible and ethical business.

Creating value in halal business also involves contributing to the well-being of the broader community. The Prophet Muhammad (PBUH) said, "The best among you are those who bring the most benefit to the people" (Daraqutni). For halal businesses, this means ensuring that their operations have a positive impact on society, both through their products and services and through their broader social responsibility initiatives.

One way businesses can contribute to the community is by supporting local economic development. This might involve sourcing materials from local suppliers, providing employment opportunities to members of the community, or partnering with local organizations to support charitable initiatives. By supporting local communities in this way, businesses not only strengthen their own resilience but also contribute to the economic and social well-being of the areas in which they operate.

For example, a halal fashion brand might partner with local artisans to create unique, handmade products that reflect the cultural heritage of the community. By promoting these products, the brand not only provides customers with high-quality, ethically produced items but also supports the livelihoods of local artisans and contributes to the preservation of traditional crafts.

In addition to supporting local communities, halal businesses can also create value by promoting environmental sustainability. The Quran teaches, "And do not commit abuse on the earth, spreading corruption" (Quran 2:60). For businesses, this means ensuring that their operations minimize harm to the environment and contribute to the preservation of natural resources. By adopting eco-friendly practices, businesses can reduce their environmental footprint while also meeting the growing demand for sustainable products.

For instance, a halal food company might commit to using recyclable packaging, reducing food waste, and sourcing ingredients from sustainable farms. By aligning its operations with the principles of environmental sustainability, the company can create value for both its customers and the planet, ensuring that its business practices are in harmony with Islamic values.

Resilience in halal business also involves building strong relationships with regulators and industry bodies. The Quran teaches, "O you who have believed, obey Allah and obey the Messenger and those in authority among you" (Quran 4:59). For halal businesses, this means ensuring that they comply with all relevant regulations, both locally and internationally, while also working closely with halal certification bodies to ensure that their products and services meet the highest standards of halal compliance.

Maintaining strong relationships with regulators and industry bodies is essential for ensuring that the business operates within the legal framework and that its products are recognized as halal by customers around the world. This might involve working with halal certification bodies to obtain and maintain certification, staying informed about changes in regulatory requirements, and participating in industry discussions about best practices for halal compliance.

For example, a halal food company might collaborate with halal certification bodies to ensure that its products are certified in multiple countries, allowing the company to expand its market reach while maintaining the trust of its customers. By working closely with regulators and certification bodies, businesses can ensure that their products meet the highest standards of quality and compliance, building a resilient reputation in the global halal market.

In building resilience, halal businesses must also focus on creating a brand that resonates with customers on a deeper level. The Quran advises, "And speak to people good words" (Quran 2:83). For businesses, this means crafting a brand message that reflects their values and speaks to the ethical and spiritual concerns of their customers. A brand that aligns with the values of its target audience is more likely to foster loyalty and trust, creating a resilient customer base that supports the business even in challenging times.

Building a resilient brand involves communicating the business's commitment to halal compliance, ethical governance, and social responsibility. For example, a halal beauty brand might emphasize its use of cruelty-free, ethically sourced ingredients and its dedication to promoting ethical beauty standards that respect both Islamic values and modern ethical concerns. By aligning the brand with values that resonate with consumers, the business can create a loyal customer base that shares its vision and supports its mission.

Brand resilience also involves consistency in communication and customer experience. Customers expect that their interactions with a brand will reflect its core values at every touchpoint, from marketing materials to customer service. Businesses that consistently deliver on their brand promise are more likely to build lasting relationships with their customers, fostering loyalty and trust that contribute to long-term resilience.

A resilient and sustainable halal business is one that maintains a strong, enduring connection with its customers. The Quran reminds us, "And those who have believed and done righteous deeds – We will surely assign to them of Paradise [elevated] chambers beneath which rivers flow, wherein they abide eternally. Excellent is the reward of the [righteous] workers" (Quran 29:58). In a business context, this verse can be interpreted as the value of consistently doing good, providing benefit, and building relationships that last. For halal businesses, this means maintaining customer trust by adhering to the highest standards of ethical governance, halal compliance, and social responsibility.

To build resilience through customer relationships, businesses must go beyond simply selling products and services. They must create experiences that resonate with their customers on an emotional level, fostering loyalty and encouraging repeat business. One way to achieve this is by developing a customer loyalty program that rewards customers for their continued support. For example, a halal restaurant might offer a points-based system where customers earn rewards for every purchase, which they can redeem for free meals, discounts, or exclusive offers. By incentivizing repeat business, the restaurant builds a loyal customer base that feels valued and appreciated.

Customer engagement is another critical aspect of building resilience. Engaging with customers through social media, email newsletters, and other channels allows businesses to maintain an ongoing dialogue with their audience, gathering valuable feedback and keeping them informed about new products, promotions, and updates. For instance, a halal fashion brand might regularly engage with its customers on Instagram, sharing behind-the-scenes content, style tips, and stories that highlight the brand's commitment to ethical fashion. By creating a community of engaged customers, the brand not only strengthens its relationship with its audience but also increases its visibility and reach.

Customer engagement also provides an opportunity to educate consumers about the values and principles that guide the business. Many consumers today are increasingly conscious of the ethical and environmental impact of their purchases, and they seek out brands that align with their values. For halal businesses, this presents an opportunity to differentiate themselves by highlighting their commitment to halal compliance, sustainability, and social responsibility. By educating customers about the halal certification process, the ethical sourcing of ingredients, or the brand's contributions to charitable causes, businesses can build deeper connections with their audience and foster long-term loyalty.

Creating a resilient halal business also involves understanding and adapting to the evolving needs of customers. The Quran teaches, "And cooperate in righteousness and piety, but do not cooperate in sin and aggression. And fear Allah; indeed, Allah is severe in penalty" (Quran 5:2). This verse highlights the importance of working together in ways that promote goodness and ethical behavior. For businesses, this means staying attuned to customer preferences, responding to their concerns, and continuously improving the customer experience in ways that reflect Islamic values.

One way to ensure that the business remains responsive to customer needs is by leveraging customer feedback to drive innovation. Feedback can be gathered through customer surveys, reviews, and direct interactions with the customer service team. For example, a halal skincare brand might introduce new products based on customer feedback about specific skin concerns, such as sensitive skin or the need for natural, halal-certified ingredients. By acting on customer input, the brand demonstrates that it values its customers' opinions and is committed to meeting their needs.

In addition to gathering feedback, businesses must also anticipate trends in consumer behavior and be prepared to adapt their products and services accordingly. For instance, the increasing demand for halal-certified vegan products is a trend that many halal food and beauty brands have capitalized on by developing plant-based alternatives that meet the dietary and ethical preferences of their customers. By staying ahead of these trends, businesses can position themselves as innovative leaders in their industry while maintaining their commitment to halal principles.

Resilience in business also means being prepared to adapt to changes in the regulatory environment. Halal businesses that operate internationally must stay informed about the halal certification requirements in different regions and ensure that their products are compliant with local laws and regulations. For example, a halal food company looking to expand into new markets might work closely with halal certification bodies to ensure that its products meet the certification standards of the countries in which it plans to operate. By proactively addressing regulatory requirements, the company can avoid potential legal issues and ensure that its products are recognized as halal by customers around the world.

As halal businesses continue to grow and evolve, it is essential that they remain focused on their core values of ethical governance, halal compliance, and social responsibility. The Quran advises, "And do not consume one another's wealth unjustly or send it [in bribery] to the rulers in order that [they might aid] you [to] consume a portion of the wealth of the people in sin, while you know [it is unlawful]" (Quran 2:188). For halal business leaders, this verse serves as a reminder that financial success must never come at the expense of ethical integrity. A resilient business is one that remains committed to fairness, transparency, and justice, even in the face of challenges.

One way businesses can maintain their ethical integrity is by ensuring that their supply chains are free from exploitation and that all materials are sourced in a way that aligns with halal principles. For example, a halal cosmetics company might work with suppliers who use ethical labor practices and avoid sourcing ingredients from areas where workers are underpaid or subjected to unsafe working conditions. By maintaining a transparent and ethical supply chain, the company not only upholds its halal certification but also builds trust with its customers, who value businesses that prioritize social justice.

In addition to maintaining an ethical supply chain, halal businesses must also focus on promoting environmental sustainability. The Quran teaches, "And do not commit abuse on the earth, spreading corruption" (Quran 2:60). For businesses, this means ensuring that their operations minimize harm to the environment and actively contribute to the preservation of natural resources. By adopting eco-friendly practices, businesses can reduce their environmental impact while also meeting the growing demand for sustainable products.

For example, a halal food company might commit to using recyclable packaging, sourcing ingredients from organic farms, and reducing food waste by donating surplus products to local charities. By aligning its operations with the principles of environmental sustainability, the company not only reduces its carbon footprint but also strengthens its reputation as a responsible and ethical business.

As halal businesses continue to grow and expand, their leaders must remain focused on the long-term sustainability of the business, ensuring that its operations, products, and services continue to reflect the values of Islam. By maintaining a commitment to ethical governance, halal compliance, and social responsibility, halal businesses can build a legacy of resilience, trust, and positive impact that will endure for generations to come.

CHAPTER 9: ETHICAL MARKETING AND PROMOTION IN HALAL BUSINESS

Marketing and promotion form the cornerstone of any successful business strategy, but in halal business, they carry a unique ethical dimension. The Quran reminds us, "And speak to people good [words]" (Quran 2:83). For halal businesses, this verse serves as a guiding principle that communication, including marketing, must always be truthful, respectful, and in alignment with Islamic values. In a marketplace filled with aggressive advertising and deceptive claims, halal businesses must distinguish themselves by promoting their products and services in a way that upholds the principles of honesty, transparency, and fairness.

Ethical marketing in halal business is not just about compliance with legal standards; it is about ensuring that every aspect of the marketing process reflects the values of Islam. Whether it's the messaging used in advertising campaigns, the channels through which the products are promoted, or the way in which the business interacts with its customers, halal marketing must embody integrity. The Prophet Muhammad (PBUH) said, "The honest and trustworthy merchant will be with the prophets, the truthful, and the martyrs" (Tirmidhi). For Muslim entrepreneurs, this hadith serves as a reminder that the rewards of honesty in business extend beyond financial success and into the realm of spiritual fulfillment.

To create effective yet ethical marketing strategies, halal businesses must first focus on understanding their target audience. Marketing must not only meet the needs and expectations of the customers but also respect their beliefs and values. For example, a halal fashion brand targeting Muslim women might focus on promoting modesty, comfort, and empowerment through its advertising campaigns. By aligning its messaging with the values of modest fashion, the brand builds a strong connection with its audience while promoting its products in a way that is both ethical and culturally relevant.

Another key aspect of ethical marketing in halal business is ensuring that all claims made about the products or services are truthful and transparent. The Quran advises, "And do not mix the truth with falsehood or conceal the truth while you know [it]" (Quran 2:42). For businesses, this means avoiding exaggerated or misleading claims, particularly in areas related to health, safety, or halal certification. For example, a halal food company must ensure that any claims about the nutritional benefits or halal status of its products are backed by verifiable evidence and certification. By maintaining transparency in its marketing, the business builds trust with its customers and fosters long-term loyalty.

In addition to truthful messaging, ethical marketing in halal business also involves using channels that align with Islamic principles. The Prophet Muhammad (PBUH) said, "Whoever calls people to righteousness, there will be a reward for him like the rewards of those who follow him, without their rewards being diminished at all" (Muslim). For businesses, this hadith serves as a reminder that the way in which a message is delivered matters as much as the content itself. Marketing strategies must avoid using unethical channels or methods that promote haram activities, such as gambling or immodest behavior.

For example, a halal cosmetics brand might choose to advertise its products through social media platforms that are popular with its target audience, but it must be mindful of the types of influencers or celebrities it partners with for promotions. If an influencer promotes behaviors or values that contradict Islamic teachings, the association could damage the brand's reputation. Instead, the brand should seek out partnerships with influencers who share its commitment to ethical living and halal principles, ensuring that the promotion aligns with both Islamic values and the expectations of its audience.

Moreover, ethical marketing in halal business involves creating campaigns that promote not only the benefits of the products but also the ethical and spiritual values behind them. For instance, a halal skincare brand might emphasize its commitment to cruelty-free practices, ethical sourcing, and natural ingredients in its marketing materials. By highlighting these ethical considerations, the brand not only appeals to consumers who prioritize sustainability and ethical consumption but also reinforces its alignment with Islamic principles of kindness and respect for all of Allah's creations.

One of the most effective ways to promote ethical values through marketing is by telling stories that resonate with the audience. The Quran teaches through stories, reminding us of the importance of narratives in conveying deeper moral and spiritual lessons. For halal businesses, storytelling can be a powerful tool for building emotional connections with customers and communicating the brand's values in a way that is authentic and impactful. For example, a halal food brand might share the story of how its products are sourced, from farm to table, emphasizing the care and ethical practices involved at every step. By using storytelling to promote the ethical foundation of the business, the brand can create a compelling narrative that inspires trust and loyalty.

Another important aspect of ethical marketing in halal business is the concept of *barakah*—the divine blessing that comes from conducting business in accordance with Islamic principles. The Prophet Muhammad (PBUH) said, "Wealth does not decrease by giving in charity" (Muslim). This hadith emphasizes the spiritual reward of generosity and ethical conduct in business. For halal businesses, this means that marketing efforts should not solely focus on maximizing profits but should also consider how the business can contribute to the well-being of society and promote positive values.

One practical way to incorporate the concept of *barakah* into marketing strategies is by promoting charitable initiatives or corporate social responsibility (CSR) programs. For example, a halal business might dedicate a portion of its profits to supporting charitable causes, such as providing food to underprivileged communities during Ramadan or sponsoring educational programs for disadvantaged youth. By promoting these initiatives in its marketing campaigns, the business not only demonstrates its commitment to social responsibility but also aligns itself with the Islamic principle of giving back to the community. This can create a sense of shared purpose between the brand and its customers, fostering a deeper emotional connection and encouraging customer loyalty.

In addition to promoting charitable initiatives, halal businesses can also use their marketing platforms to raise awareness about important social and environmental issues. The Quran advises, "And do good; indeed, Allah loves the doers of good" (Quran 2:195). For businesses, this means using their influence and resources to promote positive change in the world. For example, a halal fashion brand might use its marketing campaigns to raise awareness about the environmental impact of fast fashion and encourage consumers to make more sustainable, ethical choices. By aligning its marketing with broader ethical causes, the brand not only enhances its reputation but also contributes to the greater good.

Furthermore, ethical marketing in halal business involves being mindful of cultural sensitivities and respecting the diverse backgrounds of the target audience. The Quran teaches, "O mankind, indeed We have created you from male and female and made you peoples and tribes that you may know one another" (Quran 49:13). This verse encourages mutual understanding and respect among different cultures and communities. For halal businesses operating in diverse markets, this means ensuring that marketing campaigns are culturally appropriate and respectful of the values and beliefs of different communities.

For example, a halal food company that exports its products to multiple countries might create localized marketing campaigns that reflect the cultural norms and preferences of each region. By tailoring its messaging to the specific needs of each market while maintaining its commitment to halal principles, the business can build stronger connections with its audience and expand its reach globally.

Ethical marketing in halal business also extends to the way businesses handle customer feedback and complaints. The Prophet Muhammad (PBUH) said, "The best of people are those who are most beneficial to others" (Daraqutni). For businesses, this hadith serves as a reminder that their primary goal should be to provide value and benefit to their customers. In the context of marketing, this means that businesses must be responsive to customer concerns and complaints, addressing them in a way that is fair, respectful, and aligned with Islamic values.

One practical way to demonstrate responsiveness and ethical customer service is by creating clear, accessible channels for customers to provide feedback. Whether through social media, email, or customer service hotlines, businesses should make it easy for customers to share their experiences and voice any concerns they may have. For example, a halal restaurant might encourage customers to leave reviews on its website or social media pages, providing an opportunity for the business to respond to feedback and address any issues that arise. By actively engaging with customers and showing a genuine commitment to improving the customer experience, the restaurant builds trust and fosters long-term loyalty.

In addition to responding to feedback, businesses should also take proactive steps to ensure that their marketing materials are inclusive and accessible to all members of their target audience. This includes making sure that marketing content is available in multiple languages, where necessary, and that it is accessible to individuals with disabilities. For example, a halal skincare brand might include subtitles or sign language interpretation in its video marketing campaigns, ensuring that the content is accessible to a broader audience. By prioritizing inclusivity in their marketing efforts, businesses demonstrate their commitment to serving the needs of all their customers, regardless of their background or abilities.

Furthermore, ethical marketing in halal business involves ensuring that advertising does not exploit vulnerable individuals or groups. The Quran teaches, "And cooperate in righteousness and piety, but do not cooperate in sin and aggression" (Quran 5:2). For businesses, this means being mindful of the impact of their advertising on children, the elderly, and other vulnerable populations. For example, a halal confectionery company might be careful to avoid using marketing tactics that target young children in a way that encourages excessive consumption of sugary snacks. Instead, the company might focus on promoting its products as occasional treats that can be enjoyed in moderation, aligning its messaging with Islamic principles of balance and moderation.

Another key consideration in ethical marketing is the use of data and customer information. In today's digital age, businesses have access to vast amounts of data about their customers, including their purchasing habits, preferences, and online behaviors. However, the Quran advises, "And do not spy or backbite each other. Would one of you like to eat the flesh of his brother when dead? You would detest it" (Quran 49:12). For halal businesses, this verse serves as a reminder that privacy and trust are sacred, and that customer data must be handled with the utmost care and respect.

Ethical marketing involves being transparent about how customer data is collected, stored, and used. Businesses must ensure that they have the explicit consent of their customers before collecting any personal information and that this information is used only for legitimate business purposes. For example, a halal e-commerce company might use customer data to personalize product recommendations, but it must ensure that customers are aware of how their data is being used and have the option to opt out if they choose. By maintaining transparency and respecting customer privacy, the business builds trust and fosters a positive relationship with its audience.

In addition to transparency, businesses must also ensure that they are using customer data in a way that aligns with Islamic principles of fairness and justice. For example, a halal financial institution might use customer data to offer personalized financial advice or products, but it must ensure that these offerings are genuinely beneficial to the customer and not designed to exploit their financial situation. By using data ethically and with the customer's best interests in mind, the business not only upholds Islamic values but also strengthens its reputation as a trustworthy and responsible organization.

Finally, ethical marketing in halal business requires a long-term perspective. The Quran teaches, "And whatever good you put forward for yourselves—you will find it with Allah. It is better and greater in reward" (Quran 73:20). For businesses, this means recognizing that the true measure of success is not just short-term profits but the long-term relationships they build with their customers, employees, and the community. Ethical marketing is about creating value that lasts, both for the business and for society as a whole.

Ethical marketing in halal business is not just a strategy; it is a reflection of the business's core values and principles. The Quran advises, "O you who have believed, fear Allah and speak words of appropriate justice" (Quran 33:70). For halal businesses, this means ensuring that every aspect of their marketing, from the language used in advertisements to the way products are presented, reflects a commitment to honesty, fairness, and respect for others.

In an increasingly competitive marketplace, where aggressive marketing tactics and exaggerated claims are commonplace, halal businesses have the opportunity to stand out by promoting their products with integrity and sincerity.

In addition to maintaining honesty in marketing, halal businesses must also focus on promoting products and services that genuinely add value to the lives of their customers. The Prophet Muhammad (PBUH) said, "None of you truly believes until he loves for his brother what he loves for himself" (Bukhari). This hadith serves as a reminder that ethical business practices, including marketing, are grounded in the principle of mutual benefit. For businesses, this means ensuring that the products they promote are beneficial, not harmful, and that they are marketed in a way that encourages responsible consumption.

For example, a halal pharmaceutical company might focus its marketing efforts on promoting products that support health and well-being, while also educating consumers about the importance of using medications responsibly. Rather than simply pushing for higher sales, the company emphasizes the ethical responsibility of using its products in a way that promotes health, aligns with halal principles, and avoids overconsumption. By taking this approach, the business not only builds trust with its customers but also fosters a sense of shared responsibility for promoting good health and ethical living.

Similarly, a halal food brand might focus its marketing on promoting healthy eating habits, offering products that are not only halal but also nutritious and beneficial to the body. By educating consumers about the health benefits of its products and providing tips for maintaining a balanced diet, the brand demonstrates its commitment to promoting both physical well-being and spiritual purity. This holistic approach to marketing aligns with the Islamic principle of maintaining balance in all aspects of life and helps the brand establish itself as a trusted provider of products that contribute to overall wellness.

In addition to promoting ethical consumption, halal businesses must also be mindful of the environmental impact of their marketing efforts. The Quran reminds us, "And do not commit abuse on the earth, spreading corruption" (Quran 2:60). For businesses, this means ensuring that their marketing practices do not contribute to environmental harm, and that they actively seek out ways to reduce their carbon footprint and promote sustainability.

One way businesses can align their marketing efforts with environmental sustainability is by adopting eco-friendly practices in the production and distribution of promotional materials. For example, a halal fashion brand might choose to use recycled paper and environmentally friendly inks for its print advertisements or opt for digital marketing campaigns that reduce the need for physical materials altogether. By minimizing waste and reducing the environmental impact of their marketing efforts, businesses not only contribute to the preservation of the planet but also appeal to consumers who value sustainability and ethical consumption.

In addition to reducing waste, businesses can also use their marketing platforms to raise awareness about environmental issues and encourage their customers to adopt more sustainable habits. For instance, a halal beauty brand might launch a campaign promoting the benefits of using natural, organic ingredients that are less harmful to the environment, while also educating consumers about how to properly dispose of cosmetic packaging to reduce plastic waste. By using their marketing platforms to promote environmental responsibility, businesses not only contribute to positive change but also enhance their reputation as leaders in ethical and sustainable practices.

Moreover, ethical marketing in halal business involves being transparent about the environmental impact of the products themselves. The Quran advises, "And establish weight in justice and do not make deficient the balance" (Quran 55:9), emphasizing the importance of fairness and accountability. For businesses, this means being upfront about the environmental impact of their products, from the sourcing of raw materials to the production and distribution processes. For example, a halal food company might provide information about the carbon footprint of its supply chain and the steps it is taking to reduce its environmental impact. By maintaining transparency in this way, businesses build trust with environmentally conscious consumers and demonstrate their commitment to ethical governance.

In addition to promoting environmental sustainability, ethical marketing in halal business also involves promoting social responsibility. The Prophet Muhammad (PBUH) said, "The best of people are those who bring the most benefit to others" (Daraqutni). For businesses, this means using their marketing platforms to promote not only their products but also their contributions to the well-being of society. Whether through charitable initiatives, community involvement, or ethical business practices, halal businesses have the opportunity to make a positive impact on the communities they serve.

One way businesses can promote social responsibility through marketing is by highlighting their corporate social responsibility (CSR) programs. For example, a halal restaurant chain might launch a marketing campaign that highlights its efforts to provide meals to underprivileged communities during Ramadan or its partnership with local food banks to reduce food waste. By promoting these initiatives, the business not only enhances its brand image but also encourages its customers to support causes that align with Islamic values of charity and social justice.

Another aspect of social responsibility in marketing is ensuring that advertising does not perpetuate harmful stereotypes or exploit vulnerable groups. The Quran teaches, "And do not defraud people of their things and do not commit abuse on the earth, spreading corruption" (Quran 26:183). For businesses, this means being mindful of the messages they convey through their marketing campaigns and ensuring that these messages are inclusive, respectful, and free from bias.

For example, a halal beauty brand might ensure that its marketing materials feature models of diverse ethnic backgrounds, body types, and ages, reflecting the diversity of its customer base and promoting a message of inclusivity and self-acceptance. By promoting diversity and inclusivity in its marketing efforts, the brand not only appeals to a broader audience but also reinforces its commitment to ethical business practices and social justice.

Moreover, halal businesses can use their marketing platforms to educate consumers about important social issues and encourage them to take positive action. For instance, a halal travel company might launch a campaign promoting ethical tourism, encouraging customers to choose travel experiences that support local economies, respect cultural traditions, and minimize environmental impact. By aligning its marketing with ethical causes, the business not only enhances its brand reputation but also contributes to positive change in the world.

Another important element of ethical marketing in halal business is the responsible use of digital marketing tools, particularly in the age of social media and data-driven advertising. The Quran teaches, "And do not spy or backbite each other. Would one of you like to eat the flesh of his brother when dead? You would detest it" (Quran 49:12). For businesses, this verse serves as a reminder that privacy is sacred, and customer data must be handled with the utmost respect and care.

In today's digital landscape, businesses have access to vast amounts of personal data about their customers, including their online behavior, purchasing habits, and preferences. However, ethical marketing requires that businesses use this data responsibly and in a way that respects the privacy and autonomy of their customers. For example, a halal e-commerce platform might use customer data to personalize product recommendations or offer tailored promotions, but it must ensure that customers are fully informed about how their data is being used and have the option to opt out if they wish.

In addition to maintaining transparency, businesses must also ensure that they are not using customer data in ways that exploit their vulnerabilities or manipulate their behavior. For example, a halal financial institution might use data to offer personalized financial products, but it must ensure that these products are genuinely beneficial to the customer and not designed to take advantage of their financial situation. By using data ethically and with the customer's best interests in mind, businesses can build trust and strengthen their relationships with their customers.

Moreover, halal businesses must be mindful of the content they share on social media and other digital platforms, ensuring that it aligns with Islamic values and does not promote unethical behavior. The Prophet Muhammad (PBUH) said, "Whoever believes in Allah and the Last Day should speak what is good or remain silent" (Bukhari). For businesses, this means ensuring that all digital marketing content is respectful, truthful, and free from offensive or inappropriate material. For example, a halal fashion brand might use its social media platforms to promote modest fashion, but it must ensure that the content is presented in a way that respects the values of modesty and decency.

In ethical marketing, halal businesses must also focus on building long-term relationships with their customers, rather than simply driving short-term sales. The Quran teaches, "Indeed, Allah loves those who are fair and just" (Quran 49:9). For businesses, this means ensuring that their marketing strategies are focused on creating value for their customers and building trust, rather than employing aggressive sales tactics that prioritize profit over customer satisfaction.

One way businesses can build long-term relationships with their customers is by focusing on customer education. Rather than simply promoting products, businesses can use their marketing platforms to provide valuable information that helps customers make informed decisions and understand the benefits of halal products. For example, a halal food company might create content that educates customers about the importance of halal certification, the health benefits of certain ingredients, or how to incorporate halal foods into a balanced diet. By providing valuable information, the business positions itself as a trusted source of knowledge and builds a loyal customer base.

In addition to customer education, businesses must also focus on delivering excellent customer service. The Prophet Muhammad (PBUH) said, "The most beloved of people to Allah are those who are most beneficial to people" (Daraqutni). For businesses, this means ensuring that their marketing efforts are supported by a commitment to providing exceptional service to their customers. Whether through responsive customer support, flexible return policies, or personalized assistance, businesses that prioritize customer satisfaction are more likely to build long-lasting relationships with their audience.

Finally, ethical marketing in halal business requires a commitment to transparency and accountability. The Quran advises, "O you who have believed, fulfill [all] contracts" (Quran 5:1). For businesses, this means ensuring that they deliver on the promises they make in their marketing campaigns and that they are accountable for the quality and ethical integrity of their products. By maintaining transparency in their marketing efforts and being accountable to their customers, businesses build trust and foster long-term loyalty.

Ethical marketing in halal business extends beyond customer relationships; it also involves how a business positions itself within the broader community and the world. The Quran advises, "Cooperate in righteousness and piety, but do not cooperate in sin and aggression. And fear Allah; indeed, Allah is severe in penalty" (Quran 5:2). For businesses, this means not only avoiding unethical practices but also actively seeking opportunities to contribute to the well-being of society. A truly ethical marketing strategy is one that reflects the business's role as a positive force in the community.

One way halal businesses can align their marketing with social responsibility is by promoting initiatives that give back to the community. For example, a halal cosmetics company might launch a campaign in support of women's empowerment, with a portion of its profits being donated to organizations that provide education and resources to women in underserved communities. By aligning the brand with a cause that resonates with its audience, the business not only enhances its ethical image but also fosters a deeper connection with its customers.

Another example is a halal food company that promotes food security by working with local charities to provide meals to those in need. By integrating social responsibility into its marketing strategy, the company demonstrates its commitment to ethical practices while also highlighting the positive impact it has on the community. This kind of marketing not only builds goodwill but also reinforces the brand's values, making it more appealing to consumers who prioritize ethical consumption.

In addition to promoting charitable initiatives, businesses can also use their marketing platforms to raise awareness about important social issues, encouraging their customers to take positive action. For example, a halal travel agency might launch a campaign promoting ethical tourism, encouraging travelers to choose destinations and activities that respect local cultures, support local economies, and minimize environmental impact. By using its marketing to promote ethical behavior, the business not only builds a strong brand identity but also contributes to the greater good.

Moreover, ethical marketing involves ensuring that businesses remain transparent about their own practices. The Prophet Muhammad (PBUH) said, "Whoever cheats us is not one of us" (Muslim). For halal businesses, this hadith serves as a reminder that transparency is essential for maintaining trust with customers and stakeholders. Businesses must ensure that their marketing materials accurately represent their products and that any claims made about the benefits, sourcing, or halal status of their offerings are truthful and verifiable.

Transparency in marketing also involves being honest about the challenges and limitations of the business. Customers appreciate businesses that are open about their processes, including any efforts they are making to improve sustainability, product quality, or ethical practices. For example, a halal fashion brand might be transparent about its supply chain challenges, explaining the steps it is taking to ensure that its materials are sourced ethically and sustainably. By being open about both its successes and its areas for improvement, the brand builds credibility and trust with its customers, who are more likely to support a business that demonstrates a commitment to continuous improvement.

In addition to transparency, businesses must also prioritize authenticity in their marketing efforts. The Prophet Muhammad (PBUH) said, "The truthful merchant is rewarded" (Tirmidhi). For halal businesses, this means ensuring that their marketing reflects the true values and mission of the company, rather than adopting messaging or tactics that simply chase trends or attempt to capitalize on consumer sentiment. Authentic marketing is about staying true to the core principles of the business and communicating them in a way that resonates with the audience.

For example, a halal skincare brand that promotes natural, ethically sourced ingredients must ensure that these values are genuinely reflected in its products and practices. If the brand claims to be environmentally friendly but fails to implement sustainable sourcing or packaging, customers will quickly lose trust. Authenticity requires that businesses consistently align their marketing messages with their actual practices, ensuring that there is no disconnect between what is promised and what is delivered.

Moreover, authenticity in marketing involves building relationships with customers that go beyond transactional interactions. Ethical businesses seek to create meaningful connections with their audience by sharing stories, values, and experiences that resonate on a deeper level. For example, a halal food company might share the stories of the farmers who supply its ingredients, highlighting their dedication to halal practices and ethical farming methods. By telling these stories, the company not only promotes its products but also creates a sense of community and shared values that strengthens the bond with its customers.

Building authentic relationships with customers also involves being responsive to their needs and feedback. The Quran teaches, "And consult them in the matter. And when you have decided, then rely upon Allah" (Quran 3:159). For businesses, this verse emphasizes the importance of consultation and collaboration, reminding them to actively seek input from their customers and stakeholders. Ethical marketing is not just about promoting products; it is about creating a dialogue with customers, listening to their concerns, and continuously improving the business based on their feedback.

One practical way to foster this kind of dialogue is through interactive marketing campaigns that encourage customer participation. For example, a halal fashion brand might invite its customers to share their own stories about what modest fashion means to them, using social media platforms to create a community conversation around the brand's values. By involving customers in the brand's storytelling, the business not only strengthens its connection with its audience but also creates marketing content that feels authentic and personal.

In addition to encouraging customer participation, businesses must also be proactive in responding to customer feedback, both positive and negative. The Prophet Muhammad (PBUH) said, "Make things easy for people and do not make them difficult" (Bukhari). For businesses, this means making it easy for customers to provide feedback and ensuring that any concerns are addressed in a timely and respectful manner. Whether through social media, email, or customer service hotlines, businesses must demonstrate their commitment to customer satisfaction by being responsive and attentive to their needs.

For example, a halal restaurant chain might use its social media platforms to address customer reviews, responding to both praise and criticism in a way that shows a genuine commitment to improving the customer experience. By engaging with customers in this way, the business not only builds trust but also fosters a sense of community, where customers feel valued and heard.

In addition to fostering strong relationships with customers, ethical marketing in halal business also involves building positive relationships with other stakeholders, including suppliers, partners, and the broader community. The Quran advises, "And fulfill [every] commitment. Indeed, the commitment is ever [that about which one will be] questioned" (Quran 17:34). For businesses, this means ensuring that all relationships are built on trust, transparency, and mutual benefit.

One way to build positive relationships with suppliers is by promoting ethical sourcing practices and ensuring that all materials used in the production of halal products are sourced in a way that aligns with Islamic principles. For example, a halal food company might work closely with its suppliers to ensure that all ingredients are sourced from farms that follow ethical farming practices, such as fair labor conditions and environmentally sustainable methods. By promoting transparency and ethical governance in its supply chain, the business builds trust with its suppliers and ensures that its products meet the highest standards of halal compliance.

In addition to building relationships with suppliers, halal businesses can also use their marketing platforms to foster partnerships with other ethical brands or organizations. For example, a halal beauty brand might partner with a charity that supports environmental conservation, using its marketing campaigns to promote both its products and the charitable cause. By aligning its brand with ethical partners, the business not only enhances its reputation but also creates opportunities for collaboration that benefit both parties.

Moreover, ethical marketing in halal business involves promoting collaboration and cooperation within the industry. The Prophet Muhammad (PBUH) said, "None of you will have faith until he loves for his brother what he loves for himself" (Bukhari). For businesses, this means promoting a spirit of cooperation, rather than competition, with other halal businesses. For example, a halal fashion brand might collaborate with other halal brands to create joint marketing campaigns that promote the broader concept of halal fashion, rather than focusing solely on individual products. By working together, businesses can create a stronger, more unified message that resonates with a wider audience.

Another important aspect of ethical marketing in halal business is ensuring that the messaging is culturally sensitive and inclusive. The Quran teaches, "O mankind, indeed We have created you from male and female and made you peoples and tribes that you may know one another" (Quran 49:13). For businesses, this means recognizing the diversity of their customer base and ensuring that their marketing campaigns reflect an understanding and respect for different cultures, traditions, and values.

One practical way to ensure cultural sensitivity is by creating localized marketing campaigns that are tailored to the specific needs and preferences of each market. For example, a halal food company that exports its products to different countries might create separate marketing campaigns for each region, using language, imagery, and messaging that resonate with the local culture. By taking the time to understand and respect the cultural context of each market, the business not only strengthens its connection with its customers but also avoids any potential misunderstandings or cultural insensitivity.

In addition to tailoring marketing campaigns for different regions, businesses must also ensure that their messaging is inclusive and representative of the diverse communities they serve. This might involve featuring models of different ethnic backgrounds, ages, and body types in advertising campaigns, ensuring that the brand reflects the diversity of its customer base. For example, a halal cosmetics brand might create a marketing campaign that celebrates the beauty of women from different cultures, promoting a message of inclusivity and empowerment. By promoting diversity in their marketing efforts, businesses not only appeal to a broader audience but also reinforce their commitment to ethical and inclusive practices.

Moreover, businesses must be mindful of the potential for cultural appropriation in their marketing efforts. The Prophet Muhammad (PBUH) said, "The best among you are those with the best manners and character" (Bukhari). For businesses, this means ensuring that their marketing materials are respectful of different cultures and do not exploit or misrepresent cultural symbols or traditions for commercial gain. By approaching cultural representation with sensitivity and respect, businesses can avoid offending their audience and instead create marketing campaigns that celebrate diversity in a positive and ethical way.

Ethical marketing in halal business is deeply rooted in the values of justice, honesty, and respect. The Quran teaches, "And do not mix the truth with falsehood or conceal the truth while you know [it]" (Quran 2:42). For businesses, this means ensuring that their marketing strategies are always truthful, transparent, and reflective of the actual qualities of their products and services. In a world where deceptive advertising is common, halal businesses have the opportunity to set a higher standard by promoting their products in a way that prioritizes truth and integrity.

One key aspect of maintaining transparency in marketing is ensuring that all claims about the products are accurate and verifiable. For example, if a halal food company advertises its products as being organic or sustainably sourced, it must be able to provide evidence to back up these claims. By maintaining transparency in this way, the business not only builds trust with its customers but also sets itself apart as a reliable and ethical brand.

Another important element of transparency is being upfront about the limitations or potential risks associated with the products. For instance, a halal pharmaceutical company might provide clear information about any possible side effects of its medications, ensuring that customers can make informed decisions about their health. By providing this level of transparency, the company demonstrates its commitment to honesty and customer well-being, fostering long-term loyalty and trust.

In addition to transparency, halal businesses must also focus on maintaining fairness in their marketing strategies. The Quran advises, "And give full measure when you measure, and weigh with an even balance. That is the best [way] and best in result" (Quran 17:35). For businesses, this means ensuring that their marketing practices are fair and do not take advantage of vulnerable individuals or groups. Ethical marketing requires that businesses avoid using manipulative tactics or exaggerated claims that could mislead customers.

For example, a halal beauty brand must avoid using imagery or messaging that promotes unrealistic beauty standards or exploits consumers' insecurities. Instead, the brand might focus on promoting natural beauty, self-confidence, and the ethical qualities of its products, such as being cruelty-free or made with halal-certified ingredients. By promoting a message of self-acceptance and ethical living, the brand not only attracts a loyal customer base but also contributes to a positive and uplifting narrative that aligns with Islamic values.

In addition to promoting fairness in messaging, halal businesses must also ensure that their pricing strategies are ethical and transparent. The Quran teaches, "And those who, when they buy a measure from the people, demand full measure, and when they give by measure or by weight to others, give less than due" (Quran 83:2-3). For businesses, this verse emphasizes the importance of fairness and equity in all transactions, including pricing.

One practical way for businesses to maintain fairness in pricing is by ensuring that prices accurately reflect the value of the products and services being offered. Halal businesses must avoid inflating prices for the sake of maximizing profits, particularly in situations where customers may have limited options or where demand is artificially high. For example, during times of crisis or scarcity, a halal food company might commit to keeping its prices stable, rather than raising them in response to increased demand. By maintaining fair pricing, the business demonstrates its commitment to ethical governance and social responsibility, fostering trust with its customers.

In addition to fairness in pricing, businesses must also ensure that their promotional offers and discounts are transparent and accessible to all customers. For instance, a halal e-commerce platform might offer seasonal discounts or loyalty rewards, but it must ensure that these promotions are clearly communicated and do not contain hidden terms or conditions that could mislead customers. By being transparent about the terms of any promotions, the business builds trust and ensures that its marketing practices remain aligned with Islamic principles of fairness and justice.

Moreover, ethical marketing in halal business involves ensuring that advertising does not create unnecessary consumerism or encourage wasteful behavior. The Quran teaches, "Indeed, the wasteful are brothers of the devils, and ever has Satan been to his Lord ungrateful" (Quran 17:27). For businesses, this means ensuring that their marketing strategies promote responsible consumption and discourage excessive or wasteful behavior.

For example, a halal fashion brand might promote its products in a way that encourages customers to make thoughtful, long-lasting purchases, rather than participating in fast fashion cycles that contribute to environmental waste. By promoting the idea of investing in high-quality, ethically made garments that can be worn for years, the brand fosters a more sustainable approach to fashion consumption while aligning with the Islamic principle of avoiding waste.

In addition to promoting responsible consumption, halal businesses must also focus on building long-term relationships with their customers based on mutual respect and trust. The Prophet Muhammad (PBUH) said, "The best of people are those who are most beneficial to others" (Daraqutni). For businesses, this hadith serves as a reminder that their primary goal should be to provide value and benefit to their customers, rather than simply focusing on short-term profits.

One way to build long-term relationships with customers is by focusing on customer education. Rather than simply promoting products, businesses can use their marketing platforms to provide valuable information that helps customers make informed decisions and understand the benefits of halal products. For example, a halal financial institution might create content that educates customers about the principles of Islamic finance, the importance of avoiding riba (interest), and how to manage their finances in a way that aligns with Islamic teachings. By providing valuable information, the business positions itself as a trusted source of knowledge and builds a loyal customer base.

In addition to customer education, businesses must also focus on delivering excellent customer service. The Quran advises, "And lower your wing to those who follow you of the believers" (Quran 26:215). For businesses, this means ensuring that their marketing efforts are supported by a commitment to providing exceptional service to their customers. Whether through responsive customer support, flexible return policies, or personalized assistance, businesses that prioritize customer satisfaction are more likely to build long-lasting relationships with their audience.

For example, a halal e-commerce platform might implement a customer service chatbot that provides real-time support to customers who have questions about their orders, halal certification, or product availability. By offering responsive and helpful customer service, the platform not only enhances the customer experience but also builds trust and loyalty, encouraging repeat business.

Another key aspect of ethical marketing in halal business is the responsible use of technology and data. In today's digital age, businesses have access to vast amounts of data about their customers, including their online behaviors, preferences, and purchasing habits. However, the Quran teaches, "And do not spy or backbite each other" (Quran 49:12), emphasizing the importance of respecting privacy and protecting personal information.

For halal businesses, this means ensuring that customer data is handled with the utmost care and that all data collection practices are transparent and ethical. Businesses must obtain explicit consent from customers before collecting their personal information, and they must ensure that this data is used only for legitimate business purposes. For example, a halal food delivery service might collect data on customers' dietary preferences in order to offer personalized meal recommendations, but it must ensure that customers are fully informed about how their data is being used and have the option to opt out if they wish.

In addition to maintaining transparency in data collection, businesses must also ensure that customer data is protected from unauthorized access or misuse. This might involve implementing strong data encryption measures, regularly updating security protocols, and providing customers with tools to manage their privacy settings. By taking these steps, businesses demonstrate their commitment to protecting customer privacy and build trust with their audience.

Moreover, ethical marketing in halal business requires that businesses avoid using data in ways that exploit customers' vulnerabilities or manipulate their behaviors. For example, a halal financial institution might use data to offer personalized financial advice, but it must ensure that these recommendations are genuinely beneficial to the customer and not designed to take advantage of their financial situation. By using data ethically and with the customer's best interests in mind, businesses build trust and strengthen their relationships with their customers.

In addition to ethical data usage, halal businesses must also focus on promoting inclusivity and accessibility in their marketing efforts. The Quran teaches, "O mankind, indeed We have created you from male and female and made you peoples and tribes that you may know one another" (Quran 49:13). For businesses, this means ensuring that their marketing materials are inclusive, respectful of diversity, and accessible to all members of their target audience.

One practical way to promote inclusivity is by featuring diverse models, voices, and perspectives in marketing campaigns. For example, a halal fashion brand might create advertisements that showcase models from different ethnic backgrounds, body types, and age groups, reflecting the diversity of its customer base. By promoting diversity and inclusivity, the brand not only appeals to a broader audience but also reinforces its commitment to ethical practices and respect for all people.

In addition to promoting diversity, businesses must also ensure that their marketing materials are accessible to individuals with disabilities. This might involve creating marketing content that includes subtitles or sign language interpretation for video advertisements, or ensuring that websites and online platforms are designed to be navigable by individuals with visual impairments or other accessibility needs. By prioritizing accessibility, businesses demonstrate their commitment to serving the needs of all their customers, regardless of their abilities.

Moreover, halal businesses must be mindful of cultural sensitivity in their marketing campaigns. The Prophet Muhammad (PBUH) said, "None of you will have faith until he loves for his brother what he loves for himself" (Bukhari). For businesses, this means ensuring that their marketing messages are respectful of different cultures, traditions, and values, particularly when operating in diverse or international markets. By taking the time to understand and respect the cultural context of each market, businesses can avoid misunderstandings or offense and build stronger connections with their customers.

As businesses grow and expand into new markets, maintaining ethical consistency in marketing becomes even more crucial. The Quran advises, "And do not incline toward those who do wrong, lest you be touched by the Fire, and you would not have other than Allah any protectors; then you would not be helped" (Quran 11:113). This serves as a reminder for businesses that regardless of external pressures or incentives, they must stay true to the principles of justice and righteousness in all of their dealings, including marketing.

For halal businesses entering new regions, this means adapting marketing strategies to reflect local values while maintaining the core principles of Islamic ethics. For example, a halal food brand entering a market with different cultural norms around food might tailor its marketing campaigns to highlight the ethical sourcing, sustainability, and nutritional benefits of its products, while ensuring that halal certification remains central to its messaging. By striking the right balance between localization and ethical consistency, the brand maintains its commitment to halal standards while appealing to the unique needs of its new audience.

One key challenge for businesses expanding into global markets is navigating varying advertising regulations, particularly in countries where Islamic practices may not be as well understood. In such cases, businesses must be diligent in ensuring that their marketing materials do not mislead consumers or compromise on halal integrity. This may involve working closely with local halal certification bodies and regulatory agencies to ensure that all promotional materials meet both local advertising laws and international halal standards. By maintaining transparency and consistency, businesses not only avoid potential legal issues but also reinforce their reputation as ethical and trustworthy brands.

Another important aspect of marketing consistency across different markets is the management of online platforms, especially social media. The Prophet Muhammad (PBUH) said, "Whoever believes in Allah and the Last Day should speak what is good or remain silent" (Bukhari). For halal businesses, this means ensuring that the content shared on social media and other digital platforms reflects the ethical values of the business and does not promote inappropriate or harmful messages. As businesses grow, it becomes essential to maintain a unified tone and message across all platforms to prevent any miscommunication or ethical breaches.

For example, a halal beauty brand that uses Instagram and YouTube for product promotion must ensure that the influencers or content creators they collaborate with uphold the same ethical standards as the brand itself. If an influencer promotes behaviors or products that contradict Islamic values, this could harm the brand's reputation. Therefore, it's important for businesses to carefully vet their partners and ensure that all online content aligns with the ethical principles of halal marketing.

In addition to maintaining consistency in ethical practices, halal businesses must also focus on fostering long-term relationships with their stakeholders. The Quran advises, "And hold fast, all of you together, to the rope of Allah and do not become divided" (Quran 3:103). For businesses, this highlights the importance of unity and collaboration, not only with customers but also with employees, suppliers, and partners. Ethical marketing is not just about promoting products; it's about creating an ecosystem of trust and cooperation that benefits all stakeholders.

One practical way to strengthen relationships with suppliers and partners is by fostering open communication and mutual respect. For example, a halal food company might work closely with its farmers and suppliers to ensure that all raw materials are sourced ethically and sustainably, with clear communication about halal requirements. By maintaining transparency and fostering collaboration, the business ensures that its entire supply chain upholds the same ethical values, which in turn strengthens the credibility of its marketing messages.

Similarly, businesses must also focus on nurturing strong relationships with their employees. The Prophet Muhammad (PBUH) said, "Your employees are your brothers, whom Allah has placed under your authority" (Bukhari). For halal businesses, this means ensuring that employees are treated with respect, fairness, and dignity, and that their well-being is prioritized. Ethical marketing can be an opportunity to highlight the company's commitment to employee welfare, promoting initiatives such as fair wages, professional development, and inclusive workplace policies.

For example, a halal fashion brand might use its marketing campaigns to showcase the artisans and workers who contribute to its products, highlighting their skills and the ethical working conditions provided by the company. By humanizing the people behind the products and demonstrating a commitment to social responsibility, the business not only enhances its brand reputation but also fosters loyalty and trust among consumers who value ethical practices.

In addition to employee welfare, halal businesses can use their marketing platforms to promote ethical governance and responsible business practices. The Quran teaches, "And consult them in the matter. And when you have decided, then rely upon Allah" (Quran 3:159). For businesses, this verse emphasizes the importance of consultation and transparency in decision-making. Ethical marketing involves being open about the company's governance structure and the measures taken to ensure accountability and fairness in all business dealings.

Transparency in governance is particularly important for businesses that operate in industries with complex supply chains, such as food production, fashion, or cosmetics. By providing customers with clear information about how products are made, where materials are sourced, and what steps are taken to ensure halal compliance, businesses can build trust and foster a sense of accountability. For example, a halal food company might create a marketing campaign that highlights its traceability system, allowing customers to see exactly where their food comes from and how it has been handled at each stage of production. By offering this level of transparency, the company reassures customers that its products meet the highest standards of halal integrity.

In addition to transparency in production, businesses must also ensure that their marketing campaigns promote fairness and justice in the way they engage with the broader community. The Prophet Muhammad (PBUH) said, "He is not a believer whose stomach is filled while the neighbor to his side goes hungry" (Bukhari). For halal businesses, this hadith serves as a reminder of the responsibility they have to contribute to the well-being of the communities in which they operate.

One way businesses can demonstrate this commitment is by integrating social responsibility into their marketing strategies. For example, a halal financial institution might launch a campaign promoting its interest-free loans or profit-sharing models, highlighting the positive impact these products have on the financial well-being of its customers. By aligning marketing messages with broader social objectives, the business not only promotes its products but also reinforces its commitment to ethical governance and social justice.

In addition to promoting ethical products, businesses can use their marketing platforms to support charitable initiatives that align with Islamic values. For instance, a halal restaurant chain might partner with local charities to provide meals for those in need, promoting these efforts through its marketing channels. By actively engaging in charitable work and promoting these initiatives, the business demonstrates its commitment to giving back to the community and contributing to the greater good.

Ethical marketing in halal business also involves promoting environmental responsibility. The Quran teaches, "And do not commit abuse on the earth, spreading corruption" (Quran 2:60). For businesses, this means ensuring that their operations and marketing practices do not contribute to environmental degradation and that they actively promote sustainability in all aspects of their business.

One practical way businesses can integrate environmental responsibility into their marketing strategies is by promoting eco-friendly products and practices. For example, a halal beauty brand might use its marketing campaigns to highlight its use of natural, organic ingredients, biodegradable packaging, and cruelty-free testing methods. By focusing on sustainability, the brand not only appeals to environmentally conscious consumers but also aligns its operations with Islamic principles of stewardship and care for the planet.

In addition to promoting eco-friendly products, businesses can use their marketing platforms to raise awareness about broader environmental issues and encourage responsible consumption. For instance, a halal food company might launch a campaign promoting the benefits of plant-based or locally sourced foods, encouraging customers to make more sustainable food choices. By aligning their marketing efforts with environmental objectives, businesses contribute to positive change while also enhancing their ethical reputation.

Moreover, ethical marketing involves ensuring that all promotional materials, including packaging, advertising, and product displays, are designed with sustainability in mind. This might involve reducing the use of plastic, opting for recyclable or reusable materials, or minimizing waste in the production process. For example, a halal fashion brand might create packaging that is both eco-friendly and reusable, offering customers an added incentive to support the brand while also reducing its environmental impact.

In addition to reducing waste, businesses can also promote sustainability by encouraging customers to adopt eco-friendly habits. For example, a halal home goods company might offer tips on how to reduce energy consumption or waste in the home, using its marketing platforms to educate customers about the importance of environmental responsibility. By providing valuable information and promoting sustainable behaviors, businesses not only enhance their brand image but also contribute to the broader goal of protecting the environment.

As halal businesses continue to grow and evolve, their marketing strategies must remain aligned with the core values of honesty, transparency, and social responsibility. The Quran teaches, "Indeed, Allah commands you to render trusts to whom they are due and when you judge between people to judge with justice" (Quran 4:58). For businesses, this verse serves as a reminder that ethical marketing is not just about promoting products; it's about building trust, fostering justice, and contributing to the well-being of society.

One of the most important aspects of ethical marketing is the ability to build long-term relationships with customers based on mutual respect and shared values. Halal businesses that prioritize ethical practices, both in their marketing and in their operations, are more likely to foster loyalty, trust, and customer retention. By consistently delivering on their promises, promoting responsible consumption, and contributing to the greater good, these businesses can build a lasting legacy of ethical excellence that resonates with customers for generations to come.

In conclusion, ethical marketing in halal business is about more than just selling products—it is about promoting a way of life that aligns with Islamic values of fairness, justice, and compassion. By focusing on transparency, inclusivity, environmental responsibility, and social impact, halal businesses can create marketing campaigns that inspire trust, foster long-term relationships, and contribute to positive change in the world. As they continue to grow and evolve, halal businesses have the opportunity to set a new standard for ethical marketing, one that reflects the true spirit of Islam and promotes the well-being of all.

CHAPTER 10: FINANCIAL INTEGRITY AND HALAL BUSINESS OPERATIONS

Financial integrity is the backbone of any successful halal business. As the Quran teaches, "O you who have believed, do not consume one another's wealth unjustly or send it [in bribery] to the rulers in order that [they might aid] you [to] consume a portion of the wealth of the people in sin, while you know [it is unlawful]" (Quran 2:188). For halal businesses, financial integrity is not merely about compliance with legal standards; it is about adhering to the ethical principles outlined in Islam, ensuring that wealth is generated, managed, and distributed in a manner that is just, transparent, and free from exploitation.

At the heart of financial integrity is the concept of halal earnings. Halal businesses must ensure that their revenue streams are derived from permissible sources and that their business dealings are free from haram elements such as riba (interest), gambling, fraud, and deceit. This requires a commitment to maintaining ethical practices in all aspects of financial operations, from sourcing capital and managing investments to pricing products and compensating employees.

For instance, a halal financial institution must ensure that its lending practices are free from riba by offering profit-sharing models, such as *mudarabah* or *musharakah*, rather than traditional interest-based loans. By structuring its financial products in accordance with Shariah law, the institution not only maintains its ethical integrity but also provides value to its customers by offering them ethical alternatives to conventional banking.

In addition to avoiding haram elements, financial integrity in halal business involves maintaining fairness and transparency in all financial transactions. The Prophet Muhammad (PBUH) said, "Give to the worker his wages before his sweat dries" (Ibn Majah). For businesses, this means ensuring that employees are paid fairly and promptly for their work, that suppliers and partners are compensated justly, and that customers are charged a fair price for products and services. By maintaining transparency and fairness in financial dealings, halal businesses build trust with their stakeholders and create a solid foundation for long-term success.

One of the key challenges faced by halal businesses is navigating the complexities of modern finance while adhering to Islamic principles. The Prophet Muhammad (PBUH) warned against the dangers of riba, saying, "Allah has cursed the one who consumes riba, the one who gives it, the one who writes it down, and the two who witness it" (Muslim). For businesses, this means avoiding any form of interest-based transactions, which can be particularly challenging in an economic system that is largely built on riba.

To overcome this challenge, halal businesses must explore alternative financing options that align with Islamic principles. One such option is equity-based financing, where investors provide capital in exchange for a share of the profits rather than interest. This model, known as *mudarabah*, allows businesses to raise capital in a way that is both halal and beneficial to all parties involved. In a *mudarabah* arrangement, the investor provides the capital, while the business owner contributes expertise and management. Profits are shared according to a pre-agreed ratio, but any losses are borne solely by the investor, as long as the business owner has acted in good faith and with due diligence.

Another ethical financing model is *musharakah*, where both the business owner and the investor contribute capital and share in the profits and losses according to their respective contributions. This model fosters a sense of partnership and shared responsibility, aligning the interests of both parties and promoting fairness in financial dealings. By adopting these halal financing models, businesses can ensure that their financial operations are free from riba and are in line with Islamic values.

In addition to equity-based financing, halal businesses can also explore Islamic bonds, known as *sukuk*. Unlike conventional bonds, which involve interest payments, *sukuk* represent ownership in an underlying asset or project, with investors receiving returns based on the performance of that asset. This structure ensures that the returns are tied to real economic activity, rather than speculative gains, and that the financing arrangement is in line with Shariah law. By offering *sukuk*, halal businesses can raise capital for expansion while maintaining their financial integrity.

Financial integrity also extends to the way businesses manage their cash flow and working capital. The Quran advises, "And those who, when they spend, are neither extravagant nor stingy, but hold a medium [way] between those [extremes]" (Quran 25:67). For businesses, this means maintaining a balanced approach to financial management, ensuring that resources are used efficiently and that spending is aligned with both business goals and ethical principles.

One practical way to maintain financial integrity in cash flow management is by adopting a conservative approach to debt. Halal businesses must be mindful of the risks associated with debt and should avoid taking on excessive liabilities that could jeopardize the financial stability of the business. Instead, businesses should focus on building strong reserves and managing their working capital in a way that promotes long-term sustainability.

For example, a halal retail company might implement a cash flow forecasting system that allows it to anticipate future expenses and revenues, ensuring that it always has sufficient liquidity to meet its obligations. By carefully managing its cash flow and avoiding unnecessary debt, the company can maintain its financial integrity and avoid the risks associated with over-leveraging.

Another important aspect of financial integrity is the proper management of zakat, the obligatory almsgiving that is one of the Five Pillars of Islam. Zakat is not just a personal obligation; it is also a corporate responsibility for businesses that generate wealth. The Quran commands, "And establish prayer and give zakat" (Quran 2:110), emphasizing the importance of giving back to the community and supporting those in need.

For businesses, zakat represents an opportunity to align financial operations with Islamic values by allocating a portion of their wealth to charitable causes. Zakat is typically calculated as 2.5% of the company's excess wealth, which includes profits, inventory, and cash reserves. By fulfilling this obligation, businesses not only purify their wealth but also contribute to the well-being of society, supporting initiatives such as poverty alleviation, education, healthcare, and community development.

In addition to zakat, halal businesses can also demonstrate financial integrity through corporate social responsibility (CSR) initiatives. The Quran teaches, "The example of those who spend their wealth in the way of Allah is like a seed [of grain] that sprouts seven ears; in every ear is a hundred grains. And Allah multiplies [His reward] for whom He wills" (Quran 2:261). For businesses, this verse serves as a reminder that ethical financial management goes beyond profit generation; it also involves using wealth to create positive social impact.

One way businesses can integrate CSR into their financial operations is by setting aside a portion of their profits for charitable initiatives. For example, a halal manufacturing company might allocate a percentage of its annual profits to support education programs in underprivileged communities or to provide healthcare services in rural areas. By incorporating philanthropy into their business model, halal businesses not only fulfill their religious obligations but also enhance their brand reputation and foster goodwill among customers and stakeholders.

In addition to charitable giving, businesses can also promote financial integrity by adopting sustainable and ethical business practices. The Quran advises, "Do not waste [resources], for Allah does not love the wasteful" (Quran 6:141). For businesses, this means ensuring that their financial operations are efficient, environmentally responsible, and aligned with the principles of stewardship and sustainability.

For example, a halal fashion brand might implement sustainable sourcing practices, ensuring that all materials are ethically sourced and that production processes minimize waste and environmental impact. By adopting these practices, the business not only aligns its operations with Islamic principles but also creates long-term value for its customers and the environment.

Financial integrity in halal business also involves maintaining accurate and transparent financial records. The Quran advises, "O you who have believed, when you contract a debt for a specified term, write it down. And let a scribe write between you in justice" (Quran 2:282). For businesses, this means ensuring that all financial transactions are properly documented and that financial statements are prepared in accordance with both legal and ethical standards.

Accurate record-keeping is essential for maintaining transparency and accountability in financial operations. For example, a halal food company might implement an internal auditing system to ensure that all financial transactions are accurately recorded and that any discrepancies are addressed promptly. By maintaining clear and transparent financial records, the company can build trust with its investors, customers, and regulatory bodies, ensuring that its financial operations are beyond reproach.

In addition to internal record-keeping, businesses must also ensure that they comply with all relevant financial regulations, including tax laws and reporting requirements. The Prophet Muhammad (PBUH) said, "Give to everyone who has a right what is rightfully his" (Bukhari). For businesses, this means ensuring that they fulfill all of their legal obligations, including paying taxes and providing accurate financial reports to regulatory authorities. By maintaining compliance with legal standards, businesses demonstrate their commitment to ethical governance and financial integrity.

Furthermore, halal businesses must ensure that their financial statements are prepared in accordance with Islamic accounting principles, which emphasize transparency, fairness, and accountability. Islamic accounting differs from conventional accounting in that it places a greater emphasis on social responsibility, environmental stewardship, and the equitable distribution of wealth. For example, Islamic accounting principles prohibit the recognition of interest income, as riba is considered haram in Islam. Instead, businesses must focus on profit-sharing arrangements and ethical investments that promote real economic activity and social welfare.

Another important aspect of financial integrity is the ethical management of investments. The Quran advises, "And whatever good you put forward for yourselves—you will find it with Allah. It is better and greater in reward" (Quran 73:20). For businesses, this means ensuring that their investments are aligned with Islamic principles and that they contribute to the well-being of society.

One key principle of halal investing is avoiding haram industries, such as alcohol, gambling, and pork production. Instead, businesses must focus on investing in sectors that promote ethical and socially responsible activities, such as healthcare, education, renewable energy, and sustainable agriculture. By aligning their investment strategies with Islamic values, businesses not only avoid haram activities but also create long-term value for their shareholders and society.

In addition to avoiding haram industries, halal businesses must also ensure that their investments are free from excessive speculation, which is considered *gharar* (uncertainty) in Islamic finance. For example, a halal investment fund might avoid investing in high-risk financial instruments, such as derivatives or speculative real estate ventures, which involve a high degree of uncertainty and risk. Instead, the fund might focus on stable, income-generating assets, such as real estate or infrastructure projects, that provide tangible benefits to society.

Furthermore, halal businesses must ensure that their investments are based on ethical principles of risk-sharing and mutual benefit. The Prophet Muhammad (PBUH) said, "Allah will bless a business transaction that is honest and fair" (Bukhari). For businesses, this means structuring their investments in a way that promotes fairness and shared responsibility, rather than seeking to maximize profits at the expense of others. By focusing on ethical investments, businesses can maintain their financial integrity while also contributing to the greater good.

Financial integrity in halal business is also closely tied to the concept of *tawakkul* (reliance on Allah). While businesses must take practical steps to ensure sound financial management, they must also recognize that ultimate success and provision come from Allah alone. The Quran teaches, "And whoever fears Allah—He will make for him a way out. And will provide for him from where he does not expect. And whoever relies upon Allah—then He is sufficient for him" (Quran 65:2-3). This verse serves as a reminder that while businesses must act responsibly and ethically, they must also trust in Allah's provision and maintain a sense of humility in their financial dealings.

For businesses, *tawakkul* means adopting a balanced approach to financial management that combines strategic planning with faith. For example, a halal business might develop a comprehensive risk management strategy that includes contingency plans for economic downturns, market fluctuations, or supply chain disruptions. At the same time, the business recognizes that no matter how well-prepared it may be, the ultimate outcome rests in the hands of Allah. This approach not only strengthens the business's resilience but also ensures that its financial decisions are grounded in humility and trust in Allah's wisdom.

One practical way businesses can demonstrate *tawakkul* in their financial operations is by avoiding speculative activities that involve high levels of uncertainty and risk. The Prophet Muhammad (PBUH) warned against excessive speculation, saying, "Avoid that which makes you doubt, and adhere to what is certain" (Tirmidhi). For businesses, this means focusing on investments and financial activities that are rooted in real economic value, rather than engaging in speculative ventures that could lead to financial instability.

For example, a halal real estate company might prioritize investments in long-term, stable projects, such as residential housing developments or commercial properties, rather than speculative real estate flipping or high-risk ventures. By focusing on sustainable investments that provide tangible benefits to society, the company maintains its financial integrity while also demonstrating reliance on Allah's provision.

In addition to *tawakkul*, financial integrity in halal business also involves fostering a culture of accountability and ethical leadership. The Quran advises, "And say, 'Do [as you will], for Allah will see your deeds, and [so will] His Messenger and the believers. And you will be returned to the Knower of the unseen and the witnessed, and He will inform you of what you used to do'" (Quran 9:105). For business leaders, this verse emphasizes the importance of accountability in all financial dealings, reminding them that their actions are ultimately judged by Allah and that they have a responsibility to uphold ethical standards.

Ethical leadership in financial management requires a commitment to transparency, honesty, and fairness in all transactions. For example, a halal business leader might implement a clear code of conduct that outlines the company's commitment to ethical financial practices, such as fair pricing, prompt payment to suppliers, and responsible debt management. By creating a culture of accountability, the leader sets the tone for the entire organization, ensuring that financial integrity is embedded in every aspect of the business.

One key aspect of ethical leadership is ensuring that financial decisions are made with the well-being of all stakeholders in mind, including employees, customers, suppliers, and the broader community. The Prophet Muhammad (PBUH) said, "The best of people are those who are most beneficial to others" (Daraqutni). For businesses, this means ensuring that financial decisions are not solely driven by profit but also consider the impact on the people and communities involved.

For instance, a halal retail company might prioritize paying its employees a living wage, even if this means reducing its profit margins. By ensuring that its financial decisions reflect a commitment to social justice and fairness, the company not only maintains its financial integrity but also fosters loyalty and trust among its employees and customers.

In addition to ethical leadership, financial integrity in halal business also involves promoting a culture of *amanah* (trustworthiness) within the organization. The Quran teaches, "Indeed, Allah commands you to render trusts to whom they are due and when you judge between people to judge with justice" (Quran 4:58). For businesses, this means ensuring that all financial transactions are conducted with honesty and transparency and that the business fulfills its financial obligations with integrity.

One way to promote *amanah* in financial management is by implementing clear and transparent financial policies that are communicated to all employees. For example, a halal financial institution might establish strict guidelines for how funds are managed, ensuring that all transactions are properly documented and that there is no room for unethical behavior, such as embezzlement or fraud. By creating a culture of trust and accountability, the institution ensures that its financial operations are aligned with Islamic principles.

In addition to internal policies, businesses can also promote *amanah* by ensuring that they are transparent with their customers and stakeholders about their financial practices. For instance, a halal investment firm might provide detailed reports to its investors, outlining how funds are being managed and what steps are being taken to ensure compliance with Islamic principles. By maintaining transparency in its financial dealings, the firm builds trust with its investors and demonstrates its commitment to ethical governance.

Furthermore, financial integrity in halal business requires a commitment to social responsibility in financial practices. The Quran advises, "And cooperate in righteousness and piety, but do not cooperate in sin and aggression. And fear Allah; indeed, Allah is severe in penalty" (Quran 5:2). For businesses, this means ensuring that their financial decisions contribute to the well-being of society and do not harm others.

One practical way to promote social responsibility in financial practices is by adopting ethical investment strategies that prioritize social impact. For example, a halal investment fund might focus on supporting projects that promote education, healthcare, or renewable energy, ensuring that its investments contribute to positive social change. By aligning its financial decisions with the broader goal of social responsibility, the fund not only maintains its financial integrity but also creates long-term value for both its investors and society as a whole.

Financial integrity in halal business is also closely linked to the concept of *ihsan* (excellence). The Prophet Muhammad (PBUH) said, "Allah loves that when one of you does something, he does it with excellence" (Muslim). For businesses, this means striving for excellence in all financial operations, ensuring that financial management is conducted with the highest level of professionalism, accuracy, and ethical rigor.

One way to achieve *ihsan* in financial management is by investing in professional development and training for employees involved in financial operations. For example, a halal business might provide ongoing training for its finance team, ensuring that they are well-versed in both conventional financial practices and Islamic finance principles. By equipping employees with the knowledge and skills needed to manage finances ethically and effectively, the business ensures that its financial operations are conducted with excellence.

In addition to employee training, businesses can also promote *ihsan* by adopting best practices in financial management, such as implementing robust financial controls, conducting regular audits, and using advanced financial management software. For instance, a halal logistics company might implement a comprehensive financial management system that allows it to track expenses, revenues, and cash flow in real-time, ensuring that financial decisions are based on accurate and up-to-date information. By striving for excellence in financial management, the company not only maintains its financial integrity but also enhances its overall operational efficiency.

Furthermore, financial integrity in halal business involves a commitment to continuous improvement. The Quran advises, "And do not pursue that of which you have no knowledge. Indeed, the hearing, the sight, and the heart—about all those [one] will be questioned" (Quran 17:36). For businesses, this means continuously seeking to improve financial practices by staying informed about industry trends, technological advancements, and changes in regulatory requirements.

For example, a halal financial institution might regularly review its investment portfolio to ensure that it remains aligned with Islamic principles and that it continues to generate value for both the institution and its customers. By continuously evaluating and improving financial practices, businesses ensure that they remain compliant with both Islamic principles and industry standards, while also fostering a culture of excellence.

Another key aspect of financial integrity is the ethical management of customer relationships. The Quran teaches, "And speak to people good [words]" (Quran 2:83). For businesses, this means ensuring that financial interactions with customers are conducted with kindness, fairness, and respect, and that customers are treated with dignity in all financial dealings.

One practical way to promote ethical customer relationships is by ensuring that pricing practices are transparent and fair. For example, a halal e-commerce platform might provide clear and detailed information about the cost of products, including any additional fees or taxes, ensuring that customers are fully informed before making a purchase. By maintaining transparency in pricing, the platform builds trust with its customers and fosters long-term loyalty.

In addition to transparent pricing, businesses must also ensure that their financial practices do not exploit or deceive customers. The Prophet Muhammad (PBUH) said, "The honest and trustworthy merchant will be with the prophets, the truthful, and the martyrs" (Tirmidhi). For businesses, this means ensuring that financial transactions are conducted with honesty and integrity, and that customers are not subjected to unfair practices, such as hidden fees or deceptive advertising.

For instance, a halal travel agency might ensure that all fees and charges are clearly communicated to customers before booking, avoiding any last-minute surprises that could damage the trust between the business and its customers. By ensuring that all financial interactions are conducted with honesty and transparency, the agency fosters a positive relationship with its customers and upholds its commitment to ethical business practices.

Moreover, businesses must also be proactive in addressing any financial disputes or issues that arise with customers. The Quran advises, "And if you disagree over anything, refer it to Allah and the Messenger" (Quran 4:59). For businesses, this means taking a fair and just approach to resolving financial disputes, ensuring that customers are treated with respect and that any issues are resolved in a manner that aligns with Islamic principles of fairness and justice.

Financial integrity is more than just maintaining accurate records and lawful financial practices; it's about fostering an environment where ethical considerations are interwoven with every financial decision. The Quran teaches, "O you who have believed, do not consume one another's wealth unjustly or send it [in bribery] to the rulers in order that [they might aid] you [to] consume a portion of the wealth of the people in sin, while you know [it is unlawful]" (Quran 2:188). This highlights that financial integrity includes a steadfast commitment to fairness, transparency, and the avoidance of unjust gain.

One way that halal businesses can maintain financial integrity is by implementing rigorous financial accountability measures. This includes regular audits and transparent financial reporting to stakeholders, whether internal or external. For example, a halal investment firm might conduct quarterly audits of its portfolio to ensure that all investments are aligned with Islamic principles, such as avoiding industries linked to alcohol, gambling, and interest-based lending. These audits not only serve as an internal checkpoint but also reassure investors that their funds are being managed responsibly and ethically.

In addition to formal audits, businesses can foster a culture of financial accountability by encouraging employees at all levels to report any discrepancies or unethical practices. This can be done by establishing clear whistleblower policies that protect employees who come forward with concerns about financial integrity. By creating an environment where ethical issues are openly addressed, halal businesses reinforce the importance of accountability in financial operations.

Another important aspect of financial integrity is the way businesses manage their relationships with financial partners, including banks, investors, and creditors. The Prophet Muhammad (PBUH) said, "The best among you are those who repay their debts in the best manner" (Bukhari). For businesses, this means ensuring that all financial obligations are met in a timely and fair manner. For instance, a halal business that borrows funds through a *musharakah* or *mudarabah* agreement must ensure that profits are distributed fairly and that any losses are shared according to the terms of the agreement. By maintaining fairness in financial partnerships, businesses not only uphold Islamic principles but also foster trust and long-term cooperation with their partners.

Financial integrity also involves ensuring that businesses maintain the highest standards of transparency in their dealings with shareholders and investors. The Quran advises, "And let those who oppose His order beware, lest trial or a painful punishment befall them" (Quran 24:63). This verse emphasizes the importance of adhering to ethical guidelines and avoiding actions that could lead to harm or injustice. For halal businesses, this means providing investors with clear and accurate information about the financial performance of the company, as well as any risks associated with their investments.

One practical way to promote transparency is by holding regular shareholder meetings where the company's financial performance, future strategies, and any potential risks are discussed openly. This allows shareholders to make informed decisions about their investments and ensures that the company's financial operations are conducted in a manner that is both ethical and transparent. For example, a halal food company might hold an annual general meeting where it presents its financial statements, discusses its halal certification process, and outlines its future expansion plans. By engaging shareholders in an open and transparent dialogue, the company builds trust and fosters long-term relationships with its investors.

In addition to transparency in financial reporting, businesses must also ensure that they are managing shareholder expectations in an ethical manner. The Prophet Muhammad (PBUH) said, "The truthful and trustworthy merchant will be with the prophets, the truthful, and the martyrs" (Tirmidhi). For businesses, this means avoiding exaggerated claims about future profits or misleading statements that could create false expectations among investors. Instead, businesses should focus on providing realistic projections that are based on sound financial analysis and market research.

For instance, a halal tech company might provide investors with a detailed analysis of its growth potential, outlining both the opportunities and challenges it faces in the market. By providing a balanced view of the company's prospects, the business ensures that investors are fully informed and that their expectations are aligned with the company's actual performance.

Another key aspect of financial integrity is ensuring that all financial practices are in compliance with local laws and regulations. The Quran teaches, "O you who have believed, obey Allah and obey the Messenger and those in authority among you" (Quran 4:59). For businesses, this means ensuring that their financial operations adhere to both Islamic law and the legal requirements of the countries in which they operate. Compliance with local regulations not only protects the business from legal penalties but also ensures that it operates in a manner that is fair and just.

One practical way to ensure compliance is by working closely with legal and financial advisors who are knowledgeable about both Islamic finance and local regulatory frameworks. For example, a halal bank might work with Shariah scholars and financial experts to ensure that its products comply with both Islamic law and the regulatory requirements of the central bank in its country of operation. By maintaining compliance with all applicable laws, the bank not only protects itself from legal risks but also upholds its commitment to financial integrity.

In addition to complying with local laws, halal businesses must also ensure that their financial practices are in line with international standards for ethical business conduct. The Prophet Muhammad (PBUH) said, "There should be neither harming nor reciprocating harm" (Ibn Majah). For businesses, this means ensuring that their financial operations do not harm others, whether through exploitation, fraud, or unethical practices. For instance, a halal export company might ensure that all of its financial dealings with international partners are conducted with fairness and transparency, adhering to international standards for trade and commerce. By maintaining ethical financial practices on a global scale, the company ensures that its operations are consistent with both Islamic principles and international norms.

Moreover, businesses must be vigilant in ensuring that their financial practices do not contribute to corruption or unethical behavior. The Quran warns, "And do not consume one another's wealth unjustly or send it [in bribery] to the rulers" (Quran 2:188). For businesses, this means avoiding any involvement in corrupt practices, such as bribery or fraud, which could undermine their financial integrity and damage their reputation. By maintaining a strict zero-tolerance policy for corruption, halal businesses can ensure that their financial operations remain ethical and aligned with Islamic values.

In addition to avoiding corruption, halal businesses must also focus on ensuring that their financial practices promote social justice and equity. The Quran advises, "Indeed, Allah commands you to render trusts to whom they are due and when you judge between people to judge with justice" (Quran 4:58). For businesses, this means ensuring that their financial decisions contribute to the well-being of society and promote fairness in all transactions.

One way businesses can promote social justice is by adopting inclusive financial practices that support underserved communities. For example, a halal microfinance institution might provide small, interest-free loans to low-income entrepreneurs, helping them to start or grow their businesses. By offering financial support to those who may not have access to traditional banking services, the institution not only promotes financial inclusion but also contributes to poverty alleviation and economic development.

Another way businesses can promote social justice is by ensuring that their pricing practices are fair and accessible to all customers. The Prophet Muhammad (PBUH) said, "The best among you are those who bring the most benefit to people" (Daraqutni). For businesses, this means ensuring that their products and services are priced in a way that is fair and that provides value to customers, particularly those from low-income or vulnerable groups.

For instance, a halal pharmaceutical company might offer discounted prices on essential medications for low-income patients, ensuring that life-saving treatments are accessible to all, regardless of their financial situation. By adopting fair pricing practices, the company not only fulfills its ethical obligations but also enhances its reputation as a socially responsible business.

Financial integrity also involves ensuring that businesses maintain a balanced approach to wealth creation and distribution. The Quran advises, "And do not make your hand [as] chained to your neck or extend it completely and [thereby] become blamed and insolvent" (Quran 17:29). For businesses, this means ensuring that their wealth is managed prudently and that profits are distributed in a way that promotes long-term sustainability.

One practical way businesses can maintain financial balance is by adopting a conservative approach to profit distribution, ensuring that sufficient reserves are maintained for future growth and stability. For example, a halal manufacturing company might set aside a portion of its annual profits in a contingency fund, ensuring that it has the financial resources to weather economic downturns or unexpected challenges. By maintaining financial reserves, the company protects itself from insolvency and ensures that it can continue to operate in a sustainable and ethical manner.

In addition to maintaining financial reserves, businesses must also ensure that profits are distributed fairly among stakeholders. The Quran advises, "And give the relative his right, and [also] the poor and the traveler, and do not spend wastefully" (Quran 17:26). For businesses, this means ensuring that profits are shared in a way that benefits not only shareholders but also employees, customers, and the broader community.

For instance, a halal tech company might implement a profit-sharing program that rewards employees for their contributions to the company's success. By sharing profits with employees, the company fosters a sense of ownership and loyalty among its workforce, while also ensuring that wealth is distributed in a fair and equitable manner. In addition, the company might allocate a portion of its profits to charitable initiatives, such as supporting education or healthcare programs in underserved communities. By adopting a balanced approach to wealth distribution, the company ensures that its financial success benefits a wide range of stakeholders, rather than being concentrated among a few.

Financial integrity in a halal business involves the mindful and balanced distribution of wealth not only within the organization but also toward social causes that contribute to societal betterment. The Quran teaches, "You will not attain righteousness until you spend in charity from that which you love" (Quran 3:92). For businesses, this verse underscores the importance of using wealth to support charitable initiatives and contribute to the well-being of those in need. Philanthropy is not an afterthought in halal businesses; rather, it is an integral part of their financial strategy.

One practical way for businesses to engage in charitable giving is by establishing a zakat program that systematically allocates a portion of their profits toward helping the less fortunate. Zakat, a pillar of Islam, requires businesses and individuals to contribute a portion of their wealth (typically 2.5% of qualifying assets) to those in need. This practice not only purifies the business's wealth but also creates a direct and tangible impact on society. For example, a halal real estate development company might allocate a portion of its annual revenue toward building affordable housing for low-income families. This act of charity is not only a fulfillment of religious duty but also a demonstration of the company's commitment to social responsibility.

In addition to zakat, halal businesses can engage in *sadaqah* (voluntary charity), which allows them to contribute additional funds toward causes they are passionate about. For instance, a halal tech company might donate funds to provide educational scholarships to students from underprivileged backgrounds. By actively participating in charitable activities, the business not only strengthens its ethical foundation but also fosters goodwill among its stakeholders, including customers, employees, and investors.

Financial integrity in halal business also involves being mindful of the impact that wealth accumulation can have on society. The Quran advises, "And those who hoard gold and silver and spend it not in the way of Allah—give them tidings of a painful punishment" (Quran 9:34). For businesses, this means avoiding the excessive accumulation of wealth at the expense of social welfare. Instead, businesses are encouraged to reinvest their profits into initiatives that promote social good, such as job creation, education, and environmental sustainability.

Reinvesting in the community is a key component of maintaining financial integrity in halal businesses. The Quran teaches, "Whatever you spend of good is [to be] for parents and relatives and orphans and the needy and the traveler. And whatever you do of good—indeed, Allah is Knowing of it" (Quran 2:215). For businesses, this means using their financial resources to create positive, lasting change in the communities where they operate. This could involve supporting local businesses, hiring from within the community, or contributing to public infrastructure projects that improve the quality of life for residents.

For example, a halal fashion brand might choose to source materials from local suppliers, ensuring that the economic benefits of its operations are felt within the community. By building strong relationships with local suppliers, the business not only strengthens its supply chain but also contributes to the economic development of the area. Additionally, the business might invest in programs that provide training and employment opportunities for young people in the community, helping to reduce unemployment and foster social mobility.

In addition to community reinvestment, halal businesses must also focus on promoting environmental sustainability in their financial operations. The Quran advises, "And do not commit abuse on the earth, spreading corruption" (Quran 2:60). For businesses, this means ensuring that their financial practices do not contribute to environmental degradation and that they actively seek out ways to reduce their ecological footprint.

One way businesses can promote environmental sustainability is by adopting green financial practices, such as investing in renewable energy projects or implementing energy-efficient technologies in their operations. For example, a halal food company might invest in solar panels to power its production facilities or switch to biodegradable packaging materials to reduce waste. By integrating environmental sustainability into their financial strategy, businesses not only fulfill their ethical obligations but also create long-term value by reducing operational costs and appealing to environmentally conscious consumers.

In addition to environmental sustainability, halal businesses must also focus on ethical governance in their financial practices. The Quran teaches, "And do not devour one another's wealth unjustly or send it [in bribery] to the rulers in order that [they might aid] you [to] consume a portion of the wealth of the people in sin, while you know [it is unlawful]" (Quran 2:188). For businesses, this means ensuring that their financial governance structures are designed to prevent corruption, fraud, and unethical behavior, and that there is a strong emphasis on accountability at all levels of the organization.

One practical way to promote ethical governance is by establishing a clear and transparent financial reporting system that allows stakeholders to monitor the company's financial performance and ensure that its operations are aligned with Islamic principles. For example, a halal financial institution might implement a system of regular financial audits, conducted by both internal and external auditors, to ensure that all financial transactions are properly recorded and that any discrepancies are addressed promptly. By maintaining transparency in its financial operations, the institution builds trust with its stakeholders and reinforces its commitment to ethical governance.

Another important aspect of ethical governance is ensuring that the business's financial decisions are guided by a commitment to social justice and fairness. The Prophet Muhammad (PBUH) said, "The honest and trustworthy merchant will be with the prophets, the truthful, and the martyrs" (Tirmidhi). For businesses, this means ensuring that all financial practices—whether related to pricing, wages, or investments—are conducted in a way that promotes fairness and benefits all stakeholders.

For instance, a halal retail company might implement a wage transparency policy, ensuring that all employees are paid fairly for their work and that there are no unjust disparities in compensation. By promoting fairness in wages, the company not only improves employee morale and retention but also demonstrates its commitment to ethical governance and social responsibility.

Financial integrity in halal business also involves ensuring that businesses manage their financial risks in a way that aligns with Islamic principles. The Quran advises, "And cooperate in righteousness and piety, but do not cooperate in sin and aggression" (Quran 5:2). For businesses, this means adopting risk management strategies that prioritize ethical decision-making and avoid unnecessary financial risks that could jeopardize the company's integrity or harm its stakeholders.

One practical way to manage financial risks in a halal business is by adopting a conservative approach to debt management. Islamic finance discourages excessive reliance on debt, particularly interest-based debt, which is considered haram. Instead, businesses are encouraged to explore alternative financing methods, such as equity financing or profit-sharing arrangements, that are more aligned with Islamic principles. For example, a halal manufacturing company might choose to finance its expansion through a *musharakah* (partnership) agreement with investors, rather than taking out an interest-based loan. By adopting these ethical financing models, the company reduces its financial risk while maintaining its commitment to halal principles.

In addition to managing debt responsibly, businesses must also ensure that they are adequately prepared for economic fluctuations and other financial challenges. The Quran advises, "And those who, when they spend, are neither extravagant nor stingy, but hold a medium [way] between those [extremes]" (Quran 25:67). For businesses, this means maintaining a balanced approach to spending and saving, ensuring that they have sufficient financial reserves to weather economic downturns or unexpected expenses.

One way to maintain financial balance is by establishing a contingency fund that can be used to cover unexpected costs or losses. For example, a halal tech company might set aside a portion of its profits each year to build a financial buffer, ensuring that it has the resources to continue operating during times of economic uncertainty. By maintaining a prudent approach to financial management, the company ensures its long-term sustainability while also upholding its commitment to financial integrity.

In addition to managing financial risks, halal businesses must also focus on promoting financial literacy and education among their employees and stakeholders. The Prophet Muhammad (PBUH) said, "The seeking of knowledge is obligatory for every Muslim" (Ibn Majah). For businesses, this means ensuring that all employees, particularly those involved in financial operations, have a clear understanding of Islamic finance principles and ethical financial practices.

One practical way to promote financial literacy is by offering regular training sessions and workshops on topics such as Islamic finance, ethical investing, and responsible financial management. For example, a halal investment firm might provide its employees with training on Shariah-compliant financial products and services, ensuring that they are well-equipped to advise clients on ethical investment strategies. By investing in financial education, businesses not only improve the skills and knowledge of their employees but also reinforce their commitment to ethical financial practices.

In addition to employee training, businesses can also promote financial literacy among their customers and investors. For instance, a halal bank might offer educational resources, such as online courses or informational brochures, that help customers understand the benefits of Islamic finance and how to manage their finances in a way that aligns with their religious values. By promoting financial literacy, the bank empowers its customers to make informed financial decisions and strengthens its relationship with the community.

Moreover, businesses can use their marketing platforms to raise awareness about the importance of ethical financial practices and encourage their customers to adopt responsible financial behaviors. For example, a halal fashion brand might launch a campaign promoting the benefits of sustainable and ethical consumption, encouraging customers to make thoughtful purchasing decisions that align with their values. By promoting financial literacy and ethical consumption, businesses not only contribute to the well-being of their customers but also enhance their reputation as socially responsible organizations.

In addition to promoting financial literacy, halal businesses must also ensure that their financial operations are conducted in a way that fosters trust and transparency with their customers and stakeholders. The Quran advises, "And fulfill [every] commitment. Indeed, the commitment is ever [that about which one will be] questioned" (Quran 17:34). For businesses, this means ensuring that all financial commitments, whether to customers, investors, or employees, are fulfilled with honesty and integrity.

One way businesses can foster trust is by ensuring that their financial transactions are conducted with full transparency and that all parties involved are fully informed about the terms of the transaction. For example, a halal e-commerce platform might provide detailed information about the costs associated with each purchase, including any applicable taxes, shipping fees, or transaction charges. By providing customers with clear and accurate information, the platform ensures that there are no hidden fees or surprises, building trust and fostering long-term loyalty.

In addition to transparency in transactions, businesses must also ensure that they are responsive to customer concerns and that any financial disputes are resolved fairly and promptly. The Prophet Muhammad (PBUH) said, "Whoever relieves the hardship of a believer in this world, Allah will relieve his hardship on the Day of Resurrection" (Muslim). For businesses, this means taking a proactive approach to resolving customer complaints or disputes, ensuring that all financial issues are handled with fairness and respect.

For instance, a halal travel agency might implement a customer service policy that guarantees a prompt resolution to any billing disputes or refund requests. By addressing financial issues in a timely and respectful manner, the agency builds trust with its customers and reinforces its commitment to ethical business practices.

Financial integrity in halal business is an ongoing commitment that requires businesses to continually assess and improve their financial practices. The Quran teaches, "And whatever good you put forward for yourselves—you will find it with Allah. It is better and greater in reward" (Quran 73:20). For businesses, this means recognizing that financial integrity is not just about achieving short-term gains, but about building a legacy of ethical governance and long-term success. This ongoing commitment to financial excellence and transparency ensures that the business remains aligned with Islamic principles and promotes trust among all stakeholders.

One way to ensure continuous improvement in financial integrity is by regularly reviewing and updating the company's financial policies and practices. For example, a halal financial institution might conduct an annual review of its financial practices to identify areas where it can enhance its compliance with Islamic finance principles, such as increasing its use of profit-sharing models or improving its transparency in customer dealings. By regularly reviewing and refining its financial practices, the institution ensures that it remains at the forefront of ethical finance, offering products and services that align with both Islamic values and customer needs.

In addition to internal reviews, businesses must also seek feedback from external stakeholders, including customers, investors, and regulatory bodies, to ensure that their financial practices meet the highest ethical standards. For instance, a halal tech company might engage with Shariah scholars and industry experts to evaluate its compliance with Islamic finance principles and identify opportunities for improvement. By seeking external input, the company ensures that it is not only compliant with internal policies but also meets the broader ethical standards of the Islamic finance community.

Moreover, businesses can promote financial integrity by adopting best practices in corporate governance. The Prophet Muhammad (PBUH) said, "The strong believer is better and more beloved to Allah than the weak believer, while there is good in both" (Muslim). For businesses, this means striving to build strong governance structures that promote accountability, transparency, and ethical decision-making at all levels of the organization.

A key component of corporate governance is ensuring that there is a clear separation of roles and responsibilities within the organization, particularly in relation to financial decision-making. For example, a halal retail company might establish a board of directors responsible for overseeing financial decisions and ensuring that they are made in accordance with Islamic principles. This board could include independent directors, Shariah advisors, and financial experts, who provide a range of perspectives on the company's financial practices and ensure that all decisions are made with the best interests of the business and its stakeholders in mind.

In addition to establishing a strong governance structure, businesses must also ensure that there is clear communication and collaboration between different departments within the organization, particularly those involved in financial operations. The Quran advises, "And consult them in the matter. And when you have decided, then rely upon Allah" (Quran 3:159). For businesses, this means fostering a culture of consultation and cooperation, where financial decisions are made collaboratively and with input from all relevant parties.

For instance, a halal manufacturing company might establish a cross-functional financial committee that includes representatives from finance, operations, marketing, and human resources. This committee would be responsible for reviewing major financial decisions, such as capital investments, pricing strategies, and profit distribution, ensuring that all decisions are made in a way that aligns with the company's ethical principles and financial goals. By fostering collaboration and consultation, the company ensures that its financial operations are transparent, fair, and in line with Islamic values.

Another important aspect of corporate governance is ensuring that businesses maintain transparency in their financial reporting and communication with stakeholders. The Quran advises, "O you who have believed, be persistently standing firm in justice, witnesses for Allah, even if it be against yourselves or parents and relatives" (Quran 4:135). For businesses, this means providing stakeholders with clear, accurate, and timely information about the company's financial performance, ensuring that all financial statements are prepared in accordance with both legal and ethical standards.

One way businesses can promote transparency in financial reporting is by adopting international financial reporting standards (IFRS), which provide a clear framework for preparing financial statements that are consistent, comparable, and transparent. For example, a halal logistics company might implement IFRS in its financial reporting to ensure that its financial statements are easily understood by investors and other stakeholders, both within and outside the company. By adopting internationally recognized reporting standards, the company ensures that its financial practices meet the highest levels of transparency and accountability.

In addition to adopting international reporting standards, businesses must also ensure that they provide clear and accessible financial information to all stakeholders, including employees, customers, and the broader community.

For instance, a halal bank might publish an annual report that outlines its financial performance, highlights its commitment to ethical finance, and provides detailed information about its products and services. By providing stakeholders with clear and comprehensive financial information, the bank builds trust and demonstrates its commitment to transparency and accountability.

Moreover, financial integrity in halal business also involves ensuring that businesses are proactive in addressing any financial challenges or issues that arise. The Quran teaches, "Indeed, Allah loves those who are constantly repentant and loves those who purify themselves" (Quran 2:222). For businesses, this means taking a proactive approach to identifying and resolving financial issues, rather than waiting for problems to escalate. By addressing financial challenges early and with integrity, businesses can maintain their financial stability and uphold their ethical obligations.

For example, a halal real estate company might regularly monitor its cash flow to identify any potential shortfalls or liquidity issues. If the company identifies a cash flow problem, it could take proactive steps to address the issue, such as negotiating extended payment terms with suppliers or securing additional equity investment. By addressing financial challenges in a timely and responsible manner, the company ensures that it maintains its financial integrity and continues to operate in accordance with Islamic principles.

CHAPTER 11: ETHICAL LEADERSHIP AND GOVERNANCE IN HALAL BUSINESS

Leadership is more than merely holding a title or position; it is a sacred trust, an *amanah*, that requires individuals to act with integrity, wisdom, and responsibility. The Quran teaches, "Indeed, Allah commands you to render trusts to whom they are due and when you judge between people to judge with justice" (Quran 4:58). For halal businesses, ethical leadership is foundational to their success. It guides the company's decision-making processes, ensures that every action is aligned with Islamic values, and sets a tone of fairness, transparency, and accountability across all levels of the organization.

At the core of ethical leadership is the principle of *taqwa* (consciousness of Allah). A leader who is mindful of their responsibilities to both Allah and those they lead is driven by more than profit or personal ambition. Such a leader is focused on ensuring that their decisions benefit not only the company but also the employees, customers, stakeholders, and the broader society. This type of leadership requires courage, humility, and a commitment to justice.

For example, a halal business leader in the financial industry may make decisions about investments, keeping in mind the Quran's injunctions against riba (interest) and speculation. Even if avoiding these practices might limit certain financial opportunities, the leader remains steadfast, knowing that adhering to Islamic principles will bring barakah (blessing) in the long run.

This type of leader sets an example for the entire organization, fostering a culture where integrity takes precedence over short-term gains.

Ethical leadership also demands that leaders are fair and transparent in all their dealings. The Prophet Muhammad (PBUH) said, "The leader of a people is their servant" (Ibn Majah). This profound statement highlights that true leadership is about serving others, not wielding power over them. A leader who embodies this principle will treat employees with kindness, offer clear communication, and make decisions that benefit everyone, not just those at the top.

One of the essential qualities of an ethical leader is fairness. The Quran teaches, "And when you judge between people, judge with justice" (Quran 4:58). In a halal business, fairness must permeate every aspect of governance, from the allocation of resources to the way disputes are resolved. Leaders are responsible for ensuring that justice is maintained at all times, regardless of the circumstances or the people involved. Whether it is addressing employee grievances or ensuring that promotions are based on merit rather than favoritism, the commitment to fairness builds trust and harmony within the organization.

In a practical sense, fairness means creating policies that apply equally to everyone. For example, a halal manufacturing company might implement a clear and transparent bonus system that rewards employees based on measurable performance indicators. By establishing objective criteria for bonuses, the company ensures that all employees are treated fairly and that favoritism does not cloud the reward system. This not only boosts morale but also reinforces the company's commitment to justice and transparency.

Another key aspect of ethical leadership is the concept of *shura* (consultation). The Quran advises, "And consult them in the matter. And when you have decided, then rely upon Allah" (Quran 3:159). Consultation is an essential aspect of Islamic leadership, and it ensures that decisions are made with the input of others, particularly those who are affected by them. In a business context, *shura* fosters collaboration, promotes transparency, and ensures that the best possible decisions are made.

For instance, a halal food company might consult its employees, stakeholders, and customers before launching a new product. By seeking feedback from these groups, the company ensures that the product meets the needs and expectations of its audience, while also staying true to its Islamic values. This approach not only improves the quality of decision-making but also builds a sense of community and shared purpose within the organization.

Ethical leadership also involves ensuring that the governance structures within a halal business are robust and aligned with Islamic principles. Governance refers to the systems, policies, and processes that guide the organization's activities and ensure that it operates ethically and efficiently.

The Prophet Muhammad (PBUH) said, "Each of you is a shepherd, and each of you is responsible for your flock" (Bukhari). For business leaders, this hadith serves as a reminder that they are accountable for the actions of their organization and must ensure that its governance reflects the values of justice, fairness, and responsibility.

One way halal businesses can promote ethical governance is by establishing a board of directors or an advisory council that includes Shariah scholars, financial experts, and representatives from various stakeholder groups. This governance body can provide guidance on key decisions, such as investments, product development, and expansion strategies, ensuring that all actions align with Islamic principles. For example, a halal pharmaceutical company might consult its advisory council before entering into a partnership with a supplier to ensure that the supplier's practices are ethical and compliant with halal standards. By involving a diverse group of advisors in the decision-making process, the company ensures that its governance is transparent, accountable, and ethically sound.

Moreover, ethical governance requires businesses to be transparent with their stakeholders about their financial performance, operational practices, and future plans. The Quran advises, "O you who have believed, fear Allah and speak words of appropriate justice" (Quran 33:70). For businesses, this means ensuring that their communication with investors, customers, and employees is truthful, accurate, and clear. By providing regular updates on the company's activities and financial health, halal businesses build trust and foster long-term relationships with their stakeholders.

In addition to transparency, businesses must also ensure that their governance structures promote accountability. The Prophet Muhammad (PBUH) said, "The best of people are those who are most beneficial to others" (Daraqutni). For business leaders, this means ensuring that their actions benefit not only the company but also the broader community. Accountability ensures that leaders are held responsible for their decisions and that any unethical behavior is addressed promptly and effectively.

Ethical leadership also requires leaders to cultivate a culture of integrity within the organization. The Quran teaches, "And do not mix the truth with falsehood or conceal the truth while you know [it]" (Quran 2:42). For business leaders, this means ensuring that honesty and integrity are at the heart of everything the company does. Leaders must lead by example, demonstrating integrity in their words and actions, and ensuring that their employees are encouraged to do the same.

One way businesses can promote a culture of integrity is by developing clear ethical guidelines that outline the company's commitment to Islamic values and ethical business practices. For example, a halal tech company might create a code of conduct that emphasizes the importance of honesty, transparency, and respect in all business dealings. This code of conduct would apply to all employees, from the top executives to entry-level staff, ensuring that everyone is held to the same high ethical standards. By promoting integrity at all levels of the organization, the company builds a reputation for ethical excellence, which can enhance its brand and attract loyal customers.

In addition to developing ethical guidelines, leaders must also ensure that their employees are provided with the training and resources they need to act with integrity. The Prophet Muhammad (PBUH) said, "Allah loves to see one's task done at the level of itqan (excellence)" (Tabarani). For businesses, this means providing employees with the tools and support they need to excel in their roles and to uphold the company's ethical values. This might include offering training on Islamic finance principles, ethical marketing practices, or conflict resolution strategies. By investing in the development of their employees, ethical leaders ensure that their workforce is equipped to make decisions that reflect the company's values.

Moreover, ethical leadership requires businesses to create a work environment that fosters collaboration, innovation, and mutual respect. The Quran advises, "And hold fast, all of you together, to the rope of Allah and do not become divided" (Quran 3:103). For businesses, this means ensuring that the workplace is a space where all employees feel valued, respected, and empowered to contribute their ideas and talents. This might involve implementing policies that promote diversity and inclusion or creating opportunities for employees to work together on cross-functional teams. By fostering a collaborative and inclusive work environment, ethical leaders encourage creativity, innovation, and a sense of shared purpose within the organization.

Another critical aspect of ethical leadership in halal business is the responsible use of power and authority. The Quran advises, "And do not incline toward those who do wrong, lest you be touched by the Fire" (Quran 11:113). For leaders, this means ensuring that their authority is used to serve others, not to exploit or oppress them. Ethical leaders understand that their power comes with great responsibility, and they use it to create positive change within the organization and the wider community.

One way leaders can ensure the responsible use of power is by promoting a culture of accountability within the organization. This means establishing clear checks and balances to prevent any abuse of power and ensuring that all decisions are subject to review and oversight. For example, a halal investment firm might implement a system of internal audits and external reviews to ensure that all financial transactions are conducted ethically and in accordance with Islamic principles. By creating a governance structure that promotes accountability, the firm ensures that its leaders are held responsible for their actions and that any unethical behavior is swiftly addressed.

In addition to promoting accountability, ethical leaders must also be willing to admit their mistakes and take responsibility for their actions. The

Prophet Muhammad (PBUH) said, "All the children of Adam are sinners, and the best of sinners are those who repent" (Tirmidhi). For business leaders, this means acknowledging when they have made a mistake and taking steps to correct it. Whether it's a financial misstep or a management error, ethical leaders are transparent about their mistakes and take immediate action to address them. This humility not only builds trust with employees and stakeholders but also strengthens the leader's credibility.

Furthermore, ethical leadership requires a commitment to continuous improvement. The Quran teaches, "And those who strive for Us—We will surely guide them to Our ways" (Quran 29:69). For leaders, this means continuously seeking ways to improve their leadership skills, governance structures, and ethical practices. This might involve seeking feedback from employees and stakeholders, attending leadership development programs, or consulting with Shariah scholars on how to better align the company's operations with Islamic values. By committing to continuous improvement, ethical leaders ensure that their organization remains adaptable, innovative, and aligned with Islamic principles.

Ethical leadership within halal businesses also involves fostering a culture of trust. Trust is a cornerstone of any successful business, and it is even more significant in Islamic business ethics, as the Quran advises, "O you who have believed, fulfill [all] contracts" (Quran 5:1). For a halal business, this means honoring commitments, being truthful in all dealings, and ensuring that promises made to customers, employees, partners, and investors are kept. Trust not only enhances the reputation of the business but also strengthens the relationships with all stakeholders, fostering loyalty and long-term partnerships.

One practical way to build trust within a halal business is through consistent and transparent communication. For example, a halal restaurant chain might regularly update its customers about the sourcing of its ingredients, ensuring that all products are halal-certified and ethically sourced. By providing transparency in its supply chain, the business builds trust with customers, ensuring them that the food they are consuming meets the highest ethical and religious standards. Similarly, the business might foster trust with its employees by maintaining open lines of communication about company policies, performance expectations, and opportunities for career advancement. Clear, honest communication prevents misunderstandings and builds a strong sense of mutual respect.

In addition to fostering trust through communication, halal business leaders must also demonstrate *amanah* (trustworthiness) in their financial dealings. The Quran teaches, "Indeed, Allah commands you to render trusts to whom they are due" (Quran 4:58). This principle is particularly important in financial transactions, where trust is essential for maintaining integrity and fairness. For instance, a halal investment firm must ensure that all funds entrusted to it by clients are managed ethically, with full transparency about how the funds are being invested and what returns clients can expect. By demonstrating *amanah*, the firm not only fulfills its religious obligations but also fosters trust and loyalty among its clients.

Moreover, ethical leadership involves fostering an environment where trust is a two-way street. The Prophet Muhammad (PBUH) said, "The truthful and trustworthy merchant will be with the prophets, the truthful, and the martyrs" (Tirmidhi). Leaders must trust their employees to make ethical decisions and to act in the best interests of the company. For example, a halal manufacturing company might empower its employees to take ownership of their work by allowing them to make decisions about production processes, quality control, and efficiency improvements. By trusting employees to take responsibility for their work, leaders create an environment where initiative and ethical decision-making are valued, which in turn fosters a culture of trust throughout the organization.

In addition to fostering trust, ethical leadership in halal business requires a commitment to fairness and justice in all dealings. The Quran teaches, "O you who have believed, be persistently standing firm in justice, witnesses for Allah, even if it be against yourselves or parents and relatives" (Quran 4:135). For businesses, this means ensuring that all decisions are made with fairness, regardless of who is involved or what the situation may be. Justice must permeate every aspect of the business, from employee relations to customer service, from pricing strategies to partnerships.

One practical example of fairness in action is in employee compensation. A halal business leader must ensure that all employees are paid fairly for their work, that wages are commensurate with the value employees bring to the organization, and that there is no discrimination based on gender, race, or other factors. For instance, a halal retail company might conduct regular salary audits to ensure that pay scales are fair and equitable across the board, and that employees who perform similar work receive comparable compensation. By ensuring fairness in wages, the company builds trust with its employees and fosters a positive work environment.

Fairness also extends to how businesses treat their customers. For example, a halal e-commerce platform might implement a clear and transparent return policy, ensuring that customers can return faulty or unsatisfactory products without difficulty. By prioritizing fairness in customer interactions, the business reinforces its commitment to ethical principles and builds long-lasting relationships with its customer base.

Moreover, fairness must be demonstrated in the way businesses engage with suppliers and partners. The Prophet Muhammad (PBUH) said, "Whoever cheats us is not one of us" (Muslim). For businesses, this means ensuring that their dealings with suppliers are transparent and just. For instance, a halal food distribution company might ensure that all suppliers are paid fairly and on time, and that there are no hidden terms or fees in their contracts. By fostering fairness in these partnerships, the business strengthens its supply chain while upholding its commitment to ethical business practices.

Another critical component of ethical leadership in halal businesses is promoting accountability. The Quran teaches, "And fear a Day when you will be returned to Allah. Then every soul will be compensated for what it earned, and they will not be wronged" (Quran 2:281). For business leaders, this means recognizing that they are accountable not only to their stakeholders but also to Allah for their actions and decisions. This accountability must be built into the governance structures of the business, ensuring that leaders are held responsible for their decisions and that any unethical behavior is swiftly addressed.

One way businesses can promote accountability is by implementing robust internal controls and governance frameworks that monitor the company's operations. For example, a halal financial institution might establish an independent audit committee responsible for reviewing financial transactions, ensuring compliance with Shariah law, and identifying any areas of concern. By implementing these checks and balances, the institution ensures that its operations are transparent and that its leaders are accountable for their actions.

In addition to formal governance structures, businesses can promote accountability by fostering a culture where ethical behavior is encouraged and rewarded. The Prophet Muhammad (PBUH) said, "The best among you are those who have the best manners and character" (Bukhari). For business leaders, this means creating an environment where employees feel empowered to speak up if they witness unethical behavior and where ethical actions are recognized and rewarded. For instance, a halal healthcare company might implement a whistleblower policy that protects employees who report unethical practices, ensuring that any concerns are addressed promptly and without retaliation. By promoting a culture of accountability, the company ensures that ethical behavior is valued at all levels of the organization.

Moreover, ethical leaders must be willing to hold themselves accountable for their own actions. The Quran advises, "And those who avoid the major sins and immoralities, and when they are angry, they forgive" (Quran 42:37). For business leaders, this means acknowledging when they have made a mistake and taking responsibility for their actions. Whether it's a poor business decision or a failure to communicate effectively with employees, ethical leaders are transparent about their mistakes and take steps to correct them. This humility not only builds trust with employees and stakeholders but also reinforces the leader's commitment to ethical governance.

Another essential element of ethical leadership in halal businesses is sustainability. The Quran teaches, "And do not commit abuse on the earth, spreading corruption" (Quran 2:60). For businesses, this means recognizing their responsibility to protect the environment and ensuring that their operations are sustainable. Ethical leaders must take proactive steps to reduce the company's environmental footprint, promote responsible resource management, and ensure that the business's growth does not come at the expense of the planet.

One way businesses can promote sustainability is by adopting eco-friendly practices in their operations. For example, a halal cosmetics company might switch to using biodegradable packaging for its products or invest in renewable energy sources to power its production facilities. By adopting sustainable practices, the company not only reduces its environmental impact but also demonstrates its commitment to ethical governance. This, in turn, can enhance the company's reputation and appeal to environmentally conscious consumers.

In addition to adopting sustainable practices within their operations, businesses must also ensure that their supply chains are aligned with their sustainability goals. The Prophet Muhammad (PBUH) said, "The earth has been made for me and for my followers as a place for praying and a means of purification" (Bukhari). For businesses, this means ensuring that their suppliers and partners share their commitment to environmental stewardship. For instance, a halal food company might prioritize working with farmers who practice sustainable agriculture or suppliers who use environmentally friendly packaging. By aligning their supply chain with their sustainability goals, the company ensures that its entire operation is consistent with its ethical values.

Moreover, ethical leaders must also promote sustainability in the broader community. This might involve supporting initiatives that promote environmental education, conservation, and renewable energy development. For example, a halal construction company might sponsor community workshops on energy-efficient building techniques or donate a portion of its profits to environmental conservation efforts. By engaging with the community on sustainability issues, the company demonstrates its commitment to the environment while also fostering goodwill and strengthening its brand.

Ethical leadership in halal business is not only about ensuring that the company operates responsibly; it is also about fostering innovation and creativity in ways that align with Islamic values. The Quran advises, "Say, 'Travel through the land and observe how He began creation'" (Quran 29:20). This verse encourages exploration, learning, and innovation. For businesses, this means constantly seeking new ways to improve products, services, and operations while ensuring that these innovations align with Islamic principles of fairness, justice, and sustainability.

One way ethical leaders can promote innovation is by fostering a culture of continuous improvement. For instance, a halal tech company might create a research and development team dedicated to exploring new technologies that enhance the user experience while maintaining ethical standards. By encouraging employees to experiment with new ideas and technologies, the company fosters innovation and ensures that it remains competitive in the marketplace.

Innovation also extends to how businesses interact with their customers. Ethical leaders must continuously seek ways to improve customer service, product offerings, and overall customer experience. For example, a halal fashion brand might introduce new lines of clothing that are both stylish and modest, appealing to modern consumers while staying true to Islamic principles. By listening to customer feedback and responding to their needs, the brand fosters innovation while ensuring that its products align with its ethical values.

Moreover, ethical leaders must be willing to embrace new business models and strategies that promote both profitability and social good. For example, a halal travel company might develop a new business model that promotes eco-friendly tourism, ensuring that travelers have a minimal impact on the environment while experiencing new cultures. By embracing innovative business models, ethical leaders can ensure that their companies remain profitable while also contributing to the well-being of society and the environment.

Innovation in halal businesses should always be guided by ethical considerations, ensuring that new products, services, and processes align with Islamic values. The Quran teaches, "And cooperate in righteousness and piety, but do not cooperate in sin and aggression. And fear Allah; indeed, Allah is severe in penalty" (Quran 5:2). For ethical leaders, this means ensuring that innovation is pursued for the benefit of society, without compromising on ethical standards. True innovation is not just about profit—it is about creating value in ways that respect people, the environment, and Islamic principles.

One area where halal businesses can innovate is in their approach to social responsibility. For example, a halal financial institution might develop new products that encourage ethical investment in socially beneficial projects, such as renewable energy, education, and healthcare. These investments not only provide financial returns but also contribute to the betterment of society. By aligning innovation with social good, the institution demonstrates its commitment to ethical leadership while positioning itself as a leader in responsible finance.

Another way halal businesses can foster innovation is by embracing technology in a way that enhances both operational efficiency and customer experience. The Quran encourages the pursuit of knowledge: "Say, 'Are those who know equal to those who do not know?'" (Quran 39:9). For businesses, this means staying at the forefront of technological advancements while ensuring that new technologies are implemented ethically. For instance, a halal e-commerce platform might leverage artificial intelligence to provide personalized shopping experiences for its customers, while also ensuring that customer data is handled securely and ethically. By using technology responsibly, the business enhances its operations while maintaining its ethical obligations to privacy and security.

Innovation also plays a crucial role in addressing social and environmental challenges. The Quran advises, "Indeed, We have made whatever is on the earth an adornment for it that We may test them [as to] which of them is best in deed" (Quran 18:7). For ethical leaders, this means using innovation to find solutions to pressing global issues, such as climate change, poverty, and inequality. For example, a halal clothing brand might develop new, sustainable materials that reduce the environmental impact of production, while also creating jobs in underserved communities. By aligning innovation with social and environmental goals, the brand not only fulfills its ethical obligations but also positions itself as a forward-thinking company committed to positive change.

Ethical leadership in halal business also requires leaders to inspire and motivate their employees, encouraging them to act with integrity and to pursue excellence in their work. The Prophet Muhammad (PBUH) said, "Verily, Allah loves that when any one of you does a job, he should perfect it" (Tabarani). For business leaders, this means fostering a work environment where employees are motivated to do their best, knowing that their efforts are valued and that they are contributing to a higher purpose. Ethical leaders understand that their role is not just to manage, but to inspire—to create a sense of shared vision and purpose that drives the entire organization toward excellence.

One practical way to inspire employees is by recognizing and rewarding ethical behavior. For example, a halal healthcare company might implement an employee recognition program that highlights individuals who have gone above and beyond in upholding the company's ethical values. This could include examples of employees who have demonstrated exceptional customer service, who have contributed innovative ideas that align with the company's ethical goals, or who have taken steps to reduce the company's environmental impact. By recognizing and rewarding ethical behavior, the company reinforces the importance of integrity and encourages other employees to follow suit.

In addition to recognizing ethical behavior, ethical leaders must also provide their employees with the resources and support they need to excel in their roles. The Prophet Muhammad (PBUH) said, "The best among you are those who bring the most benefit to people" (Daraqutni). For businesses, this means ensuring that employees have access to the tools, training, and mentorship they need to develop their skills and contribute meaningfully to the company. For instance, a halal tech company might offer ongoing professional development opportunities for its employees, allowing them to stay up-to-date with the latest advancements in their field while also reinforcing the company's commitment to ethical excellence. By investing in their employees, ethical leaders create a culture of continuous improvement and mutual benefit.

Moreover, ethical leadership requires leaders to lead by example, demonstrating the behaviors and values they expect from their employees. The Quran advises, "O you who have believed, why do you say what you do not do?" (Quran 61:2). For business leaders, this means ensuring that their actions align with their words, and that they embody the company's values in everything they do. Whether it's adhering to ethical business practices, treating employees with respect, or taking a stand on social issues, ethical leaders set the tone for the entire organization by modeling the behaviors they expect from others.

In addition to inspiring employees, ethical leaders in halal business must also ensure that they foster a sense of inclusion and diversity within the organization. The Quran teaches, "O mankind, indeed We have created you from male and female and made you peoples and tribes that you may know one another" (Quran 49:13). For businesses, this means recognizing the value of diversity and creating an environment where people of different backgrounds, cultures, and perspectives can come together and contribute to the success of the organization.

One practical way to promote inclusion is by developing policies and practices that ensure equal opportunities for all employees, regardless of their gender, race, or cultural background. For example, a halal marketing firm might implement a diversity and inclusion program that actively seeks to hire employees from underrepresented groups and provides them with mentorship and career development opportunities. By fostering a diverse workforce, the company not only benefits from a wider range of perspectives and ideas but also reinforces its commitment to fairness and equality.

Inclusion also extends to ensuring that all employees feel valued and respected in the workplace. The Prophet Muhammad (PBUH) said, "The most beloved of people to Allah are those who are most beneficial to people" (Tabarani). For businesses, this means creating a work environment where all employees are treated with dignity and respect, and where their contributions are recognized and appreciated. This might involve implementing policies that promote work-life balance, ensuring that employees have access to flexible working arrangements, or providing opportunities for employees to share their ideas and feedback with management. By fostering an inclusive and supportive work environment, ethical leaders create a sense of belonging and purpose that motivates employees to contribute their best.

Moreover, ethical leadership requires leaders to be open to new ideas and perspectives, recognizing that innovation and creativity often come from diverse viewpoints. The Quran advises, "And their affair is [determined by] consultation among them" (Quran 42:38). For business leaders, this means actively seeking input from employees, customers, and other stakeholders when making decisions, and ensuring that all voices are heard and considered. For instance, a halal food company might hold regular town hall meetings where employees can share their ideas for improving product quality, customer service, or sustainability practices. By creating a culture of openness and collaboration, the company not only fosters innovation but also ensures that its decisions are guided by a wide range of perspectives.

Ethical leadership also involves a commitment to ethical supply chain management. The Quran teaches, "O you who have believed, do not consume one another's wealth unjustly or send it [in bribery] to the rulers in order that [they might aid] you [to] consume a portion of the wealth of the people in sin, while you know [it is unlawful]" (Quran 2:188). For businesses, this means ensuring that their supply chains are free from unethical practices such as exploitation, corruption, and environmental degradation. Ethical leaders must take responsibility for the entire supply chain, from sourcing raw materials to delivering the final product to consumers.

One way businesses can promote ethical supply chain management is by conducting regular audits of their suppliers to ensure compliance with Islamic principles and ethical standards. For example, a halal apparel company might work with third-party auditors to verify that its suppliers are providing fair wages and safe working conditions for their employees. By taking proactive steps to ensure that the supply chain is ethical, the company not only protects its reputation but also ensures that its products are truly halal in every sense of the word.

In addition to auditing suppliers, ethical leaders must also work to build long-term, mutually beneficial relationships with their supply chain partners. The Prophet Muhammad (PBUH) said, "The honest and trustworthy merchant will be with the prophets, the truthful, and the martyrs" (Tirmidhi). For businesses, this means fostering relationships based on trust, transparency, and fairness, rather than seeking to maximize short-term profits at the expense of suppliers. For instance, a halal restaurant chain might work closely with local farmers to source fresh, halal-certified ingredients, providing them with fair prices and support to grow their businesses. By building strong, ethical relationships with suppliers, the company ensures that its supply chain is both sustainable and aligned with Islamic values.

Moreover, ethical supply chain management also involves ensuring that the environmental impact of the supply chain is minimized. The Quran advises, "And do not commit abuse on the earth, spreading corruption" (Quran 2:60). For businesses, this means taking steps to reduce the carbon footprint of their supply chains by adopting eco-friendly practices, such as using renewable energy, reducing waste, and minimizing transportation emissions. For example, a halal cosmetics company might switch to using recycled materials for its packaging and work with suppliers who use sustainable farming practices. By aligning supply chain management with environmental sustainability, the company not only fulfills its ethical obligations but also appeals to consumers who value eco-friendly products.

Ethical leadership in halal businesses is also about ensuring that the business's operations contribute to the broader well-being of society. The Quran teaches, "Indeed, Allah loves the doers of good" (Quran 2:195). For businesses, this means recognizing that their success is not just measured in financial terms, but also in the positive impact they have on the community, the environment, and society as a whole. Ethical leaders must ensure that their businesses contribute to the common good by promoting social justice, supporting charitable initiatives, and engaging in responsible business practices.

One way businesses can contribute to the common good is by engaging in corporate social responsibility (CSR) initiatives that align with their ethical values. For instance, a halal pharmaceutical company might donate a portion of its profits to fund healthcare programs in underserved communities or sponsor medical research into diseases that disproportionately affect low-income populations. By aligning their CSR initiatives with their ethical values, the company ensures that its success benefits society as a whole, not just its shareholders.

In addition to engaging in CSR initiatives, businesses can also promote social justice by adopting fair labor practices and ensuring that their employees are treated with dignity and respect. The Prophet Muhammad (PBUH) said, "Your employees are your brothers, whom Allah has placed under your authority" (Bukhari). For businesses, this means ensuring that employees are provided with fair wages, safe working conditions, and opportunities for career advancement. For example, a halal construction company might implement a comprehensive safety program to ensure that its workers are protected from harm, while also offering training and development opportunities to help employees grow in their careers. By treating employees with fairness and respect, the company builds a loyal and motivated workforce while upholding its ethical responsibilities.

Moreover, ethical leaders must ensure that their businesses contribute to environmental sustainability. The Quran advises, "And do not waste [resources], for indeed, He does not like the wasteful" (Quran 6:141). For businesses, this means adopting practices that minimize waste, reduce energy consumption, and promote the responsible use of natural resources. For example, a halal food packaging company might develop innovative packaging solutions that are biodegradable or recyclable, helping to reduce the environmental impact of its products. By promoting sustainability, the company not only protects the planet but also demonstrates its commitment to ethical leadership and responsible business practices.

Ethical leadership in halal businesses also involves a commitment to transparency and open communication. The Quran advises, "And do not mix the truth with falsehood or conceal the truth while you know [it]" (Quran 2:42). For businesses, this means ensuring that all communication, whether with employees, customers, investors, or other stakeholders, is honest, clear, and accurate. Transparency not only builds trust but also reinforces the company's commitment to ethical practices. Leaders who prioritize transparency create an environment where people feel informed and confident in the company's decisions, which fosters loyalty and engagement.

One way businesses can promote transparency is by providing regular updates on company performance, challenges, and goals. For instance, a halal e-commerce company might send out quarterly reports to its investors, detailing the company's financial performance, new initiatives, and progress toward its sustainability goals. By keeping stakeholders informed about the company's activities, the business builds trust and demonstrates accountability. Similarly, the company might communicate openly with employees about organizational changes, ensuring that everyone understands how these changes align with the company's long-term vision and ethical values.

Transparency is also essential in customer communication. The Prophet Muhammad (PBUH) said, "The seller and the buyer have the right to keep or return goods as long as they have not parted, and if they tell the truth and make clear [the defects of the goods], then they will be blessed in their transaction, but if they tell lies or hide something, then the blessings of their transaction will be wiped out" (Bukhari). For businesses, this means being upfront with customers about product details, pricing, and any potential limitations or risks. For example, a halal cosmetics company might clearly label all ingredients in its products, ensuring that customers know exactly what they are purchasing. By promoting transparency in customer interactions, the company fosters trust and encourages repeat business.

In addition to customer communication, transparency in governance is essential for maintaining ethical leadership. This includes being open about decision-making processes, the company's financial health, and the ethical principles guiding its operations. For example, a halal investment firm might provide detailed information about its Shariah-compliant investment strategies, allowing investors to understand how their funds are being used. By maintaining transparency in its governance, the firm reinforces its commitment to ethical leadership and ensures that its operations are aligned with Islamic principles.

Ethical leadership also demands that businesses take responsibility for their actions and decisions, particularly when mistakes are made. The Quran teaches, "Every soul will be compensated in full for what it did, and Allah is most knowing of what they do" (Quran 39:70). For business leaders, this means acknowledging when things go wrong, taking steps to correct mistakes, and learning from them to avoid repeating the same errors in the future. Leaders who take responsibility for their actions set a powerful example for their employees and create a culture where accountability is valued.

One practical way businesses can demonstrate responsibility is by implementing feedback mechanisms that allow employees, customers, and other stakeholders to raise concerns or report issues. For instance, a halal pharmaceutical company might create an anonymous reporting system where employees can voice concerns about ethical violations or workplace safety without fear of retaliation. By providing a safe space for feedback, the company demonstrates its commitment to accountability and ensures that issues are addressed proactively.

Taking responsibility also extends to how businesses handle customer complaints. The Prophet Muhammad (PBUH) said, "Whoever relieves the hardship of a believer in this world, Allah will relieve his hardship on the Day of Resurrection" (Muslim). For businesses, this means ensuring that customer complaints are taken seriously and resolved in a fair and timely manner. For example, a halal travel agency might implement a customer service policy that guarantees a prompt response to any issues related to bookings or refunds. By taking responsibility for resolving customer complaints, the business reinforces its commitment to ethical customer service and strengthens its reputation.

Moreover, ethical leadership requires businesses to take responsibility for their impact on society and the environment. The Quran advises, "And do not commit abuse on the earth, spreading corruption" (Quran 2:60). For businesses, this means recognizing that their actions have a wider impact on the planet and society and taking steps to minimize any negative effects. For example, a halal construction company might adopt sustainable building practices that reduce environmental harm, such as using eco-friendly materials or implementing energy-efficient designs. By taking responsibility for their environmental impact, businesses demonstrate their commitment to ethical leadership and contribute to the greater good.

In addition to transparency and responsibility, ethical leadership in halal businesses involves fostering resilience and adaptability. The Quran teaches, "Indeed, with hardship [will be] ease" (Quran 94:6). For business leaders, this means recognizing that challenges are inevitable but that with the right mindset and strategies, these challenges can be overcome. Resilient leaders are those who can navigate difficult situations with patience, wisdom, and a commitment to their values, ensuring that the business emerges stronger from adversity.

One way businesses can foster resilience is by developing contingency plans that allow them to respond to unexpected challenges, such as economic downturns, supply chain disruptions, or regulatory changes. For example, a halal logistics company might create a risk management plan that outlines steps to be taken in the event of a supply chain interruption, such as identifying alternative suppliers or adjusting delivery schedules. By planning ahead for potential challenges, the company ensures that it can continue operating smoothly even in the face of adversity.

In addition to contingency planning, resilient businesses are those that embrace change and innovation. Ethical leaders understand that the business landscape is constantly evolving and that staying competitive requires a willingness to adapt and explore new opportunities. The Quran advises, "And those who strive for Us—We will surely guide them to Our ways" (Quran 29:69). For businesses, this means being open to new ideas and approaches, even if they involve taking risks. For instance, a halal food company might explore new markets by developing plant-based or organic halal products, catering to consumers who are both health-conscious and committed to halal standards. By embracing innovation, the company ensures that it remains competitive while staying true to its ethical principles.

Resilience also involves maintaining a long-term perspective, recognizing that success is not achieved overnight. Ethical leaders understand that true success comes from building a sustainable business that grows steadily and responsibly over time. The Prophet Muhammad (PBUH) said, "The strong believer is better and more beloved to Allah than the weak believer, while there is good in both" (Muslim). For businesses, this means focusing on long-term goals, such as building a loyal customer base, fostering strong relationships with partners, and ensuring that the company's growth is aligned with its ethical values.

Another key aspect of ethical leadership in halal businesses is fostering collaboration and teamwork. The Quran teaches, "And cooperate in righteousness and piety, but do not cooperate in sin and aggression" (Quran 5:2). For businesses, this means creating a work environment where employees are encouraged to collaborate, share ideas, and work together to achieve common goals. Ethical leaders understand that the success of the business depends on the collective efforts of the team, and they take steps to foster a sense of unity and purpose within the organization.

One practical way to promote collaboration is by creating opportunities for cross-functional teamwork, where employees from different departments come together to work on projects or solve problems. For example, a halal technology company might create project teams that include members from engineering, marketing, and customer service, ensuring that all perspectives are considered when developing new products or services. By fostering collaboration across the organization, the company not only enhances innovation but also strengthens relationships among employees.

Collaboration also involves ensuring that employees feel empowered to contribute their ideas and talents to the company's success. The Prophet Muhammad (PBUH) said, "None of you [truly] believes until he loves for his brother what he loves for himself" (Bukhari). For businesses, this means creating a culture where employees are encouraged to support one another and work together for the collective good. For instance, a halal financial institution might implement a peer mentoring program where experienced employees help new hires develop their skills and integrate into the company culture. By promoting a sense of mutual support and teamwork, the institution fosters a positive work environment where employees feel valued and motivated to contribute their best efforts.

Moreover, ethical leaders must ensure that collaboration extends beyond the company's internal operations to include partnerships with external stakeholders, such as suppliers, customers, and the community. For example, a halal beauty brand might collaborate with local artisans to create ethically sourced, handmade products, supporting small businesses while ensuring that the brand's products align with its ethical values. By fostering collaboration with external partners, the company not only enhances its product offerings but also builds strong, mutually beneficial relationships that contribute to long-term success.

Ethical leadership in halal businesses also requires a commitment to continuous learning and development. The Quran advises, "And say, 'My Lord, increase me in knowledge'" (Quran 20:114). For business leaders, this means recognizing that there is always more to learn and that staying competitive in a fast-changing world requires a commitment to lifelong learning. Ethical leaders must invest in their own personal development, as well as in the development of their employees, ensuring that the company remains at the forefront of industry trends while maintaining its commitment to ethical values.

One way businesses can promote continuous learning is by providing employees with opportunities for professional development. For example, a halal retail company might offer training programs that help employees improve their skills in areas such as customer service, leadership, or technology. By investing in employee development, the company not only enhances its workforce but also reinforces its commitment to ethical leadership by ensuring that employees have the tools they need to succeed.

In addition to employee development, ethical leaders must also seek out opportunities for their own personal growth. This might involve attending industry conferences, participating in leadership training programs, or seeking mentorship from other successful ethical leaders. By continually improving their own skills and knowledge, business leaders ensure that they remain effective in their roles and that their businesses continue to thrive in a competitive environment.

Moreover, ethical leaders must stay informed about the latest trends and developments in their industry, particularly in areas such as technology, sustainability, and ethical business practices. For example, a halal energy company might stay up-to-date with advancements in renewable energy technology, ensuring that its operations remain environmentally friendly and aligned with Islamic principles of stewardship. By staying informed and embracing innovation, the company ensures that it remains competitive while maintaining its commitment to ethical leadership.

Ethical leadership in halal businesses is deeply intertwined with the concept of stewardship. The Quran reminds us, "It is He who has made you successors upon the earth" (Quran 35:39). For business leaders, this means recognizing that they have been entrusted with resources—whether financial, environmental, or human—that they must manage responsibly. Ethical stewardship involves making decisions that benefit the business while also considering the broader impact on society and the environment.

One way businesses can demonstrate ethical stewardship is by adopting sustainable practices that protect natural resources and minimize environmental harm. For instance, a halal agriculture company might implement water-saving irrigation systems, use organic farming methods, and reduce the use of harmful pesticides. These practices not only ensure that the company's operations are environmentally responsible, but they also contribute to the long-term sustainability of the agricultural industry. By being mindful stewards of the environment, the business ensures that it is contributing positively to the planet while aligning its operations with Islamic principles.

Stewardship also involves taking care of the people within the organization. The Prophet Muhammad (PBUH) said, "The best of people are those who are most beneficial to others" (Daraqutni). For business leaders, this means ensuring that their employees are supported, respected, and provided with opportunities for growth. This might involve offering health and wellness programs, implementing fair wage policies, or creating a positive work-life balance. For example, a halal technology company might offer flexible working hours and remote work options, allowing employees to balance their professional and personal lives more effectively. By taking care of their employees, businesses not only foster loyalty and productivity but also create a positive work culture rooted in ethical values.

In addition to environmental and employee stewardship, ethical leaders must also be mindful stewards of their company's financial resources. The Quran advises, "And do not waste [resources], for indeed, He does not like the wasteful" (Quran 6:141). For businesses, this means ensuring that financial decisions are made prudently, with a focus on long-term sustainability rather than short-term gains. For instance, a halal retail company might adopt a conservative financial strategy that involves building up reserves during profitable periods, allowing the company to weather economic downturns and unexpected challenges. By managing financial resources responsibly, the company ensures its long-term viability and maintains its commitment to ethical leadership.

Ethical stewardship also extends to how businesses interact with their local communities. The Quran teaches, "And cooperate in righteousness and piety" (Quran 5:2). For businesses, this means recognizing that they have a responsibility to contribute to the well-being of the communities in which they operate. Ethical leaders must take an active role in supporting local communities through charitable initiatives, partnerships, and community engagement.

One practical way businesses can engage with their local communities is by supporting charitable causes that align with the company's values. For example, a halal food company might partner with local food banks to provide nutritious, halal-certified meals to families in need. By contributing to local charities, the company not only fulfills its religious obligation to give back to society but also strengthens its relationship with the community. This type of engagement fosters goodwill, enhances the company's reputation, and reinforces its commitment to social responsibility.

In addition to charitable giving, businesses can also contribute to their communities by creating jobs and supporting local economic development. The Prophet Muhammad (PBUH) said, "The one who looks after a widow or a poor person is like a warrior who fights for Allah's cause" (Bukhari). For businesses, this means ensuring that their operations provide meaningful employment opportunities for people in the community, particularly those from disadvantaged backgrounds. For instance, a halal construction company might prioritize hiring local workers and offering training programs that equip them with valuable skills. By creating jobs and investing in the local workforce, the company not only supports economic development but also strengthens its ties to the community.

Furthermore, ethical stewardship involves promoting inclusivity and equality within the organization and the broader society. The Quran teaches, "And do not deprive people of their due and do not commit abuse on the earth, spreading corruption" (Quran 26:183). For businesses, this means ensuring that their policies and practices promote fairness, equity, and respect for all individuals, regardless of their background. This might involve creating an inclusive hiring process that ensures equal opportunities for all candidates or developing products and services that cater to a diverse range of customers. For example, a halal fashion brand might offer clothing lines that accommodate various cultural and religious practices, ensuring that everyone feels represented and respected. By promoting inclusivity, the company fosters a culture of fairness and equality that aligns with Islamic principles.

Ethical leadership in halal business also involves a commitment to innovation that is guided by ethical principles. The Quran encourages the pursuit of knowledge and innovation, stating, "And He has subjected to you whatever is in the heavens and whatever is on the earth—all from Him. Indeed, in that are signs for a people who give thought" (Quran 45:13). For businesses, this means embracing innovation as a way to improve products, services, and operations, while ensuring that these innovations align with Islamic values and contribute to the well-being of society.

One area where halal businesses can innovate is in the development of new, ethical products that meet the needs of modern consumers while adhering to halal standards. For example, a halal skincare company might innovate by developing eco-friendly, cruelty-free products that use ethically sourced, natural ingredients. This not only appeals to consumers who are concerned about sustainability and animal welfare but also ensures that the company's products meet both ethical and religious standards. By focusing on ethical innovation, the company can differentiate itself in the market and build a loyal customer base that values both quality and integrity.

Innovation also extends to how businesses approach their operations and business models. The Prophet Muhammad (PBUH) said, "Seeking knowledge is obligatory upon every Muslim" (Ibn Majah). For businesses, this means continuously seeking new ways to improve efficiency, reduce costs, and enhance customer satisfaction. For instance, a halal logistics company might adopt cutting-edge technology to optimize its delivery processes, reducing fuel consumption and minimizing environmental impact. By embracing innovative solutions that align with their ethical goals, businesses can enhance their operations while maintaining their commitment to sustainability.

Moreover, ethical leadership requires businesses to use innovation as a tool for addressing social and environmental challenges. The Quran teaches, "And strive for Allah with the striving due to Him" (Quran 22:78). For businesses, this means using their resources and expertise to find solutions to pressing global issues, such as climate change, poverty, and inequality. For example, a halal energy company might invest in research and development to create new renewable energy technologies that reduce dependence on fossil fuels and promote environmental sustainability. By aligning innovation with social good, businesses not only contribute to the greater good but also position themselves as leaders in ethical business practices.

In addition to fostering innovation, ethical leadership in halal businesses involves ensuring that all business practices are conducted with honesty and integrity. The Quran advises, "O you who have believed, fear Allah and speak words of appropriate justice" (Quran 33:70). For business leaders, this means ensuring that all transactions, contracts, and dealings are conducted with fairness and transparency, and that the company's reputation for integrity is upheld in every aspect of its operations.

One practical way businesses can promote honesty and integrity is by implementing clear and transparent contractual agreements with suppliers, customers, and partners. For example, a halal construction firm might create detailed, transparent contracts with clients that outline project timelines, costs, and deliverables, ensuring that there are no hidden fees or unexpected charges. By being upfront and transparent in all business dealings, the company builds trust and fosters long-term relationships with its clients.

Integrity also extends to how businesses treat their employees. The Prophet Muhammad (PBUH) said, "Give the worker his wages before his sweat dries" (Ibn Majah). For businesses, this means ensuring that employees are compensated fairly and promptly for their work, and that they are provided with safe and respectful working conditions. For example, a halal retail company might ensure that all employees receive fair wages, benefits, and opportunities for career advancement, while also promoting a positive and inclusive work environment. By treating employees with fairness and integrity, the company builds a loyal and motivated workforce.

Moreover, businesses must ensure that their marketing and advertising practices are truthful and do not mislead customers. The Prophet Muhammad (PBUH) said, "The honest and trustworthy merchant will be with the prophets, the truthful, and the martyrs" (Tirmidhi). For businesses, this means avoiding deceptive advertising, exaggerated claims, or false promises in their marketing campaigns. For instance, a halal beauty brand might ensure that all marketing materials accurately represent the benefits of its products without making unrealistic or misleading claims. By promoting honesty in marketing, the company fosters trust with its customers and reinforces its commitment to ethical business practices.

Ethical leadership in halal business also requires a commitment to ethical investment practices. The Quran advises, "And those who, when they spend, are neither extravagant nor stingy, but hold a medium [way] between those [extremes]" (Quran 25:67). For businesses, this means ensuring that their investments are aligned with Islamic principles, avoiding industries or activities that are haram (prohibited), such as alcohol, gambling, and interest-based financial transactions.

One way businesses can promote ethical investment is by adopting Shariah-compliant financial practices, such as profit-sharing models and asset-backed investments. For instance, a halal investment firm might offer clients the opportunity to invest in real estate projects that are structured as *musharakah* (partnerships), where profits and losses are shared equitably among the investors. This not only ensures that the investments are compliant with Islamic finance principles but also fosters a sense of shared responsibility and ethical governance.

In addition to promoting ethical investments, businesses must also ensure that their financial operations are transparent and accountable. The Quran teaches, "O you who have believed, do not consume one another's wealth unjustly" (Quran 4:29). For businesses, this means implementing clear financial reporting practices, conducting regular audits, and ensuring that all financial transactions are properly documented and disclosed. For example, a halal manufacturing company might work with external auditors to ensure that its financial statements are accurate and comply with both Islamic and legal standards. By maintaining transparency and accountability in financial operations, the company builds trust with its investors, customers, and stakeholders.

Finally, ethical leadership in halal business involves a commitment to creating value that benefits society as a whole. The Quran advises, "So give the relative his right, as well as the needy and the traveler. That is best for those who desire the countenance of Allah, and it is they who will be successful" (Quran 30:38). For businesses, this means ensuring that their success is not just measured in financial terms but also in the positive impact they have on the community, the environment, and society as a whole. Ethical leaders must strive to create value that extends beyond profit, contributing to the greater good and upholding the values of Islam in every aspect of their business.

ABOUT THE AUTHOR

Afjal Khan is a dedicated writer, educator, and entrepreneur passionate about guiding Muslims in building successful, halal businesses that align with their faith and values. With a deep commitment to integrating Islamic teachings into modern business practices, he empowers Muslims to navigate the complexities of the business world while staying true to the principles of the **Qur'an** and **Sunnah**.

Rooted in the authentic traditions of Islam, **Afjal Khan's** work emphasizes the importance of conducting business with integrity, transparency, and in a way that pleases Allah. Drawing inspiration from the wisdom of the Salaf and the core principles of **Tawheed**, he offers practical and actionable advice for Muslims seeking to balance worldly success with spiritual growth. His mission is to help entrepreneurs thrive in a way that not only benefits them financially but also brings barakah (blessing) to their efforts and to the Ummah as a whole.

Through his books, lectures, and content, Afjal Khan aims to bridge the gap between the timeless teachings of Islam and the evolving landscape of modern business. His goal is to empower Muslims to build wealth ethically, ensuring that their success in this life is aligned with their aspirations for the Hereafter.

"As a humble student of knowledge, I (Afjal Khan) welcome any feedback or corrections. While I strive to ensure that everything I share aligns with the Qur'an and Sunnah, I acknowledge that I am human and capable of making mistakes. If any part of my work inadvertently contradicts authentic Islamic teachings, I ask for your forgiveness. Please do not follow my words if they conflict with Islam, and I kindly request that you inform me of any errors so that I may correct them, inshaAllah, as long as I am alive. You are welcome to reach out to me at **mdafjalkhan29@gmail.com** for any corrections, insights, or questions."

Afjal Khan's vision is to inspire Muslims to pursue their entrepreneurial dreams while remaining steadfast in their faith, allowing them to build a legacy of success that benefits both themselves and their communities in this world and the next.

To stay **connected** with **Afjal Khan** and access valuable insights, free eBooks, and resources designed to strengthen your understanding of Islamic parenting, join

@IQRAJOURNEY

his community. As a special thank you for joining, you'll receive an exclusive guide to help you on your journey of raising righteous Muslim children.

www.ingramcontent.com/pod-product-compliance
Lightning Source LLC
Chambersburg PA
CBHW052147220526
45471CB00004B/1564